KILLERS ON THE LOOSE

KILLERS ON THE LOOSE

UNSOLVED CASES OF SERIAL MURDER

Antonio Mendoza

This updated edition first published in 2002 by
Virgin Books
Thames Wharf Studios
Rainville Road
London W6 9HA

First edition published 2000

Copyright © Antonio Mendoza 2000, 2001

Check out Antonio's website at *www.mayhem.net*

www.virgin.com/books

ISBN 0 7535 0681 5

Series style by Roger Kohn Designs
Design and typesetting by
TW Typesetting, Plymouth, Devon

Printed and bound by Mackays of Chatham PLC

Dedication

I would like to dedicate this book to all the innocent victims who died at the hands of these killers, especially the drug-addicted prostitutes who constitute the most disenfranchised, abused and ignored sector of our society.

CONTENTS

Acknowledgements   xi

Introduction   1

1. The Spokane Serial Killer   7

A high-risk lifestyle involving prostitution, drugs, or both, has characterized the victims of the suspected 'Spokane Serial Killer'. According to the special task force assigned to the case, eight women have been slain in the Spokane area and two others with similar profiles have been murdered in Tacoma. The task force is looking into possible links with seventeen other unsolved killings of women in the area since 1984 – the year the Green River Killer vanished.

2. The Green River Killer   35

Between 1982 and 1984 the 'Green River Killer' tallied 49 kills in the Seattle–Tacoma area, then vanished without a trace. Experts believe he may be dead, may have relocated, may be incarcerated for an unrelated crime, or institutionalized for mental illness. But no one involved in this case believes the perpetrator has 'retired' from murder. Currently, authorities are investigating the possibility that he may be linked to the recent rash of killings in San Diego, Spokane, Vancouver and Portland.

3. The Case of the Missing Vancouver Sex Workers   55

Though they have no bodies or hard evidence, civic leaders in Vancouver suspect a serial killer is responsible for the disappearance of more than 29 local sex-trade workers. Police, stumped by the disappearances, have been reluctant to acknowledge the existence of a killer. In an attempt to keep track of local sex-trade workers, two agencies started recording personal details of the prostitutes that would give police clues if the women disappeared. After much debate local business leaders decided to donate cell phones to the prostitutes and asked them to call in occasionally to let authorities know they were still breathing.

4. Getting Away with Murder in the Big Easy   69

Authorities suspect that one or several serial killers are responsible for the abduction and brutal strangulation of 24 women whose bodies have been found dumped in swamp areas outside New Orleans. To date, two suspects have been arrested. One, a police officer, was released for lack of evidence and put on temporary leave from the department. The other is awaiting his release from custody after an investigating officer was caught planting evidence against him.

5. The Spotsylvania Child Killer 81

In the summer of 1997 three girls from Spotsylvania, a small town thirty miles north of Richmond, Virginia, disappeared from their homes after school, leaving behind no signs of a struggle. Authorities believe the girls were victims of a local serial killer. The three victims had dark hair and slim, athletic builds, and lived within a ten-mile radius of each other.

6. Death Walks the Streets of Chicago 89

Chicago authorities issued a citywide warning about four separate predators stalking the windy city's South Side. Since 1993 the killers – identified by their DNA-profiles – have claimed at least thirteen lives. The victims have been mostly crack-addicted prostitutes who were strangled and/or bludgeoned to death and left inside abandoned buildings.

7. *Lustmord* in Los Angeles 109

Authorities believe there are two killers hunting black prostitutes in the urban sprawl of Los Angeles. One, the 'South Side Slasher', has killed at least fifteen 'strawberries' (crack-addicted prostitutes) in the South Central area. The second is suspected of strangling six prostitutes from the Holt Avenue area in Pomona.

8. Operation Enigma 121

Scotland Yard's Operation Enigma, in which authorities reviewed 207 unsolved murders of women since 1986, concluded that four separate serial killers were stalking Britain. Enigma was launched after the top detectives in 43 police forces in England and Wales were alerted to the alarmingly high number of prostitutes and other types of 'vulnerable women' being murdered.

9. The South Dublin Killer 135

Irish police have called the FBI for help profiling a suspected serial killer responsible for the disappearances of six women. Four of the 'Missing Six', all aged between 17 and 26, vanished within a 30-mile area of the Wicklow and Dublin mountains, south of the Irish capital. Police originally dismissed suggestions that there was an active serial killer, but, after the disappearance of an eighteen-year-old student teacher in broad daylight, officers launched a special task force to investigate the killings.

10. The Butcher of Mons 143

Belgium's 'Butcher of Mons' has been leaving garbage bags with the dismembered remains of his female victims in places with emotive names like the River Haine (Hate), the Chemin de l'Inquietude (the Path of Worry), and the River Trouille (Jitters). Authorities are baffled by this taunting killer who is thought to be a surgeon or butcher due to the 'remarkable precision' he has demonstrated in dismembering his prey.

11. The Lisbon Ripper 151

Young, drug-dependent prostitutes have been the victims of a Portuguese serial killer dubbed the 'Lisbon Ripper'. Authorities think he may be responsible for the murders of at least nine women in five different countries: Portugal, Belgium, the Czech Republic, Denmark and The Netherlands. Because of the itinerant nature of these crimes, police think the killer may be a truck driver with a pathological hatred of women. He has also been profiled as a man suffering from AIDS.

12. Rome's Gay Serial Killer 161

Italian authorities believe there is a serial killer in Rome targeting influential gay men. There have been twenty homosexual murders in the city in the last seven years, of which only ten have been solved. Many of the deaths are attributed to a new breed of violent male hustlers populating the streets of Rome. However, the deaths of an American intellectual, a Florentine aristocrat and an art-restorer in Umbria are suspected of being the work of a possible serial killer.

13. Ciudad Juárez, City of the Dead 169

This baffling case involving the deaths of more than 187 female victims in Ciudad Juárez, a border town next to El Paso, has Mexican Federales on the lookout for one or more serial killers. Authorities suspect that the majority of the women were killed by known assailants, including pimps, drug dealers, husbands and boyfriends. However, up to 35 killings are unexplained and police have no suspects. Several men have been arrested and confessions have been beaten out of them. The death toll continues unabated.

14. The Psychopath of Costa Rica 183

Costa Rican police believe a mysterious serial killer known as the 'Psychopath' is responsible for at least nineteen cold-hearted murders. Stumped by a decade of random attacks, Costa Rican police asked the FBI for help in tracking their serial killer. The Psychopath preys on young couples in secluded parks in an area known as San José's 'Triangle of Death'. The killer often waits for the couples to start making love before shooting at them with a high-caliber rifle. Authorities believe the killer could be a 'Rambo'-type former soldier or police officer, or the son of a wealthy politician or landowner.

15. The Highway Maniac 195

Since 1997 Argentina's 'Highway Maniac' has claimed at least five lives. All victims have been prostitutes who were strangled or had their throats slit. Their nude bodies were found along highways around the Argentinian city of Mar de Plata. Some of the victims had their genitals mutilated; one had the word 'Puta' (whore) carved on her chest. Police have six suspects but no evidence linking them to any of the crimes. Five more prostitutes are missing and presumed dead at the hands of the killer.

16. Serial Killing in Belize 203

There is a vicious serial killer roaming the streets of Belize City who has raped, murdered and mutilated at least four young girls. Being the first case of serial killing in the nation, local police have proven to be inadequately prepared to deal with the situation, and have called on the FBI and Scotland Yard for help.

17. The Perth Serial Killer 217

A suspected serial killer is believed to have murdered three women in the Australian city of Perth. The victims were abducted outside a popular nightspot in the affluent suburb of Claremont. Their bodies were later found twenty to forty miles from the city. Police believe the killer enjoys driving, because of the long distances he covers to bury the bodies.

18. South Africa's Serial Killer Epidemic 227

South Africa is fast becoming the serial sex-crime epicenter of the world, with up to five separate serial killers active today. One, the 'Cape Town Strangler', is responsible for killing about twenty women. Another, the 'Nasrec Strangler', is believed to have strangled fifteen women. Leading both investigations is famed female psychologist Dr Micki Pistorious who has successfully profiled several other local serial killers.

Epilogue 241

Science and technology have made huge strides in the detection and identification of serial killers. In current investigations throughout the US detectives are relying heavily on DNA-databanks and computerized systems like VICAP to shift out possible serial killers. But the slaughter continues unabated. New serial patterns are emerging in Denver, Pittsburgh, Brooklyn and France, while many other spots in the globe are grappling with uncaught serial predators. Is there any way to stop the mayhem? How many more roaming maniacs lusting for blood are still out there undetected and unknown? Before you read the rest of this book get up and close all the doors.

ACKNOWLEDGEMENTS

The author would like to thank the following people for their help researching, writing and proofreading this book. First of all I would like to thank my wife Deirdre and my children, Gala and Cassio, for their patience during the many nights I spent in the basement writing about serial killers. I am also very grateful to James Marriott and Kerri Sharp, my two editors, for not freaking out over my painfully unreliable working habits.

I would also like to thank Rui Horta Santos for his valuable research on the Lisbon Ripper, Henrik Kragh for his help with the Mons and Lisbon cases, Mark Nollinger for his timely Nexis searches, Federico Sosa for his research on Argentina's Highway Maniac, Lynn Everson from Spokane's Downtown Women's Shelter, Elaine Allan of the Women's Information Safe House in Vancouver, Jon Clarke of the West Midlands Police Department, Christy Castillo of the Belize Police Department and Karla Heusner of the Belizean Channel Five News.

Others whose help, support and advice have been instrumental in the writing of this book are Adoris Mendoza, Harvey Markowitz, Michael Newton, Eric Hickey, Jonathan Vankin, Greg Miller, Alejandra Santaolalla, Mercedes Velasco, Jose Perez de Lama, Angelica Garza, Alberto Miyares, Jesus Juárez, Jeanne Meyers and Stephen Siciliano.

Finally I would like to acknowledge the extensive use I've made of the Electric Library web site, the Joe1orbit's Serial and Mass Murder Mailing List and its vast archive of articles on everything pertaining to serial killing, and Wayne Leng's web site – www.missingpeople.net – and its list of articles concerning Vancouver's missing women.

INTRODUCTION

'We serial killers are your sons, we are your husbands, we are everywhere. And there will be more of your children dead tomorrow.'

Ted Bundy

He might be your neighbor. He might be your gardener, or the creep staring at you on the bus. He could be hunting prostitutes, drifters, hitchhikers, old widows, or young boys. He could strike any time, any place. And with horrifying regularity, he does. Yes, a serial killer living somewhere near you is looking for his next victim.

According to an FBI Behavioral Unit study, serial killing has climbed to 'an almost epidemic proportion'. Authorities estimate that presently there are between 35 and 50 serial killers on the loose in the United States. In the UK there are up to four unidentified predators. And new reports of suspected killers are constantly surfacing all over the globe. Once a rare phenomenon, serial killing has become increasingly frequent, with dozens of maniacs terrorizing different cities simultaneously. From Australia's 'Perth Killer' to Costa Rica's 'Psychopath', California's 'South Side Slasher', and Ireland's 'South Dublin Killer', serial killers have become an uncomfortably unfathomable reality of modern life.

Though a worldwide problem, the vast majority of serial killers are active in North America, particularly the US. From the chilly streets of Anchorage, Alaska, to the gay bars of Miami Beach, serial predators are getting away with murder at an unprecedented rate. In the Northwestern United States a serial killer has murdered ten prostitutes in Spokane and Tacoma. Nearby in Seattle the hunt for the dreaded 'Green River Killer', responsible for the deaths of 49, remains active and unsolved. Across the border in Canada, police officials, stumped by the disappearances of 29 sex-trade workers from Vancouver's red-light district, refuse to admit there might be a serial killer plucking them from the streets and perhaps burying them under his home.

Many cities in the US have suspected serial predators at large. Since 1982, Kansas City police suspect that a serial killer has dumped the dismembered bodies of seven prostitutes in the Missouri River. Further south in New Orleans, police formed a serial killer task force to investigate the deaths of 26 women and transsexuals whose naked bodies were found in swamps, bayous and country roads. In Charlotte, Poughkeepsie, Grand Rapids, Denver and Jersey City investigators have detected 'murder clusters' centered on prostitution and drugs, indicating the possibility of one or more active serial killers on the hunt.

In Chicago modern DNA-profiling techniques have detected four different sexual predators acting within the same South Side neighborhood, independently of each other, who have claimed at least thirteen victims. Though serial killing is nothing new in the crack- and heroin-ravaged Chicago South Side. Three more killers have recently been arrested in the same area for a combined total of 28 kills.

Police in Atlanta, Georgia, suspect three different killers are stalking the streets. One is hunting transvestites. The second is slaying prostitutes. A third has continued murdering black children since the arrest and conviction of Wayne Williams. Five more serial killers are believed responsible for the deaths of thirty gay men in New Jersey, Virginia, Maryland, New York and Texas. Senior citizens in Columbus, Mississippi have been arming themselves following a police warning that a local serial killer was targeting the elderly in the area.

Federal agents in San Diego, California, suspect a trucker of committing at least twenty murders across eight states. Up the coast in the Los Angeles metropolitan area, two separate prostitute killers are operating in different parts of the city. In southern Texas 32 women have appeared dead in what is called the 'I-45 Killing Fields', a fifty-mile stretch of highway between Houston and Galveston. Police believe multiple serial killers are responsible for the high body count. Serial killers have been arrested in New York, Virginia, California, New

Jersey, North Carolina, Kentucky, Texas, Florida and Ohio. Even the affluent community of retired FBI agents in Spotsylvania has a serial killer who has abducted three young girls. Chillingly, the killer left their corpses partly submerged in water with their pubic hair shaved off.

Europe is similarly plagued by a dramatic rise in serial murder. Irish police suspect a serial killer is hunting women in the mountains south of Dublin. In Glasgow there are fears that a serial killer has been plucking prostitutes from the streets since 1993. In 1998 Scotland Yard launched an investigation, code named Enigma, after an increase in the murder rate of known or suspected prostitutes. Studying the deaths of 207 women over a five-year period, Enigma identified four different 'murder clusters' – indicating the possible existence of four serial killers.

Police in Portugal suspect a truck driver with a deep hatred towards women is responsible for the murders of at least seven prostitutes in five European nations. This same killer, agents theorize, might also be responsible for ten more killings in New Bedford, Massachusetts, where there is a large Portuguese immigrant community. More serial killers have been identified in France, Germany, Poland and Greece. In Belgium, the 'Butcher of Mons' has baffled police by leaving garbage bags full of carefully dismembered human remains in strategic places with evocative names. In Italy there are two to four suspected predators at large. One has been hunting influential gay men in Rome and Florence. Another is killing elderly widows in the northern region of Apulia, striking only during televised soccer matches.

The Soviet Union, where until 1992 authorities denied the existence of serial killers, is now experiencing an exponential rise in serial murder. The southern city of Rostov-on-Don, which is fast becoming the serial killing capital of the world, has had 29 multiple killers arrested over the last ten years. More serial killers have been arrested in Moscow, the Ukraine and Siberia. One killer, known as the 'Terminator', tallied upwards of 52 victims over a six-year period. Others, like Sasha Spesivtsev in the Siberian town of Novokuznetsk, ate their victims' remains.

Since the dismantling of apartheid, South Africa has been swept by a wave of serial killing. Recently three serial killers have been found guilty of multiple murders and five others are still at large. One killer in Cape Town, while successfully eluding authorities, has strangled twenty women. Another, referred to by the superstitious as the 'River Monster', has killed over six people near a particular bridge. Other African nations have reported cases involving serial killers – on the run or in custody. One unidentified maniac in Zambia has killed thirty people, including the former deputy speaker of Zambia's National Assembly and his wife. In February 1999, two suspected Nigerian cannibals were arrested for killing and cannibalizing at least ten people under a bridge separating Lagos and Nigeria.

Latin America has not been immune to the global serial menace. Since August 1993, a growing number of girls and young women have turned up dead on the outskirts of Ciudad Juárez, a Mexican border town next to El Paso. Most of the 187 victims have been dark-haired girls, between fourteen and eighteen years old, who work in the surrounding American-owned *maquiladoras* factories. Authorities believe two gangs of serial killers paid off by another suspected serial killer in custody were responsible for between twenty and eighty killings.

For over a decade authorities in the Costa Rican capital of San José have been tracking a serial killer who attacks amorous couples making love in their cars. In El Salvador police suspect a cunning predator stalking transvestites. Residents of the tiny nation of Belize are in a state of shock after four young girls were abducted on their way to school, then raped, mutilated and murdered by a serial killer. In northeastern Brazil someone has been killing boys and mutilating their genitals. In Bogotá, Colombia, a predator has abducted five girls from the same street. Another maniac in Colombia was arrested and confessed to killing 140 boys. While grappling with the feared and unidentified 'Highway Maniac', Argentine police are now facing a new copycat killer.

On the other side of the world in Australia, since the arrest of Ivan Milat, the notorious 'Backpacker Murderer', there has been a marked increase in serial killer activity.

Authorities believe there are at least two active serial killers in their nation – one in Perth and another in New South Wales. The Perth killer preys on young, blonde women leaving a popular nightclub in the suburb of Claremont and enjoys washing his car after each kill. The New South Wales killer is an Ivan Milat copycat killer who has claimed the lives of three unsuspecting hitchhikers. Recent reports indicate there could be another serial killer in Sydney stalking the homeless.

Not surprisingly, Asian nations also reflect the worldwide crisis of serial murder. In the last two years Thailand, Indonesia and Japan have arrested local serial killers. In one case, the dreaded 'Kobe Decapitator' turned out to be a 'Zodiac killer-obsessed' teenager. Even the relatively crime-free republic of China has been experiencing an explosion of serial killing, with at least three multiple murderers arrested – in Beijing, Canton and Yangjiang – in the last two years.

This book tracks suspected serial killer cases from the end of the twentieth century. Alarmingly, most of the victims in this book are prostitutes. In fact, they are by and large the most victimized sector of society. Alone and forgotten, prostitutes worldwide make the perfect targets for these unidentified killers. In some of the cases featured in *Killers on the Loose* authorities are unwilling to even admit they have a serial killer. In some others, one or more suspects have been arrested and charged with some of the killings. Sometimes police are pretty sure about the identity of the killer, but lack the evidence to make the arrest. As this book was being written some suspected killers were caught and others have confessed. Their cases are included in the text as examples of how thorough police work – or mere luck – can lead to the suspect's arrest.

It's hard to imagine that there is no longer a place in the world safe from these roaming killers. The carnage speaks for itself. While law-enforcement agencies worldwide, using high-powered computers, DNA-analysis and the latest psychological profiling techniques, desperately try to stop the mayhem, the next serial killer is just one step ahead. Unchecked, undetected and addicted to murder, the predator living near you is tracking his next kill.
The hunt is on . . .

1. THE SPOKANE SERIAL KILLER

According to the Spokane Serial Killer Task Force at least ten women have been slain by the same individual operating in the northwestern cities of Spokane and Tacoma. Seven of the bodies have been found in remote areas around Spokane, Washington's second largest city with a population of approximately 190,000. Two other victims were discovered in the suburbs of Tacoma, a bedroom community of Seattle on the south end of the Puget Sound with a population of 176,000. One more Spokane woman is reportedly missing and considered the tenth victim of the suspected killer. Her body has yet to be recovered. All women except one were shot in the head, their bodies dumped in out-of-the-way places in semi-rural areas near well-traveled roads. All but one of the women were white and all led high-risk lifestyles involving prostitution, drugs, or both.

The suspected serial spree was made public in December 1997, following the grisly discovery of four dead East Sprague Avenue prostitutes in two locations outside Spokane. Authorities quickly formed a joint task force with thirteen veteran officers from the Spokane Police Department and the Spokane County Sheriff's Department to investigate the serial killings. Though the inter-agency task force has been using the latest police investigative technology, including DNA-analysis, high-powered computer databasing and a high-tech helicopter with infrared search capabilities, it is no closer to finding the killer than it was more than two years ago when the first victims were discovered.

According to the former task force lead officer, Sheriff Captain Doug Silver, a profile of the killer drafted by FBI agents from Quantico, Virginia, has been next to useless. 'The first thing [the agents] told us after they gave us the profile is not to use it,' Silver said. The profile paints the killer as a white man, between twenty and forty years old, who might be a loner – which describes most of the male residents of the state, including all the investigating officers.

The now-decrepit East Sprague Avenue area is known as the red-light district of Spokane. In the past it used to be the main east–west highway of the city carrying traffic through Spokane to Idaho. Back then it was a solid working-class neighborhood, home to many of Spokane's Italian families. But with the construction of Interstate 90 in the 1970s everything changed. Now East Sprague is the home of Spokane's underworld of prostitutes and junkies. With most of its neighborhood supermarkets, schools and churches closed and abandoned, the area has become the perfect haven for lost souls. An unforgiving four-lane thoroughfare, the avenue is dotted with used-car lots, tattoo parlors, strip clubs, adult bookstores, bars, shabby motels, crack houses, shooting galleries and prostitutes. It has also become the spot of choice from where the suspected serial killer has been plucking his victims.

The first decomposed body was found on 5 November, near the Hangman Valley Golf Course southwest of the city. With the use of dental records the victim was identified as 29-year-old Darla Sue Scott. The next victim, Shawn L. Johnson, 36, was found a month later along another road in Hangman Valley. On 26 December two more victims – Laurie Ann Wasson, 31, and Shawn A. McClenahan, 39 – were discovered in a gravel pit near the Johnson crime scene. All four women died of gunshot wounds to the head. All four lived 'highly mobile lifestyles' and had arrest histories involving drugs and/or prostitution.

On 7 December Melinda Mercer, 24, of Seattle, was found three hundred miles west, in a South Tacoma weed field. She was shot repeatedly in the head, which was found covered with a plastic bag. Because of similarities in lifestyles, methods of death and dumpsites, authorities correlated her murder with the growing victim list in Spokane. Tragically, Tacoma authorities failed to notify Mercer's mother Karyl Greenwood that her daughter was added to the Spokane Serial Killer victim list. 'Nobody has notified me of nothing,' Greenwood told the *Seattle Times*. 'This can't be right, can't be fair that others know about this before I'm notified.' According to Greenwood, Linda moved from Centralia to Seattle in search of a better life, but instead started 'running in a fast world up in Seattle, but she was the most loving girl, the most innocent victim ever. She never deserved this. Nobody deserves to be shot in the head three times.'

Over the next year, three more women in Spokane and one in Tacoma were linked to the unidentified killer. The Spokane victims were: Sunny Oster, 41, who was found on 12 February, hours after the end of a candlelight vigil in honor of the previously slain prostitutes; Linda Marie Maybin, 34, who was found on 1 April in the same gravel pit where the bodies of Wasson and McClenahan were discovered; and Michelyn Derning, 47, whose nude body was found on 10 July, dumped like garbage under a hot tub cover in a vacant lot near an area frequented by prostitutes. Unlike the other victims, Derning was seen alive a week before her body was discovered. The others were found weeks, or sometimes months, after they disappeared.

Like many of the other unfortunate victims, Oster had been trying to turn her life around. She traveled on a friend's recommendation from Auburn to Spokane to enter a drug-rehabilitation program. A mother of two, Oster had a troubled life, starting when she was seventeen when she dropped out of her high school, pregnant. Soon after, an insurmountable struggle with drugs took control of her life leading to her untimely death. 'She's had problems like this most of her life,' her father, Ed Oster, told the *Columbian* newspaper. Oster wrote a letter to her father in early October in which she talked about completing treatment, getting a job and buying a car. The day after she left treatment, she disappeared. 'It plain hurts,' said her father. 'If I had one wish, I wish she was here.'

Linda Maybin was remembered in the East Sprague neighborhood as a friendly and colorful character. Everyone in the area knew her as 'Barefoot Linda' because she refused, even in the dead of winter, to wear any shoes. Though she disappeared on 22 November, authorities found her in April in an area that had been searched in mid-February by a helicopter with infrared sensing equipment. Investigators theorize the killer, in an attempt to draw some attention to himself, moved her body from a previous location to the gravel pit where she was found.

A more horrifying scenario was posited by former Los Angeles detective Mark Furhman who believes Ms Maybin was kept alive by the killer for his own pleasure. Furhman, who says he will solve the serial killer case and write a book about the investigation, is known for his racist-laden testimony during the O.J. Simpson trial. After leaving the LAPD he relocated to nearby Idaho where he works as an electrician. He was invited by a Spokane radio station to host a talk show. Furhman's arrival in Spokane has been received tepidly by local law enforcement who wish he would keep his high-profile self away from their case. 'Furhman is not part of the official investigation,' Spokane police spokesman Dick Cottam reiterated.

Connie Lynn LaFontaine, the second and last known victim found in Tacoma, was discovered on 10 October 1998. The 35-year-old was shot in the head and dumped in a Tacoma suburb called Parkland, four miles from where Melinda Mercer was discovered. In January 1999, LaFontaine was officially added to the victim list. 'She fit the parameters,' said Spokane sheriff's office spokesman Dave Reagan. Like the others, she had a drug problem, was shot in the head, and dumped in a rural area easily accessible from a main road. One last woman, Melody Ann Murfin, is considered to be the killer's tenth victim. Though her body has not been found, authorities believe circumstantial evidence surrounding her disappearance indicates that she was murdered by the suspected killer. Like the others, the 43-year-old Spokane woman had a history of drug arrests. She was reported missing on 4 June 1998.

According to Lynn Everson, a Spokane Regional Health District AIDS outreach worker, street women in Spokane have known for a while about a predator in their midst. 'They're feeling incredibly at risk,' Everson told ABC News. 'They're trying to work in pairs because this is so scary. This [situation] is more frightening than anything else they have ever encountered.' Every Wednesday night Everson visits the ravished East Sprague area in a 28-foot health-district motor home offering condoms, food and a friendly ear to prostitutes and other street women. The motor home, Gloria, was named in honor of the famed feminist writer Gloria Steinem. It is the second mobile home used by Everson and the health district. The first one, recalls Everson, was Eleanor, named after Eleanor Roosevelt, 'because she was big, homely, and got the job done'.

Since the killings started, 'any woman who could get out did,' says Everson. But others still have to work. 'The women who are still here are often the ones who have few choices. They have children, they have an addiction.' Many of the new women on the street are very young and harder to access. 'They are out there because of the welfare cuts . . . They have lost most of what they have.' Some of the prostitutes just try to see their regular johns. But still, Everson adds: 'Prostitution isn't a job, it's done out of necessity.'

In a recent study of 475 prostitutes in five countries, psychiatrists Melissa Farley and Norma Hotaling found that most street women suffer from Post Traumatic Stress Disorder at a level comparable to treatment-seeking American Vietnam veterans. An accumulation of factors, starting with repeated sexual abuse as children and violent sexual assaults as adults, make street women the most physically and psychologically vulnerable sector of any urban population. Eighty percent of the prostitutes interviewed by Farley and Hotaling had been physically assaulted since entering prostitution and 77 percent have been raped while working. The study, conducted for Kaiser Permanente in San Francisco, showed that all prostitutes interviewed suffered from acute psychological damage, not unlike torture victims and war veterans.

'These girls, they all had a life. They have family. They have friends out here. They ain't no less than none of us,' Brandi Mitchell, a former prostitute, told ABC News.

Echoing her sentiments, Kevin Bartlett, one of the organizers of a January 1999 memorial service for the victims, told a crowd of two hundred people: 'Let's remember them as human beings, not garbage.'

In an attempt to help the women break their cycle of misery, the Coalition for Women on the Street – a group of social service providers – raised $3,000,000 to build a shelter for street women regardless of their chemical dependency, mental health and means of income. The facility, the Downtown Women's Shelter, was opened on 7 June 1999. It sleeps more than 30 women; twelve in the shelter regardless of their profession, addiction or mental health; eighteen more who live in apartments attached to the shelter meant for those women who are trying to break out of the cycle of prostitution and drugs.

Known by prostitutes as 'The Condom Lady', Everson is the closest link between the authorities and the women being murdered. Having been involved in the health district for over a decade, Everson sadly recalls several of the slain prostitutes she knew. 'Most women think it's a sick trick,' she says about the possible serial killer. 'There are people out there with guns, knives, tire irons, handsaws, handcuffs.' Everson has been compiling a list of 'bad tricks' which she updates weekly and gives to prostitutes and police. The list, now three pages long, has descriptions of more than one hundred dangerous men and their vehicles. 'Ninety-five percent of the people on the list are white males with trucks.' With 'Do Not Get Into These Cars' on top of each page, the list describes the cars, drivers, and their particular fetish: 'Strangles', 'Talked about killing', 'Robs and rapes', 'Very, very violent'. One entry mentions a man in a yellow car who holds a hacksaw to the window as he drives by the prostitutes. Another is a white male in a blue, flatbed truck who preaches and listens to religious music as he 'tries to choke you and send you to your maker'.

Fortunately, Everson says, the task force moved quickly to establish a rapport with the targeted women. Two homicide detectives have been walking the streets of East Sprague giving the women a certain sense of security. The officers have developed 'real trusting' relationships with the prostitutes, even though, by and large, both parties stand on opposite sides of the law. Everson emphasized how helpful, respectful, caring and non-judgmental the officers have been towards the street women. Several women refer to the detectives as 'their angels'. Everson estimates there are between fifty and one hundred prostitutes working the streets in Spokane, with most congregating around the run-down East Sprague Avenue area.

However, it is hard for her to gauge how many girls are still working, or if any have disappeared. Many prostitutes follow a circuit imposed by their pimps in which they travel from Spokane to Seattle, Portland, Salt Lake City, Phoenix and back to Spokane. 'The majority of them are dead,' said a former crack addict, who did not want to be identified, in an interview for *Newsday*. 'There's still a few out there, but they're new and scared. They're not leaving town; their drug habits won't allow it.' The former drug user, who says she knew many of the victims, thinks that 'whoever's doing this is doing it through drugs. The girls knew the killer and felt safe; that's how he got close to them.'

Following a one-year lull in the slayings detectives doubt that the killer has been inactive. Instead, they believe he's continued killing undetected elsewhere in the state by changing his habits or is becoming better at hiding his victims. 'We haven't had any really [solid leads] since December 1997. That concerns me,' Sheriff Silver told the *Seattle Times*. 'I'm worried the killer has changed his habits, or his location. It's bad to have a serial killer. It's worse to have one that moves around.' Health worker Lynn Everson believes the suspect is presently in jail on an unrelated offense. Once he is released, she believes the killings will start again.

Investigators say they have been trying to refocus their efforts to detect and extract useful information from the massive amount of data accumulated. Mark Sterk, who became the lead officer of the task force in January 1999, has said that he wants detectives to concentrate on finding potential links between the victims and their killer, whose name, he believes, is probably somewhere in police arrest records. Sterk, a Republican state representative and sheriff's deputy, brought to question the task force's previous approach and called for changes in the way the investigation was being managed. 'One thing I have heard is it has been kind of a shotgun approach. We're going to narrow it down a bit,'

Sterk said, advocating a more focused investigation into police records.

'Right now if a person has called us with info that would point us in the right direction, we haven't recognized that,' said Sergeant Cal Walker of the Spokane Sheriff's Department. The task force has been compiling and comparing lists of friends for each of the victims, looking for any similarities or patterns.

'I'm not sure if [the killer] is from Spokane, but I am convinced we have had contact with him,' Sterk said. 'Either the sheriff's office, Washington State Patrol or Spokane Police have had contact with this guy and he is in our database.'

In what could be a promising lead, detectives uncovered that Linda Maybin, the sixth victim, provided the address on a Department of Corrections form of the owner of a local escort service as her own. The escort service, Christine's Escorts (named after John Carpenter's killer car picture), has connections with two other victims. Furthermore, according to drug counselor Theresa Schinzel, Maybin told her at a Narcotics Anonymous meeting that she knew two of the slain prostitutes and feared that she would be next. 'She knew two of the women who had just been found,' Ms Schinzel said. 'She paced back and forth and kept saying, "That's it. I have had it. I'm not going out there again!"' Sadly, she did, and within a month, she disappeared.

Wendell L. Bonton, the man whose address Maybin used in the Department of Corrections document, took over Christine's Escorts in 1996 after its original owner, John R. 'Rick' Koesterman, was arrested for selling crack cocaine. In 1995 Darla Sue Scott, the first victim found, allegedly lived with Koesterman for an extended period of time. Court records also linked victim number four, Shawn A. McClenahan – who worked as a police informant – to Koesterman. McClenahan allegedly bought crack cocaine from Koesterman, and with the information she provided authorities, Koesterman was convicted of five felonies, including possession of crack cocaine and forgery. After pleading guilty in two of the five charges against him, Koesterman, 38, fled the Spokane area. Presently authorities have a bench warrant for his arrest but haven't been able to locate him.

Other than the Koesterman connection – which is at best tenuous considering that most women in this line of work would have contact with an escort service – the task force has no other credible leads. Task force members are looking for connections with a northern Idaho man who was arrested for abducting an exotic dancer at gunpoint and assaulting her. In custody the man admitted that he bludgeoned his mother with a baseball bat. As of this writing no links between the man and the Spokane killings have been made public. In January 2000, the task force also talked to detectives in Michigan about two admitted prostitute killers in their state. The suspects, who are nineteen and 27, are believed to be responsible for two murders in Michigan and two more in Toledo, Ohio. All victims were prostitutes and were found outside urban areas in shallow graves. Although there are no known links between these four murders and the Spokane serial killings, detectives are hoping that by comparing information they might shed new light on their case.

The task force has also been in contact with authorities in nearby Lewiston, North Dakota, where a long-time rampage killer suspect was mentioned in relation to the Spokane killings. Law-enforcement personnel in Lewiston believe a series of five killings from the late '70s and early '80s were perpetrated by the same individual who they have identified but cannot charge with the crimes for lack of evidence. The killings of Kristina Nelson, 21, and Jacqueline Miller, eighteen, and the disappearance of 35-year-old Steven Pearsall – who vanished on the same night in September 1982 – were reopened when authorities linked the suspect to evidence possibly connecting him to the Spokane slayings. Authorities believe the murders of twelve-year-old Christina White from Asotin, Washington, who disappeared in 1979, and 22-year-old Kristen David, of Lewiston, who disappeared in 1981, were also perpetrated by the same person responsible for the 1982 triple killing. However, the trip to North Dakota was described as a 'fishing expedition' by investigators who, at best, hoped that the suspect would confess to the five Lewiston murders.

At a meeting of nearly twenty Puget Sound-area police agencies at the King County Regional Justice Center in Kent,

Sheriff Silver raised the frightful possibility that the Spokane serial killer might have moved to, or at least frequents, the Seattle–Tacoma area. 'There is the possibility that our serial killer is moving,' said Sheriff Silver. 'Movement by a serial killer is a very normal process.' One theory being investigated is that the killer might have a legitimate reason, like work or a family connection, that enables him to bounce back and forth between Spokane and Washington. If detectives can uncover that reason they believe they have a better chance of cracking open the case.

Vernon Geberth, a retired New York City police homicide commander, told the *Spokesman-Review* that he suspects the killer is a street person with a criminal record who is able to quickly gain his victims' confidence. He believes the killer knows the victims, either as a pimp, customer or junkie, and that he is part of the environment, explaining why he can operate in virtual anonymity.

Former Baltimore homicide detective and FBI profiler Patricia Kirby said she thinks the killer is a seemingly harmless individual playing out his calculated and ritualistic homicidal fantasies. Both former investigators agree that although the killer travels to Tacoma, he probably still lives in Spokane. 'He's got a connection in Tacoma that has nothing to do with the murders: family, children, maybe work. The urge to kill and the situation that is the catalyst for that, is not something he can control,' Kirby said. 'When something triggers it, he can't wait until he gets back to Spokane to kill again.'

Kirby believes the killer is an ordinary-looking individual because his victims – street-smart prostitutes – seem to have let down their guard when they have come in contact with him. The lure of drugs may also account for the victim's willingness to leave with him. Another telling sign about the killer is the way the bodies are discarded. The fact that he's dumping them in fields near neighborhoods and that he is reusing previous crime scenes shows that he wants his victims found. According to Kirby, the killer dumps his victims like 'nothing more than garbage', demonstrating his profound hatred towards women. Because several of the women were found shoeless, authorities believe the killer might have taken them indoors, perhaps to his home, where they probably shared drugs before he murdered them. Another theory posits that the killer works, in some capacity, with the local methadone clinic. Several of the victims were presently in treatment or had passed through the methadone program sometime before they disappeared.

The former New York police officer and now psychic investigator Reily G announced he too was willing to help identify the Spokane Killer. Offended by the lack of response from the task force to his psychic profile, he posted his findings on a website. In the profile Reily G says the killer is around 33 to 36 years of age, male, of average height, with reddish to light brown hair. His first name is Richard (Rich) or John but he may go by a nickname; he works in a construction-related field, drives a pick-up truck and a small blue or light-colored car, has some sort of police record, and may frequent and know the prostitutes he has murdered. The psychic also theorizes that the suspect has removed fingers or a hand from some of the victims. He feels the killer's mother was murdered by his father, and might be reliving her murder each time he kills. Finally he believes the serial rampage was triggered by a separation or divorce, and with each murder the suspect is acting out his fantasy of killing his ex-wife.

Investigators are looking into possible links with eighteen other unsolved killings of area women since 1984 – the year the Green River killings in nearby Seattle came to an unexpected halt. Based on FBI analysis of the crimes, authorities said they were very confident 'that our individual, or individuals, is in no way connected to the Green River Killer'. Investigators have consulted with King County's Green River Task Force, though officially they were just looking for tips on how to handle their investigation.

Authorities admit that 1984 was set as an arbitrary trace date to start their investigation because most prostitute slayings in the area previous to 1984 have been attributed to the Green River Killer. Other unsolved killings of area women who did not fit the prostitute-and-drug pattern were, moreover, not considered or investigated. If one factors in the other seemingly unrelated cases, however, the number of unsolved murders of Spokane women since 1984 is closer to 35.

The first victim attributed to this current serial rampage was the fifth Spokane-area prostitute to be slain in 1997. Seven more women, believed to have been prostitutes, were murdered around Spokane from February 1990 to June 1996. Though none of the cases have been solved, detectives have seen no compelling evidence linking the slayings to each other, or to the emerging new cluster of killings. The other four slayings in 1997 were as follows: Margaret M. Anselmo, 45, a floral designer whose body was found on 3 January in a downtown Spokane alley; Heather L. Hernandez, twenty, and Jennifer A. Joseph, sixteen, who were both found separately shot to death on 26 August; and Teresalyn Marie Asmussen, 22, of Spokane, who was found on 17 October, bludgeoned to death in the Spokane River near downtown. All women had histories of prostitution and drug arrests. All but Asmussen were shot to death. The cases of Hernandez and Joseph, investigators noted, were strikingly similar to the slayings of five other women killed since 1990.

A second distinct serial pattern of three linked murders in 1990 indicates perhaps that the Spokane area had another serial killer, or that the current serial killer spent time in jail between 1990 and 1997. One of the detectives who investigated the 1990 slayings said authorities at the time believed a serial killer was at large. The three 1990 victims were killed with a .22-caliber handgun and dumped along the Spokane River. The killer was never identified and the cases remain open. The first of the three victims was Yolanda Sapp, a 26-year-old heroin addict who was found on 22 February, shot to death, dumped along the river bank in the eastern part of Spokane. A month later, the body of Nickie Lowe, a 34-year-old heroin addict, was discovered about two miles away. Then, two months later, on 15 May, the body of Kathy Brisbois, a 38-year-old heroin addict and prostitute, was found on the banks of the river, also shot to death. Larry Erickson, who was a Spokane County sheriff officer at the time, thinks the 1990 killings and the recent cases are probably linked. 'I think these two strings could very well be connected,' said Erickson, who now lives in Olympia and is executive director of the Washington Association of Sheriffs and Police Chiefs. 'My best guess is the person was in jail for a time, and is now back out there killing women.'

Investigators found tiny traces of greenish carpet fiber on the bodies of Sapp, Lowe and Brisbois. Lab tests led detectives to the manufacturer of a glue-down carpet, which is commonly used in SeaRay recreational boats. Police staked a boat dealership selling SeaRay boats along Spokane's East Sprague Avenue knowing that prostitutes working nearby were servicing tricks in the boats parked on streets and the adjoining lots. 'The police talked to us about that back then and asked us not to say anything about it,' recalled Bill Trudeau, the owner of the dealership. 'They even questioned my customers who had boats with that color of carpeting.' After sorting through the names of five hundred possible suspects, police identified a car salesman who worked nearby as a suspect. The man, who frequently hired prostitutes, was eventually released and taken off the suspect list. The boat dealership was also taken off surveillance and the owner installed a high fence around his lot and started keeping his boats locked at night.

The earliest cases being reviewed are: Debbi Finnern, 30, found on 22 June 1984, in East Spokane, stabbed to death; Ruby Jean Doss, 27, found on 30 January 1986, strangled and bludgeoned to death; and Mary Ann Turner, 30, found strangled on 4 November 1986. One more victim, Cindy C. Butler, 26, was found west of Spokane in October 1984. Because Butler was visiting from Texas at the time she was murdered, she has not been officially included in the Spokane victim list. However, some crime analysts list her as a possible victim of the Green River Killer.

On 26 September 1998, police released a sketch of a suspect and received about 150 new tips within a 24-hour period. The sketch was produced in 1995 by detectives investigating the unsolved murder of a woman who disappeared from downtown Seattle and whose body was found in Kitsap County. Detectives have been distributing copies of the sketch in Spokane's East Sprague, hoping that someone might recognize the suspect. The man is believed to be white, in his mid to late 30s, about six feet tall with strawberry-blond hair. The Kitsap County victim was identified as Patricia Barnes, 60, a transient who was last seen alive in Seattle on 22 August 1995. She was known as the 'Towel Lady' because she often wore a bandanna or towel on her head. Her body was found three days after her disappearance in a ditch in a remote area near Port Orchard. Like the victims in the Spokane area, she was shot in the head. No one was ever arrested for her killing. Authorities have not released why they believe the Barnes murder is connected to the current Spokane slayings. Victim-wise Barnes is very different from the Spokane women; she is much older than the other victims and was an alcoholic rather than a drug addict.

In December 1999, Spokane's acting Police Chief Roger Bragdon announced that he was pulling five police detectives from the task force and returning them to their regular assignments because of budget constraints. The move resulted from the statewide measure Initiative 695 that set the motor vehicle excise tax to a flat $30 fee. 'There are ten women dead, and there's still a lot of work to do,' Bragdon told the *Seattle Times*. 'But [the department] can't absorb that kind of hit.' The decision disappointed Spokane County sheriff's officials, who are leading the serial killer investigation.

'It's a concern to us, a major concern,' Sheriff Silver said. 'It was understood right up front that this was going to be a three- to five-year investigation. This decision will slow that up. I'll tell you this, though: I still believe we're going to catch this killer.' Investigators realize that the depleting of the task force can only be good news for the killer if, indeed, he remains in Spokane.

'Well, I'm sure that it hasn't brought a lot of fear into his heart, knowing that the task force has been cut back,' said Captain John Simmons of the Sheriff's Department.

Trying to solicit help from the public, officers held a public forum on 28 February 2000, to discuss the progress, or lack thereof, of their case. 'We're going to put up pictures of the victims, with the dates the bodies were found and the timespan between,' Sheriff Mark Sterk announced. 'We hope somebody out there is going to look at that and say, "That's a pattern." '

At the meeting Sheriff Sterk announced investigators had DNA evidence of the killer. 'There are some unique identifiers we have in terms of evidence. When we come across the right person, we're going to solve this case,' Sterk said. 'Unlike the Green River case . . . we have good physical evidence.'

'We do feel the suspect is in our databases,' Sterk explained to the 100 people attending the forum. 'This guy has killed upwards of eighteen women – he's left this community before, I am convinced of it – and he's come back,' he added, alluding to the fourteen-month break since the last victim was discovered. So far investigators have received 6,000 tips, 2,000 of which have been examined. The task force has also collected 1,000 pieces of evidence. Though the Task Force was drastically downsized because of departmental funding cuts, Police Chief Roger Bragdon said: 'It's a priority we can't fund. We're embarrassed we can't do that.'

Charles Mandigo, head of the FBI operations in Washington State, announced the bureau had officially become involved in the investigation, adding that they will be looking at all possible suspects, including those involved in law enforcement. Federal agents, it was revealed, have already conducted interviews with suspects in Idaho, Montana and South Dakota. They have also interviewed a possible witness in Tennessee, checked the military records of a potential suspect in Missouri and looked into a similar series of unsolved killings in Germany.

ROBERT LEE YATES TIMELINE
18 April 2000 – At 6:23 a.m. Spokane County sheriff's deputies arrested Robert Lee Yates for the 1997 murder of Jennifer Joseph, a sixteen-year-old Spokane prostitute. Detectives said they were in the process of obtaining a search warrant to draw blood from Yates and compare it to DNA samples of the Spokane serial killer. Spokane Sheriff's spokesman Reagan said: 'We are very optimistic. This is really our first big break in our investigation.'

20 April 2000 – The three-year investigation into the serial murders of up to eighteen Spokane, Tacoma and Kitsap

County area prostitutes seems to have come to an end with the arrest of 47-year-old Robert Yates, a balding husband of 24 years, father of five, aluminum worker and Desert Storm veteran. Yates was charged with the 1997 murder of Jennifer Joseph and is suspected of being responsible for up to seventeen more deaths. An army veteran of nearly twenty years, Yates was stationed in New York, Massachusetts and Alabama, as well as Germany and Somalia, before retiring and moving to Spokane. In 1997 he joined the National Guard where he served as a helicopter pilot. As a guardsman he spent one weekend a month training at Fort Lewis south of Tacoma. 'He came to us very, very qualified. In the three years he was assigned to us, he was a good performer. He did an excellent job,' said a spokesman of the National Guard.

Like in so many serial killer cases, friends and neighbors of Yates were shocked by the suspect's newfound infamy. 'Bob Yates, he was a great guy. He really was,' said Gary Berner, an Oak Harbor dentist who's been his friend since high school. Neighbors said he frequently played catch on his front lawn with his eleven-year-old son. He also enjoyed washing and tinkering with his cherished white 1977 Corvette.

The affidavit of Joseph's murder states that the young prostitute was last seen in Spokane's East Sprague neighborhood, getting into a white Corvette driven by a white man thought to be between 30 and 40 years old. Five weeks after her disappearance Yates was stopped in his Corvette near East Sprague. A year later, after he had sold the Corvette, Yates was stopped in another car after picking up a prostitute. At the time he said he was just giving the woman a ride. In September 1999, that same woman told detectives Yates had agreed to pay her $20 for oral sex the night they were stopped. Acting on the evidence they had collected, two task force officers interviewed him. According to sheriff Captain John Simmons, Yates 'was just one of many, many names that had apparent potential'. After the interview both detectives remarked that he sweated a little too much. Otherwise, they didn't think much of him as a suspect.

In January 2000 police tracked the new owners of the Corvette and obtained permission to search the car. In it they found a mother-of-pearl cuff button missing from Joseph's jacket, as well as carpet fibres matching those found on her shoes and a blood stain on the seat-belt buckle matching her parent's DNA. 'The white 'Vette was really the link to Mr Yates,' Sheriff Sterk said.

21 April 2000 – Authorities announced the identities of nine women believed to have been shot to death by Robert L. Yates Jr between 1997 and 1998. The victims are Darla Scott, Melinda Mercer, Shawn Johnson, Laurie Wasson, Shawn McClenahan, Sunny Oster, Linda Maybin, Michelyn Derning and Jennifer Joseph. Police said they linked Yates to six of the cases by DNA evidence and to three others by physical evidence that has not yet been disclosed.

Investigators sealed off eight square blocks around Yates's home and took over everything inside the house. Authorities have combed through every inch of the property using a 'total station mapping' system that utilizes lasers and the Global Positioning System (GPS) to create an accurate 3-D map of the crime scene.

Yates's family, for obvious reasons, was moved to an undisclosed location where police had to buy them new clothing. Authorities have also impounded and searched seven of his vehicles – three Hondas, a Ford pickup truck, two vans and the white 'Vette – two of which he no longer owned. Five of his alleged victims were dumped within a mile and a half radius of the house. In an attempt to leave no stone unturned, the task force set up two hot lines to obtain information about the hardware and grocery stores Yates patronized, as well as clues about his lifestyle, hobbies and activities, and whether he had a storage locker or rented garage.

25 April 2000 – German police said they were investigating whether Yates was involved in any crimes while he was stationed in Germany. 'It is possible the former US soldier could be linked to unsolved murders in Germany, although we have nothing concrete as yet,' a police spokesman said. Police in Watertown, New York, where Yates was stationed after returning from Germany, are also looking for links between an unsolved prostitute murder there and the suspect.

26 April 2000 – Spokane County Sheriff Mark Sterk asked county commissioners for more money to continue the investigation into Robert Lee Yates. Sterk requested additional storage space for the nine vehicles Yates owned or had previously owned. He also requested funds to pay for the vehicles confiscated from new owners.

30 April 2000 – The Spokane task force investigating serial killer suspect Robert Yates have uprooted a twelve-foot blue spruce tree next to his home. Spokane County Sheriff's Office spokesman Captain David Reagan said they also sifted soil from another site where neighbors said Yates removed a hedgerow and filled in the area with new soil. Yates said he replanted the tree after it was knocked over by a drunken driver.

12 May 2000 – The FBI sent a genetic profile and other identifying material of Robert Lee Yates to Germany, where authorities are investigating the deaths of nearly two dozen women. Yates, the suspected Spokane serial killer, served two tours of duty in Germany as a helicopter pilot in the US Army. He was at a base in Hanau from August 1980 to February 1984, the Pentagon said. He returned to Germany in May 1988 and was stationed at a base near Goeppingen until 1991. German authorities are particularly interested in any evidence found in a 1988 Chevrolet van that Yates had shipped to Germany.

17 May 2000 – Investigators revealed they have found a woman who survived an attack by Robert Lee Yates. 'That was a surprise and it was a stroke of good luck,' Spokane County Sheriff's Office spokesman Dave Reagan said. 'This has been a case of miracles.'

18 May 2000 – The surviving victim of suspected serial killer Robert Yates was identified as 32-year-old Christine L. Smith. She is believed to have been shot at by Yates in August 1998.

Smith said Yates allegedly picked her up in a black van near East Sprague and drove her behind a clinic, where she agreed to perform oral sex on him on a mattress in the back of the van. On the way there she asked him if he was the 'psycho killer' who was killing prostitutes, to which he answered no, adding that he had five kids and wasn't into that type of thing. Then he allegedly shot her in the head when he was unable to become aroused and asked for his $40 back. Unaware that she had been shot, Smith noticed she was bleeding from the back of her head, and climbed out of the van. She then ran to a rehabilitation center and was taken to a hospital where doctors closed the wound with three stitches. Shortly after, she reported the incident to police.

A year later, after Smith was in an automobile accident, an X-ray revealed bullet fragments in her head. On 18 May, Smith recognized Yates as her attacker from a mugshot published in the *Spokesman-Review*. Since the emergence of Smith as a potential witness, detectives have searched a van formerly owned by Yates that matches the one described by her, and found it contained blood stains inside. A .25-caliber casing was found on the floor and a spent bullet was discovered in the roof track above the windshield. Tests on the casing and bullet are pending. Smith has agreed to remove the bullet fragments from her head to see if they match any of the bullets recovered from the other victims.

18 May 2000 – On the day of his 48th birthday, suspected Spokane serial killer Robert L. Yates Jr was charged with eight counts of aggravated first-degree murder, one count of attempted murder and one count of robbery. The indictment upgraded the previous first degree murder charge in the case of sixteen-year-old Jennifer Joseph to aggravated murder. The other aggravated murder charges are for the deaths of Darla Sue Scott, Shawn L. Johnson, Laurel A. Wasson, Shawn A. McClenahan, Sunny G. Oster, Linda Maybin and Michelyn Derning. The attempted murder and robbery charges are for the August 1998 attack on Christine L. Smith.

Prosecutor Steve Tucker and Sheriff Mark Sterk revealed that Yates left plastic bags over most of the victims' heads. The bags became the 'signature' which alerted investigators to the fact that the rash of prostitute murders in Spokane and Tacoma were the work of the same individual. Tucker and Sterk added that, since his arrest, DNA and other physical evidence has linked Yates to the crimes.

23 May 2000 – Detectives in Spokane wrapped up their investigation into the home of alleged Spokane serial killer Robert Lee Yates Jr and returned family possessions that were taken from the house. Since his arrest more than a month ago the house has been surrounded by a blue tarp while investigators searched every inch of the property. The search yielded evidence in the yard matching clippings and detritus found near the dump sites of three of his alleged victims. Having already been charged with eight murders, Spokane authorities are preparing two more cases – the deaths of Heather Hernandez and Shannon Zelinski.

24 May 2000 – Investigators from Vancouver contacted Spokane authorities to determine if suspected serial killer Robert Lee Yates could be involved in the disappearance of 29 Vancouver sex-trade workers. In fact more than 30 juristictions have contacted the Spokane Sheriff's Department for information on Yates and his whereabouts as a military careerist before setting in Spokane.

28 May 2000 – Pointing at a new trend of profiting from high-visibility murder cases, Spokane's Superior Court announced that they will sell copies of Robert Lee Yates's 462-page indictment at a dollar a page. According to Gary Berg, chief deputy court clerk, four news outlets have already bought the whole stack of court documents. With $1,848 in their coffers, perhaps the county will now auction off pieces of evidence on EBay to the highest bidder.

7 June 2000 – Investigators are still waiting to search Robert Yates's locker at the military base in Ft Lewis. The Pentagon apparently did not accept the search warrant presented by Spokane detectives and ordered the locker to be shut with a safety wire until they received a federal warrant. Not wanting to risk any tainting of evidence, detectives have decided to wait until a federal search warrant allows them to open the locker. 'It's secure. It's locked up. But it's safe and it's documented that no one can get in there for now,' said Sheriff Mark Sterk. 'Hopefully we'll get inside very soon.'

17 June 2000 – Following the arrest of serial killer suspect Robert Lee Yates, the Downtown Women's Shelter in Spokane has been forced to close its doors. The 21-bed shelter, which opened a year ago when local prostitutes were being hunted by an unidentified predator, was unique in that it accepted the women who fit the killer's victim profile: alcoholic and drug-addicted prostitutes. Even though the suspected killer has been arrested, these women still need a safe place to sleep. A greedy landlord – who for reasons unknown doubled the rent – and community apathy led to the center shutting its doors. Hopefully, Lynn Everson, president of the Coalition for Women on the Street, will obtain funds to reopen the shelter.

12 July 2000 – Spokane County sheriff's detectives searched the two lockers used by serial killer suspect Robert Lee Yates Jr when he performed helicopter flights at Fort Lewis near Tacoma. Investigators did not say what evidence, if any, was found. Richard Fasy, Yates's attorney, said the search was expedited with Yates's consent. 'It's my expectation that nothing of evidentiary value was found in the lockers,' Fasy said.

19 July 2000 – Pierce County prosecutors charged Robert Lee Yates with two counts of aggravated first-degree murder in the December 1997 slaying of Melinda Mercer and the September 1998 killing of Connie LaFontaine Ellis, bringing the total of murder counts against him up to ten. In charging papers filed in Pierce County, prosecutors said Mercer, 24, was shot in the head twice. Her nude body was found in Tacoma with four plastic grocery bags tied over her head – the serial killer's 'signature'. Furthermore, DNA from semen found on Mercer's body matched DNA from a blood sample provided by Yates.

Like Mercer, Ellis was shot in the head and had plastic grocery bags tied over her head and her blood was found inside a van owned by Yates. Because of the decomposition of her body, no DNA analysis could be performed on her remains. In both cases, forensic scientists were able to recover bullet fragments and match them to a .25 caliber Raven model semi-automatic pistol. Court documents showed Yates owned two pistols of that caliber and model.

20 July 2000 – The Rotary Club 21 of Spokane donated $1,000 to the family of serial killer suspect Robert L. Yates. Donations for the family totaling nearly $7,000 have trickled in since his 18 April arrest. The family, which was forced out of their home in an upper-middle-class neighborhood on Spokane's South Hill, has had to deal with several unanticipated expenses, while having no means of making an income. One has to wonder where these generous souls were when Yates was hunting down street women with impunity and investigators were running out of funds.

18 October 2000 – In a deal that would spare him the death penalty Spokane serial killer Robert Yates pleaded guilty to thirteen murders – including three that were previously not linked to him – and directed investigators to a body buried outside his bedroom window. According to the agreement, prosecutors would not consider the death penalty only if the body found in the yard was that of Melody Murfin, 43, a suspected victim who had been missing for over two years. However, even if the Spokane agreement is honored, Pierce County Prosecutor John Ladenburg said he intends to pursue aggravated first-degree murder charges in the two Tacoma killings which are not included in the Spokane charges.

Yates pleaded guilty to the seven Spokane slayings he was charged with and three slayings in which he was the primary suspect. Furthermore, he pleaded guilty to the 1975 slaying of a young couple in Walla Walla County and the 1998 murder of a woman in Skagit County. The young couple – Patrick Oliver, 21, and Susan Savage, 22 – crossed paths with Yates, who was 23 years old at the time, while they were picnicking on Mill Creek, just east of Walla Walla. Back then, the soon-to-be serial killer worked as a guard at the Washington State Penitentiary in Walla Walla. He said he was hunting when he saw the college graduates and decided to kill them. The 1988 murder he confessed to is believed to have been the first prostitute killing of his serial killing career. Yates told investigators he killed 23-year-old Stacy Elizabeth Hawn, who was last seen alive in Seattle on 7 July 1988. Her skeletal remains were found five months later in Skagit County.

Spokane County prosecutor Steve Tucker said he agonized over the plea agreement, but felt he didn't have enough evidence to prove the aggravating circumstances he needed to convince a jury to impose the death penalty. Under state law, if the prosecution wanted to go for the death penalty they would have had to prove that the victims were killed to cover up a robbery, which was not the case in the Yates slayings. Strangely, Tucker said he agreed to the plea to give peace to the victims' families. However, all but one of the victims' families would have preferred to see Yates on death row. Perhaps the decision was grounded more on the fact that the victims were prostitutes and Yates is a white, middle-class family man.

23 October 2000 – Police agencies around the state of Washington are trying to determine if confessed serial killer Robert L. Yates Jr is responsible for more deaths than the fifteen already attributed to him. 'We're not convinced we have all the victims,' said State Attorney General Christine Gregoire. Investigators from Washington, Oregon and British Columbia met recently to discuss two large gaps – from 1975 to 1988 and from 1988 to 1996 – in Yates's murderous timeline.

In Island County near where he grew up, Yates is a suspect in the 1977 unsolved slaying of nineteen-year-old Tracy Hesslegrave on Whidbey Island. 'He grew up in this area, knew the area, and was seen frequenting the area during this time period,' said Island County Sheriff Mike Hawley. Snohomish County detectives suspect Yates could also be connected to the 1987 deaths of a British Columbia couple, Sheriff Rick Bart said. Tanya Van Cuylenborg, eighteen, was found on 24 November 1987, shot to death and dumped in a wooded area near Burlington in Skagit County. The body of her boyfriend, Jay Roland Cook, 20, was discovered two days later, about two miles south of Monroe. Yates admitted dumping one of his victims' bodies in Skagit County, just months after the Cook-Van Cuylenborg murders. Yates is also being investigated in the death of Patricia Barnes, whose body was found in Kitsap County in 1995.

The special task force that caught Yates will continue to investigate the 1990 shooting deaths of Yolanda Sapp, Nickie Lowe and Kathy Brisbois and the 1992 shooting death of Sherry Palmer. Sapp, Lowe and Brisbois were all heroin-addicted prostitutes whose bodies were left along the Spokane River. They were all shot and dumped from a car. Yates, who at the time was stationed in Germany, is believed to have returned to Spokane on a regular basis. The bodies of Sapp, Lowe and Brisbois did not bear Yates's signature: plastic bags pulled over their heads. However, the bodies of Palmer and Barnes were found with plastic grocery bags over their heads.

25 October 2000 – Spokane County Prosecutor Steve Tucker said DNA testing has failed to match two blood stains found in his truck to any of the victims Yates confessed to killing. Tucker added that a lie detector test taken by Yates suggested he was not lying when he said there were no more victims.

26 October 2000 – Spokane serial killer Robert Yates was sentenced to 408 years in prison after striking a plea bargain and confessing to thirteen killings. 'I pray that God will right the wrongs that I have committed and that justice will bring closure,' the repentant prostitute-killer told a small courtroom packed with sobbing relatives of his victims. Spokane County Superior Judge Richard Schroeder also fined Yates $60,000, and signed him over to the custody of the Pierce County sheriff.

Several family members of the victims confronted Yates during the sentencing hearing. 'Do you have any idea what it's like to go to a cemetery for a family reunion for 25 years?' said Chris Oliver, brother of victim Patrick Oliver killed in Walla Walla in 1975. 'He has disgraced and dishonored every uniform he ever wore,' said John Joseph, father of victim Jennifer Joseph.

1 November 2000 – Though having admitted to thirteen murders in Spokane, Walla Walla and Skagit counties, Robert Lee Yates pleaded innocent to two murder charges in Pierce County Superior Court in Tacoma. Explaining his innocent plea is the fact that Pierce County prosecutors rejected the plea bargain that spared him the death penalty for thirteen killings. If found guilty of the murders of Melinda Mercer and Connie Ellis, the former helicopter army pilot could be sentenced to death. Pierce County Superior Court Judge John McCarthy, who will preside over Yates's Tacoma Trial, ordered Yates held without bail in the Pierce County Jail pending a pretrial hearing on 16 November.

11 November 2000 – The wife of serial killer Robert L. Yates Jr said she asked her husband why he killed all those women. 'I said, "Do you know why you killed these women?" ' Linda Yates recalled saying in an interview aired on NBC. 'How you could have done this, and still be married to me?' Yates did not answer. However, in court, his lawyer tried to blame his mania on a neighbor who sexually molested him as a young boy.

During her 'Dateline' interview Linda also talked about what can now be seen as tell-tale signs of her husband's extracurricular activities. 'Especially when he said he was going hunting, and he was dressed up nice, and had cologne on,' she said. 'You don't go out hunting with cologne on.' She added that she confronted her husband about having extramarital affairs. 'He always had answers to everything,' she said. 'Already prepared in his mind, I think.'

26 November 2000 – The Spokane serial killer task force asked to use the Army Guard's helicopters to check out 70 sites recorded in a Global Positioning System device owned by confessed killer Robert Yates. The sites were logged on to a Magellan 2000 GPS computer device that was found by detectives during a search of Yates's South Hill home after his arrest. Sergeant Cal Walker hopes the Army Guard will facilitate the task force detectives personally visiting the sites 'to see what Mr Yates saw when he recorded these locations'.

Detectives want to make sure the geographic coordinates Yates recorded are airstrips or airports, and not hiding places that may have been used by the serial killer. When Walker initially asked the Army Guard for use of its helicopters, he was told there must be a 'drug connection' for the military to become involved. However, a year before Yates' arrest, the Army Guard authorized use of helicopters equipped with heat-detecting equipment to look for the bodies of missing prostitutes. Curiously, now that they are investigating one of their own the Army Guard is not so willing to cooperate.

9 January 2001 – The Spokane County Sheriff's Office, Spokane Police Department, Washington State Patrol and the Spokane County Prosecutor's Office announced they will share a two million dollar federal grant over three years to help make up money spent on the investigation that led to the arrest and conviction of serial killer Robert Lee Yates. The money, which comes from the Byrne Discretionary Grant Program, was attached to an appropriations bill by Republican US Representative George Nethercutt that was signed by President Clinton.

11 January 2001 – Pierce County prosecutors said they will seek the death penalty against Yates for the murders of two Tacoma prostitutes. 'I'll be honest with you, we didn't agonize over it,' said Pierce County Prosecutor Gerald Horne. 'This is a compelling case to ask for the death penalty.' Assistant Public Defender Richard Fasy, who represented Yates in Spokane, said he was 'deflated, disappointed and depressed by the decision'. Fasy said it made no sense for the state to make a 'spiteful and costly decision' to seek the death penalty against a man who's already condemned to die in prison. However, the victims' families applauded the decision. Fasy added he wasn't surprised about how Yates received the news. 'He's got that military bearing. He's a model prisoner.'

25 January 2001 – A life trail of confessed serial killer Robert Lee Yates is being assembled by the Spokane homicide task force. Once the time line is complete, the task force will host a national conference to share the information with other law enforcement agencies. More than 50 police agencies – from Vancouver, British Columbia, to Dothan, Alabama – have expressed interest in Yates as a possible suspect in their unsolved homicides. Detective Cal Walker said that the date and location of the national briefing haven't been chosen. A site in the central United States is being discussed, so it can be convenient for everyone. The single briefing and information exchange will save time and money for the Spokane task force, which would otherwise have to brief each individual agency separately.

The tedious task of tracing the killer's whereabouts for the past four decades is being done through receipts, employment, military records and family members. The job became more difficult when Spokane task force investigators lost their power to subpoena certain records. That power ended after Yates pleaded guilty in Spokane to thirteen murders and one attempted murder. But authorities in Pierce County are actively investigating Yates, and therefore still have subpoena power.

12 April 2001 – Pierce County prosecutors say Robert Yates's previous convictions in the Spokane serial killings will shed light for jurors on the two murders he's charged with in this county. Defense attorneys, though, have promised to try to keep details of Yates's thirteen murder convictions secret, in order not to prejudice the jury against him. Pierce County Superior Court Judge John McCarthy is expected to hear arguments on the issue later this month.

Pierce County's chief criminal deputy prosecutor, Jerry Costello, said prosecutors have to prove that the Pierce County murders were part of a common scheme because that's one of the 'aggravating factors' prosecutors allege.

Prosecutors say that the common scheme was a killing spree of drug-addicted prostitutes, that included Ellis and Mercer as well as ten more women in Spokane.

Robert Yates will most probably be found guilty of two murders in Tacoma and will receive the death penalty. Unless he starts cutting deals and uncovering more bodies, Yates will soon meet his maker inside prison walls, without ever acknowledging any other murders he might have committed.

2. THE GREEN RIVER KILLER

The Green River Killer case has been the longest, costliest and most frustrating investigation in American history. For fifteen years, detectives in the Seattle–Tacoma area have been trying to track down the killer, an unidentified man believed to be responsible for the murders of 49 women in King County between 1982 and 1984. A task force, formed in January 1984 to investigate the killings, was originally made up of two lieutenants, four sergeants, a dozen detectives and 22 plain-clothes officers from Seattle, Tacoma and King County. At its peak in 1985, the number of officers involved in the investigation was 56. At the time, with only one percent of evidence processed, investigators realized it would take fifty years to examine everything they had. As the investigation itself became buried under a mountain of files, the task force itself came under fire for their lack of results. 'We were confident that the whole thing would be over in a few months,' one of the original task force members recalled. 'None of us believed it would take any longer than that.'

By November 1986, after a series of frustrating high-profile missteps and an incoming new police administration, the task force was drastically cut. Two years after the last killing, even politically correct Seattle residents began to forget a killer remained on the loose. By 1989, seven and a half years after the first known victim was fished out of the Green River, the case had all but vanished from the fickle public mind. Now, after spending fifteen million dollars, compiling more than a room full of evidence and files on more than half a million people, only one officer, King County Police Major Crimes Division Detective Tom Jensen, is left searching for the elusive killer.

In retrospect, some say, the only good thing to come out of the Green River investigation was the experience the Seattle Police Department gained as it became the top police department in the US, evaluating forensic evidence and crime scenes. Now detectives in Spokane, Portland, Vancouver and New Bedford have sought the help of their Seattle counterparts as they try to unravel data patterns in their own serial killer investigations.

The horror was first uncovered on 15 July 1982, when two young boys riding their bicycles across a bridge over the Green River – a mere stream in southeastern King County, south of the Seattle–Tacoma Airport – discovered a woman's naked body in the water. The victim, identified as sixteen-year-old Wendy Lee Coffield, had been strangled with her own jeans, which were still tightly knotted around her neck. Coffield, a known prostitute, was last seen a week before in the Tacoma area, fifteen miles to the south of the Green River.

Less than a month later, on 12 August, a worker on his afternoon break at a meatpacking company just south of the Coffield crime scene found the nude body of 23-year-old Debra Bonner on the riverbank. Three days later a man rafting down the Green River in search of bottles and cans found two more bodies submerged in the water. The two corpses, identified as 31-year-old Marcia Chapman and seventeen-year-old Cynthia Hinds, were weighted underwater with rocks. By sunset investigators had found a third corpse hidden in the grass thirty feet away from the two submerged victims. The victim in the grass, sixteen-year-old Opal Mills, also had her pants wrapped tightly around her neck.

With five victims found within a quarter-mile of each other, King County police, suffering from what law-enforcement officers call 'linkage blindness', said they saw no obvious connections between the killings. Instead, they suggested the deaths were the result of a 'pimp war'. But the links between the murders could not be ignored: the victims were all about the same age, they were killed within a month of each other, they were found in close proximity, they were strangled, two still had their pants wrapped around their necks, three had prostitution arrests, and two – the coroner's office discovered – had pyramid-like rocks inserted in their vaginas.

Serial killer expert Bob Keppel was the first to officially voice his concerns that they had a serial killer on the loose. 'I can tell you one thing,' he said at a 16 August meeting with investigators from Seattle, Tacoma and King County. 'This probably isn't the first time this guy has killed, and not only that, he's not going to stop until he is caught or dies.' Keppel, a special investigator for the Washington State Attorney General's Office, was instrumental in the case against Seattle's 'other' serial killer, Ted Bundy. Backing Keppel's claims Seattle police had a number of missing persons reports from a known prostitute area called the Strip, just south of the Sea-Tac Airport.

Keppel couldn't have been more right. For the next five years King County Police Officers found themselves recovering the remains of young women in isolated spots to an unfathomable total of 49 victims. The women were all of similar ages and backgrounds. Many of them disappeared from the Strip. Their bodies were found with frightening regularity in logging trails, behind Little League fields, in water, up mountains and down ravines. With each find new patterns of evidence emerged, new clues in an endless jigsaw puzzle that would form a clear picture of the killer without ever revealing his identity.

The most telling signifier of the killer was his choice of dumpsites, which he tended to use repeatedly. In all he gravitated towards four prominent clusters around Seattle: north and south of the Sea-Tac Airport, the Green River, and the Star Lake area. Most dumpsites showed evidence of illegal dumping of household garbage, suggesting the killer could be involved in garbage disposal. At times the killer used more than one site simultaneously. In general the killer used wooded areas next to isolated roads with good views in both directions. The victims were usually naked or had little clothing on. Some of the victims were buried in shallow graves, some covered with branches, and some were theatrically displayed. Sometimes he would leave the victims close to homes or well-traveled areas, which suggests that he wanted them found.

The locations of many of the dumpsites are connected by a network of secondary state highways to Highway 18. Evidence at the crime sites suggests that the killings involved only one person. Details from the various dump-sites paint a picture of a man playing a cat and mouse game with the law. For instance, there are the theatrically placed bodies found in the river, such as 21-year-old Carol Christensen, who was found with two skinned fishes draped on her body, and a sausage and a bottle of wine carefully laid out next to her. Another victim, Sandra Gabbert was found next to a large dead dog. Another victim was eight months pregnant. She was one of the first found buried, suggesting the killer felt remorse for killing the baby. He picked up at least two women in Seattle and traveled to Portland to dump their remains. In the case of Denise Bush, the killer left some of her remains outside Portland, and some near Sea-Tac Airport.

According to retired LA detective Pierce Brooks, the bodies of the victims were valuable to the killer. In August 1985 Brooks, famous for his work in the Atlanta Child Killer Investigation and Chicago's Tylenol Murders, was contracted to review the investigation. Facing the mountains of data accumulated, Brooks suggested that the killer's name was already in the records. 'The odds are that his name is in there, probably more than once,' said Brooks. 'You just have to dig it out.' Brooks profiled the killer as a sexual psychopath with a deep hatred towards women, whom he considered nothing more than trash. The roots to his rage, Brooks believes, lie somewhere in his childhood psyche, when he might have been abused by his mother. 'Control is a big thing with him,' Brooks told *People* magazine. 'He's got to have control. Serial killers are the biggest cowards in the criminal subculture. These victims are teenagers, some of them fifteen or sixteen years old. He's got to be physically stronger than his victims.' Brooks believed the killer previously visited the dumpsites for other reasons before using them to hide his victims. The remoteness of the spots indicated that the killer was intimately familiar with the area.

Using a library of missing persons' dental charts, the King County Police Department was able to identify 40 of the 49 sets of human remains they recovered. All the slain women were young, some in their early teens. Racially they were white, black and Native American. Many were runaways, some hitchhikers, but mostly they were involved in prostitution and drugs and worked the Sea-Tac Strip. Since the women abducted by the killer were so mobile and were not in regular contact with relatives and friends, sometimes the exact times of their disappearances are hard to pin down.

By most accounts, the last woman slain by the killer was seventeen-year-old Cindy Anne Smith, who disappeared from the Sea-Tac Strip area on 21 March 1984. Her remains were never found. After that, investigators have said, the killer may have been imprisoned for some other crime, died, fallen ill, or moved somewhere else where he continued with his lust for blood. 'Why did the guy stop killing people?' asked Detective Tom Jensen in an interview for APB Online. 'Who knows? And we may never find out.' At the time of the last murder the total number of victims was 40. Today the number stands at 49.

Jensen, who has spent more than a decade trying to solve the cases of the murdered prostitutes and is the remaining officer on the case, does not believe there's any evidence connecting the Green River slayings with other more recent slayings. 'I was aware of these cases,' the detective said. 'If we have multiple victims at some dumpsite then we could safely say the same person was responsible for all these cases.' Others are not as sure.

According to author Tomas Guillen: 'Officially, King County police took the position that the Green River Killer stopped killing in early 1984. Investigators in the 1990s revealed it was very possible and maybe likely that he killed into the late '80s.' The task force, at its investigative peak, reviewed 38 other unsolved murders from between 1973 and 1982 in King, Pierce and Snohomish Counties with identical traits to the Green River killings. However, these cases were never included in the 'official' Green River victim list.

King County Police Captain Frank Adamson said, 'I don't believe for a minute that these crimes started with the bodies found in the river in 1982.'

From the start of the investigation, interagency rivalry between the different police departments from different jurisdictions and the task force severely crippled the progress of the investigation. Airport officers, who literally had their precinct handed over to the task force, accused the investigating agents of being secretive and clannish. Looking at the Green River investigation with the advantage of time, one cannot help but think that the rivalry and stubbornness of several departments and agencies greatly contributed to the killer's escape from justice.

Vice officers, who resented the attention and funding given to task force members, refused to lend any help and made a point of not sharing information with them. Instead, they passively sabotaged the investigation by never recording the license plate numbers of johns seen leaving the Strip and refusing to interview arrested prostitutes about the murders. At one point the task force raised the suspicion that the killer could be working in the Vice Squad. Of the 46 disappearance dates known, Vice Squad officers had not arrested anyone on 41 of them. Otherwise, the squad rarely went for two days without making an arrest.

Also, once the task force started keeping the Strip under surveillance, the killings stopped, suggesting the killer might have had inside information from the department. The Vice Squad theory was quickly scrapped when no officer was unaccounted for on all dates of the disappearances. The only way Vice officers could be involved would be if they formed a deadly cadre, which would be a next to impossible feat to get away with.

Adding to the investigative chaos, serial confessor Henry Lee Lucas told authorities in Texas that he committed some of the Green River killings. The claim was quickly dismissed when it was noted that Lucas and his cannibal partner, Ottis Toole, also confessed to several murders on the Easy Coast that took place around the same time as the King County killings. From jail in Florida, Ted Bundy, Seattle's most infamous serial killer, implied that he knew the identity of the killer. In an attempt to delay his execution, Bundy wrote to special investigator Bob Keppel suggesting he had pertinent information about the case. Bundy thought authorities should keep the known dump-sites under surveillance since most killers enjoyed returning to them for kicks. Keppel believes Bundy was cynically motivated to offer his help because he wanted the Green River suspect caught before he passed his own record-setting number of 22 kills.

By the time the murders stopped in Seattle police said the killer might have moved to Portland, Oregon – three hours away – where they had seven unsolved prostitute murders, four of which had striking similarities to the Green River killings. Oregon police officers were skeptical about the Seattle officer's assertion that the killer had relocated there. Proving that the killer did indeed have connections to Portland, two of his victims abducted from the Sea-Tac Strip in 1982 were found south of Portland in 1985. Then an attack on a fifteen-year-old Portland prostitute on 6 September 1985, was also linked to the Green River suspect. Like the other victims she was young, was picked off the street, and was taken to a remote area where she was raped and left dying in a ditch. But this time the victim survived and provided police with a description of her attacker which was used to make what is believed to be the most accurate composite picture of the Green River fiend.

The Green River composite describes a white male in his late twenties or early thirties, about five-feet-nine to six-feet tall, with a corpulent build, short curly blond hair, moustache, ruddy complexion, roundish face and acne scars all around it. The fifteen-year-old said her attacker drove a blue station wagon with the name of a taxi company stencilled on the door and a taxi sign on top. Other composites of the suspected killer had described him as thinner, younger and with straight blond or reddish hair. Conveniently, the two most widely circulated composite pictures match two of the three most prominent 'persons of interest' identified by investigators.

Many of the complications that arose from not having access to cross-jurisdictional information during the Green River investigation led to the development and creation of the National Center for the Analysis of Violent Crime and the Violent Criminal Apprehension Program (VICAP). With the VICAP computer database, unsolved violent crimes from different parts of the country could be analyzed together to search for possible correlation. The VICAP system, which is now fifteen years old, has become a standard tool in serial crime investigation, helping officers nationwide solve what previously were unsolvable crimes. Using the VICAP system, officers input a multi-page event sheet highlighting all aspects of the crime, which then becomes part of the national database that might correlate the information with other similar crimes pointing at the possibility of an emerging serial killer.

In 1984 the task force spent $200,000 on a VAX minicomputer and, for the next two years, entered more than a million bits of information about the case into a database. Using software customized by the CIA, detectives, in an attempt to find new leads in the investigation, were able to wade through enormous amounts of data about evidence and similar homicides across the country. 'The computer is the heart of the investigation,' said Crime Analysis Supervisor Chuck Winters. 'But it's old-fashioned police work that will solve this case.'

In 1998 the investigation reached a high-tech plateau when scientists at the Pacific Northwest National Laboratory (PNL) ran all data collected from the case through a powerful Cray computer developed for the US Army Intelligence and Security Command. The software, called Starlight, searches for word similarities and extracts data patterns from the millions of documents accumulated in the investigation. Still, no new results pointed at the identity of the killer.

In an attempt to figure out what happened to their killer, task force members theorized that he might have resurfaced down the western coast in San Diego where, since 1984, there was a marked upsurge of prostitute killing. San Diego, a Southern California city with a population of 900,000, is in many ways a sunnier version of Seattle. Like Seattle, San Diego has an extensive aerospace industry, sizeable fishing and merchant fleets, and nearby military bases, which might have provided a job base for the relocated killer.

Between 1984 and 1988 up to 25 bodies were found outside San Diego city limits in isolated areas of unincorporated sections of the county. Most of the dumpsites were easily accessible from the I-80 Freeway. San Diego Police, wishing that the Seattle Task Force kept their problems up north, chose to ignore the increase of violence surrounding prostitutes, noting that prostitution was a dangerous job and violence came with it. In 1988 the Metropolitan Homicide Task Force – consisting of up to 32 investigators from San Diego's Police Department, District Attorney's office, Sheriff's Department and the California Attorney General's office – was formed to solve a growing list of 45 vagrant and prostitute-related murders starting in 1984.

At first investigators focused on the possibility of two separate multiple serial killers operating in the area. Both killers were suspected of hunting prostitutes, particularly those working the El Cajon Boulevard strip. One killer, police noted, was dumping his victims in trash containers near the downtown area, two of which he had set ablaze. The other, not unlike the Green River Killer, was murdering the women in his vehicle and dumping them in rural areas outside the city. 'You have bodies dumped in the county that take weeks or months to find, and you can't even identify some of the victims. To try and identify a suspect is difficult, and to establish a case and try to prove someone did it is a monumental task,' said Gary Schons, a deputy state attorney general from the San Diego office who became part of the Metropolitan Task Force.

In 1990 investigators announced they were considering possible police involvement in the prostitute slayings. In the first press conference ever given by the task force, authorities disclosed that one of the three divisions of the force would look into possible police misconduct, specifically allegations of officers' involvement in the death of 22-year-old Donna Gentile. Gentile, an alleged prostitute, was found in 1985 off Sunrise Highway in East County with her mouth stuffed with stones. She had recently testified at a police civil service hearing against two officers who were disciplined for engaging in improper conduct with a prostitute. One officer, Larry Avrech was fired and the other, Lieutenant Carl Black, demoted. According to Gentile, Avrech provided her with confidential police information in return for sexual favors. Some investigators interpreted the stones in her mouth as meaning she had been killed in retaliation for her testimony.

Four months before her death, Gentile tape recorded a message in the Las Colinas women's jail, where she was serving a prostitution conviction. 'In case I disappear somewhere or am missing, I want my lawyer to give this to the press,' she said on the tape. 'I have no intention of disappearing or going out of town without letting my lawyer know first. Because of the publicity that I have given a police scandal, this is the reason why I'm making this . . . I feel someone in a uniform with a badge can still be a serious criminal.' Eventually the Gentile murder was pinned on Ronald Elliott Porter, who was convicted of one murder and is suspected of fourteen others, and no police misconduct was found to have lead to her untimely death.

Porter, an ex-Marine and former Escondido auto mechanic, was first arrested in 1988 on rape and battery charges. By September 1991 – when he was a week away from his parole hearing – he was charged with the killings of Sandra Cwik, 43, a transient from Florida, and Carol Gushrowski, 26, an El Cajon mother of two. Deputy District Attorney Dick Lewis, who led the task force, said Porter was linked to as many as fourteen crimes by fibers, bloodstains, possessions and at least two witnesses. But prosecutors were only able to convict him of one charge of second-degree murder. 'He was working in a tire store when he was doing the murders,' said San Diego's Deputy District Attorney Jeff Dusek. 'He liked to drive, especially in the back country and he would drive back roads.'

Many of the women died of neck fractures that were possibly inflicted by a kind of hand-to-hand combat strangulation technique that was regularly taught in the Marine Corps. 'When we got [arrested] Porter in October 1988, we didn't have a killing or attack after that,' Lewis said. 'There are no bodies showing up on Interstate 8. There were no more ladies showing up at El Cajon Hospital begging for treatment.' Several prostitutes who survived Porter's attacks described him as a pleasant-looking individual. One victim said he reminded her of a minister. Another thought he was a soldier. According to a surviving witness Porter, who was friendly and unthreatening, would invite them to go to Arizona. Once they reached the desert, he would pull off the road and turn violent. On 26 October 1992, Porter was sentenced to 27 years to life. Because there was no solid link establishing a connection between Porter and the Green River killings, he was never considered a viable suspect up in Seattle.

In a separate case Brian Maurice Jones was charged with four of the San Diego killings and given the death penalty for two. He was charged with the killings on 25 June 1992, while he was serving a 22-year sentence for sexual assault at Corcoran State Prison. The suspected serial killer was returned to San Diego where he was arraigned on four counts of murder, two counts of attempted murder, and single counts of rape and sodomy. Jones is believed to have left his four victims in dumpsters within a two-block area in East San Diego.

Another suspected multiple San Diego killer was identified as Blake Raymond Taylor, 27, of Lemon Grove. Taylor, who is already serving nine years to life in prison for the attempted murder of a prostitute, is believed to have killed three more prostitutes, although authorities lack evidence to successfully charge him with any of the killings. In addition to the sixteen murders attributed by Lewis to Porter and Taylor, ten other murders have resulted in fourteen more arrests.

The task force also obtained a successful murder conviction for Allan Michael Stevens, 48, who was charged with killing 26-year-old Cynthia McVey. The nude and beaten body of McVey was found hog-tied in a remote area on the Pala Indian Reservation on 29 November 1988. Stevens, known as 'Buzzard' by his biker buddies, is believed to be responsible for three more killings. The lethal biker was linked to the strangulation murder of McVey by fingerprints, fibers and an eyewitness. She was discovered with a folded sock in her mouth held in place by masking tape which had three fingerprints belonging to Stevens. Some forty fingerprints and three palmprints belonging to McVey were found on a mirror in a San Marcos storage space that Stevens was renting.

One final suspect, Richard Allen Sanders, was posthumously linked to both the San Diego and Green River cases.

Sanders was killed in March 1989, by two close-range shotgun blasts to the back. While detectives investigated his murder, he himself became a suspect in several of the San Diego killings. Not Mr Nice, Sanders was allegedly involved in making 'snuff' films and dealing narcotics. His name also appears as a low-priority suspect in early files of the Green River investigation.

After a five-year investigation at an additional cost of nearly one million dollars, San Diego's Metropolitan Homicide Task Force was disbanded with the satisfactory resolution of 26 murders. The task force, called 'the most successful serial killer task force in US history', incarcerated three, perhaps four, suspected serial killers. All in all, no real evidence linked the killings in San Diego with the Green River cases. Authorities no longer consider the killer's relocation to Southern California a viable option.

Considering that most large cities in the US have ongoing prostitute killings, the Green River Task Force was not hard pressed to locate other emerging serial patterns that might reflect the killer's new playground. Another series of killings that looked promising to Seattle detectives was in Honolulu. Between 1985 and 1987 seven women had been strangled in what is considered Hawaii's first case of serial murder. Most of the victims were young. Several were found in or near water. Some were raped. Others had their hands tied behind their back. Because the victims were not prostitutes, investigators thought it was highly unlikely that the perpetrator was the Seattle killer. Other serial patterns in Oakland, Vancouver, Spokane and Los Angeles were reviewed by the task force and dismissed. 'Most every big town has prostitutes being killed; it's a dangerous profession,' said Jeff Dusek of the San Diego's District Attorney.

Haunted by failure, task force officers made several costly high-profile mistakes that marred the public perception of the investigation. Because of its failure to quickly wrap up the case, the task force itself became the victim of a fickle public. Three times in three years the task force focused the investigation on three individuals – raiding their homes, taking car paint and clothing fiber samples, bringing them in for questioning – and, in the end, the three were let go.

The first person of interest named by the task force was Melvyn Foster, a Seattle cabdriver. Foster brought the task force's attention onto himself in September 1982 when he contacted detectives to discuss his theory that the killer was, like himself, a cab driver. Officers, knowing that serial killers like to inject themselves into the investigation, decided to investigate him instead. Soon detectives became intrigued by his close relationship to one of the victims found in the river. In February 1985, undercover agents surreptitiously bought Foster's aging sedan, then had it dismantled and processed in search of usable evidence. The high-tech analysis of his car yielded no matching fibers, paint chips or fingerprints linking him to any of the known victims.

Foster was kept under surveillance for a large portion of the killings. Not all investigators believe there was only one killer responsible for the Green River cases. Former FBI agent and true crime author, John Douglas, suggested there could be two distinctive killers: one killer responsible for the victims found in the river which were elaborately staged murders, and another who went to great lengths to conceal his victims in the woods. If one were to consider this scenario, then Foster would be a viable suspect in the five river killings. Otherwise, it would have been impossible for Foster to commit so many murders while under surveillance.

The second high-profile suspect was a fur trapper. He became a person of interest after he was suspected by park and game officials of trapping illegally near many of the dumpsites. The trapper, who had an arrest history for burglary, was put under surveillance weeks before he was taken in for questioning. On 6 February 1986, when he was taken into custody, the suspect asked officers: 'What took you so long?' Following his arrest, in a typical media feeding frenzy, the *Seattle Post-Intelligencer* decided to print his name and a package of articles portraying him as the worst serial killer in American history. After several hours of questioning it became apparent that the trapper was not the feared killer. He was released the next morning as the local papers, taking an enormous hit in credibility, came out with screaming headlines heralding his guilt.

For obvious reasons the trapper, furious with the task force and with the media, claimed his rights were violated and his privacy invaded, and filed suit against several newspapers. His wife was even angrier. She had been taken to FBI headquarters in Seattle and asked to give blood and hair samples. All the lawsuits resulting from his unfortunate bungled arrest were settled out of court. Following the embarrassing turn of events, one local editorial cartoonist dubbed the investigation the 'Task Farce'.

The last 'viable suspect', William Jay Stevens II, was arrested by Spokane police at his parents' house in January, 1989, following a series of phone tips resulting from the airing of the TV program, 'Manhunt Live: A Chance to End a Nightmare'. Eerily reminiscent of Ted Bundy, Stevens was in his last year at Gonzaga University Law School in Spokane at the time of his arrest. The President of the student's Bar Association, Stevens promptly issued a statement denying any wrongdoing. 'I am not the Green River Killer. They have made me out to be a very bad person, and I am not,' he declared.

Because a series of alibis placed him on trips with his parents out of the Seattle area at the time of some of the murders, Stevens was released and taken off the list of suspects. Stevens died of cancer on 30 September 1991. Nearly ten years later, his adoptive brother, Robert Stevens, has been managing a website claiming that his older brother was indeed the elusive Green River Killer. In the website the younger Stevens states that his older brother would disappear for a couple of days during the family trips, then would rejoin the family before they returned to Seattle. During these disappearances, the younger brother believes Stevens would return to Seattle where, with one or two accomplices, he would murder the women. According to the website, the accomplices are still living in the Seattle area and, in effect, have got away with the killings.

In any case, with or without accomplices, Stevens was a 'great suspect'. Police searching his parents' home where he lived found a box full of driver's licenses with his picture and credit cards issued to different names. In fact, Stevens used up to thirty different aliases. Some of them were of dead family friends, others were from stolen wallets or simply made up. The search also yielded 29 firearms, one hundred police badges – three from the Spokane Police Department – and fifty Polaroid pictures of naked women. Some of the women were Spokane-area prostitutes. Police also found about 1,800 videotapes, many of them pornographic.

Detectives found receipts showing that Stevens was an avid police-paraphernalia collector and had spent a large amount of money buying police equipment. Among his toys that piqued the task force's interest was a fully equipped Washington State Patrol motorcycle, an ambulance, and a customized police cruiser with radio, radar unit, and blue emergency grill light. Authorities in Spokane discovered that Stevens had applied for a government-authorized license plate for his police cruiser saying that he was the Emergency Services Director of the city of Spangle, which does not exist. Tellingly, the task force often described the killer as someone who could be a law officer or was posing as one, which seemed to be one of Stevens's favorite pastimes.

In 1979 Stevens and another man were charged with burglarizing a uniform store in Spokane. At the time Stevens was a pharmacological student at the University of Washington where, during his freshman year, he coincided with Ted Bundy. Stevens also had a degree in psychology and, when he was in the military service, had been an MP. Coincidentally, the investigating officer in the burglary charge was task force member Tom Jensen. At the time of the arrest Stevens said he wanted to join the Seattle Police Department but was rejected for having a bad driving record. In 1981, two years after being convicted of robbery, Stevens somehow managed to walk out of the King County jail work release program and was never seen or heard of again.

Stevens was brought back to the attention of Detective Tom Jensen when an investigator in the Veteran's Administration Fraud Detection Unit called asking about the 1979 burglary charge. According to the VA officer the former burglary partner tried to open a VA claim under Stevens's name, but Stevens himself had already opened his own claim while he was at Gonzaga.

A forty-page affidavit prepared by the task force to obtain a search warrant of his home traced Stevens' whereabouts following the prison escape. Police had him living around the Portland area until May 1985, when he moved back to Spokane to attend Gonzaga University Law School. A trail of credit-card receipts under four aliases showed that between 1981 and 1985 he traveled extensively between Seattle, Portland, Spokane and Vancouver, placing him in proximity to seventeen of the Green River crime scenes. The affidavit also suggests that, as well as the Green River killings, Stevens may have been responsible for at least a dozen other murders in Seattle, Portland and Tacoma.

Stevens, according to informants, frequently talked 'about serial killer Ted Bundy and appeared to be quite knowledgeable of Bundy's methods and victims.' A source quoted in the affidavit said that the suspect claimed to work 'undercover' with Seattle vice detectives. His duties, he told acquaintances, meant he 'often was involved in the torture of prostitutes'. Stevens also reportedly said he would like to have a videotape of 'cutting up prostitutes'. Informants added that Stevens insinuated he worked for a secret government agency and went on secret 'missions'. According to friends, Stevens knew an inordinate amount of information about the Green River killings. He once told an acquaintance he was part of the task force and was investigating links between the killings and snuff films.

Sirena Caruso, a tenant who lived in Stevens's house between 1981 and 1985, said her neighbor 'was very bizarre'. Caruso moved out when she discovered bullet holes in Stevens's room. According to Caruso, Stevens had a collection of mannequins, videotaping equipment and a secret room hidden behind a moving bookcase. She allegedly told police that she and her boyfriend used to joke about Stevens being the Green River Killer. One day she asked him about it to which he reportedly answered: 'Don't start that rumor; people around here think I'm weird enough.'

One of the guns in Stevens's possession was traced back to a former law school classmate, Dale Wells. According to the police affidavit, Stevens told Wells that he blamed prostitutes for the rapid spread of AIDS. Spokane police discovered that in 1986, days before the strangled body of a prostitute was found in a field, Wells had been searching for the woman. Wells killed himself while Stevens was in custody. In his home police found a letter addressed to crime writer Anne Rule in which he talked about an unnamed friend who was like Ted Bundy. In fact, the similarities between Stevens and Bundy are uncanny. Both attended the University of Washington, both were law students, both were obsessed with pornography and both collected police badges. Whether like Bundy Stevens also killed numerous women is merely speculative.

As profiled by then FBI agent John Douglas, the Green River Killer was a combination of an organized and disorganized serial killer. On the one hand, the suspect was able to think in an organized manner during his post-offense behavior as reflected by the amount of time he spent at the crime scenes. He also organized himself before entering his fantasy murder construct by scouting dump-sites. The weighing down of the river victims showed that the killer was comfortable at the dumpsite and was capable of thinking clearly. His simultaneous use of several dump-sites at once showed his probable awareness and tracking of police surveillance at the locations. On the other hand his disorganized behavior was demonstrated by the random way he picked victims and used items found at the crime scenes as murder weapons.

Douglas described the killer as an opportunistic killer, someone whose murderous mechanism might be triggered by something like a conversation with the victim. At first the victim might feel she had the suspect under control, then somehow he would gain control of the situation and enter in his fantasy construct that would lead to murder. 'Serial murderers commit a series of murders for the same reasons,' said Les Davis, a spokesman for the FBI's behavioral science unit. 'It may be hatred, it may be sexual gratification, they may hear voices inside their head . . . They are harder to track because of motive and the patterns might not be so quickly recognizable.'

The killer, Douglas believes, might feel locked in competition with the police. In a sense the killer could be making a statement, showing the world that he has control of the situation. 'He's a very angry person,' Douglas told detectives. 'He enjoys the power he has over the victims and all the publicity he's getting.' Douglas theorized the killer relished humiliating the women. He dumped them like trash because of the inadequacy of his own relationships with them. Like other prostitute killers, the Green River suspect believed he was somehow justified in killing, as if the victims brought it on themselves and he was ridding the world of their corruption.

Typically serial killers are unemployed or underemployed, especially after reaching such a feverish pitch of murdering. Studies show that the fantasy life of serial killers tends to grow with each killing, leaving less and less time for actual working and normal living. Each time he passes by a location that related to any of the crimes, the suspect would relive his murderous fantasies, prompting him to perhaps search for a new victim.

Ed Schau, a clinical psychologist from Bellevue, said at the American Psychological Association annual conference in Boston that the pattern of clues left by the Green River Killer revealed he was a religious fanatic. A psychologist who holds a doctorate from the University of Washington, Schau believes the killer focused on prostitutes because he thought they were evil. The killer also left signs indicating some sort of religious ritual in at least eight of the crime scenes.

According to Schau, the five bodies found in the Green River indicated the killer's wish to give them some sort of post-mortem baptism. The triangular rocks found in two victims represented symbols of the trinity placed inside them. Another of his posed victims, Carol Christensen, exemplified the killer's religious convictions. She was found with two cleaned fish on her body, with a bottle of wine and a sausage next to her. Schau interprets the staging of the props as symbols for the Eucharist. Detective Jensen, who's heard it all, dismissed Schau's theory suggesting that Christensen was coming from the store when she was abducted. According to the detective, every nut has a theory about who is the killer. And Schau's theory is no different than many other ones.

With seemingly all investigative avenues explored, there seems to be no new tracks for Detective Tom Jensen to search for the killer. Though, not surprisingly, new tidbits of evidence keep surfacing surrounding the investigation. For instance, nearly sixteen years after her death, Jensen was able to conclusively identify the bones of one of the victims. Using a type of DNA-test only used by the military, he was able to genetically match the bones of nineteen-year-old Tracy Ann Winston to her mother's mitochondrial DNA, making her the 42nd Green River victim accounted for. As of this writing there are still four more sets of unidentified human remains in the King County Medical Examiner's office.

To identify the Winston remains Detective Jensen used a process called mtDNA-Testing, which uses mitochondrial parts of the cell rather than the nucleus to examine remains where there's a limited amount of nuclear DNA. The technique is commonly used to identify the remains of MIA soldiers brought back from Southeast Asia. MtDNA is only passed on from mothers to their children. Though testing it is considered less conclusive than testing nuclear DNA, it is done as a last resort. In the fall of 1999 Jensen collected blood samples from eleven mothers of missing area women and the daughter of another missing woman. Eight of the daughters of the women were on the Green River Killer victim list.

The FBI's forensic lab positively connected the blood from one of the samples to the Winston skeletal remains at the King County morgue. No other matches were made between the ten remaining blood samples and the other sets of bones. Jensen believes the identification of other sets of remains would provide a 'tremendous sense of closure' for the victim's families but would not significantly advance the investigation. 'It's still a full-time job. Lots of tips are still coming in,' he told the APB News. 'As long as the calls come in, you need someone to listen to them and follow up on them. You don't want to miss what could be the big one.'

Now, nearly sixteen years after the last known murder, the only things known about the killer are that he wears size ten or eleven shoes, drives a pick-up truck with a camper shell, is probably now in his forties or fifties and has curly hair. He might have been involved in garbage disposal, or worked as a security guard or as a police officer. He is familiar with the outskirts of Seattle and Tacoma and works occasionally with fiberglass. He probably worked at or near the Sea-Tac airport around 1982–83. Since 1983 he's been dead, in prison for an unrelated offence, or has moved elsewhere were he has continued killing. And, of course, he has a deep, psychopathic hatred of women and especially those working the streets. Perhaps we will never know for certain who the infamous Green River Killer turned out to be. Or if in fact there ever was only one single killer. Detective Tom Jensen, the last investigator on the case, hopes one day the puzzle will be solved, and someone will be brought to justice for the grisly murders of 49 innocent women.

3. THE CASE OF THE MISSING VANCOUVER SEX WORKERS

Though they have no corpses or hard evidence to back their claims, prostitutes and social workers suspect a serial killer is responsible for the disappearance of 29 local sex-trade workers from Vancouver's Downtown Eastside. Police are less certain. 'We have no crime scenes, we have no bodies . . . It's very frustrating,' Vancouver police spokeswoman Constable Anne Drennan told the press. 'It's one of the most difficult files we've ever worked because of the lack of clear evidence.'

Patricia Gay Perkins was the first to disappear in 1978, but she was not reported missing until 1996. Six more women vanished between 1978 and 1995. The pace picked up in 1995 with three new disappearances, three more in 1996, eight in 1997, and six more in 1998. As of this writing, two prostitutes have been reported missing in 1999. The victims range in age from nineteen to 46. Most are described as known drug users and prostitutes frequenting Vancouver's ravaged Downtown Eastside.

The missing women reportedly sold sex to feed their intravenous cocaine and/or heroin habits. Some had HIV, hepatitis or both. They all left behind their belongings, bank accounts, their children in foster care, and uncashed welfare checks. 'You're talking about women on welfare who didn't pick up their last welfare check, who left their belongings in a dingy hotel room,' said Constable Drennan. 'It's not as though they could just jump on a plane and fly to Toronto.'

One missing woman, Angela Jardine, disappeared in her bright pink formal gown, leaving in her hotel room an eerie reminder of her possible untimely death – an unmailed Easter card addressed to her parents saying: 'Know how much I love you, Mother and Dad? A whole bunch!' Stephanie Lane disappeared, leaving her child with her mother and an uncashed welfare check. Despite a life of prostitution and drugs, Lane always kept in contact with her mother, calling her for birthdays and holidays. It's been three years since she last called.

The issue of the missing women was brought to national prominence in March 1999, when Jamie Lee Hamilton, a transsexual and former prostitute now director of a drop-in center for sex-trade workers, called a news conference to bring the disappearances to public attention. At the news conference Hamilton and others were highly critical of the Vancouver Police Department's lackadaisical attitude towards the missing prostitutes.

'Prostitutes are great victims because they are invisible. If someone victimizes prostitutes they can get away with it longer than if they victimize school children,' said Robert Ressler, a former FBI behavioral sciences unit agent and the man who coined the term 'serial killer'. 'Schoolchildren are immediately noticed missing and there is public furore. Even with a body, there isn't so much noise with a prostitute.'

At first, friends and relatives of the missing women blamed authorities for ignoring the situation. Some families, disenchanted by the police investigation, hired detective agencies to look into the situation. Six months after repeated protest marches and memorial services for the missing women, local authorities changed their tune and stepped up their investigative efforts. 'You can always say somebody is not doing enough,' Drennan said. 'We are doing everything literally we can think of that we can do. We're not afraid to acknowledge there could be a serial killer or multiple killers.'

During a phone conversation on 8 December 1999, Constable Drennan said emphatically that nothing pointed towards a serial killer being involved: 'Nothing at all suggests the existence of a serial killer.' When asked for an interview for this book, Constable Drennan said the situation in Vancouver was 'not suited for a book on serial killers considering there is no evidence or bodies'.

The women on the streets and those closest to them disagree with the Constable's opinion. 'The women here don't talk about it very much because they're so scared,' said Elaine Allan, executive director of the Women's Information Safe House, a drop-in center for sex-trade workers. Surprised by the Constable's position, Allan remarked on the fact that no missing women have been reported since the case started receiving attention from the press. Some women believe it's a border-hopper, perhaps even the infamous Green River Killer, coming from the US to satisfy his murderous lust. Some think it is a snuff film ring, or a lethal merchant marine cadre kidnapping the women and murdering them at sea. Others, according to Allan, try not to think. The alternatives are too grim.

Reaching investigative overdrive, the Canadian Ministry of the Attorney General and the Vancouver Police Board authorized a $100,000 reward for information leading to the resolution of the case. Using the mass publicity of prime-time television on both sides of the border, investigators featured the case in the crime-busting TV program, *America's Most Wanted*. The show aired on 31 July 1999, fanfaring a $100,000 reward. It prompted over one hundred calls to the program's Washington headquarters. 'Only twenty were thought to be useful; the task force is investigating them,' said Constable Drennan. Adding to the effort, one of Vancouver's largest private detective agencies, CPA Confidence Group, offered four of their 'cadaver' dogs to search selected areas, looking for decomposing human remains. There was even an attempt spearheaded by local business leaders to give cell phones to prostitutes with 911 on the speed dial. The idea was quickly dismissed because of fears that the sex-trade workers would use their new toys to conduct their age-old business.

Police say that Vancouver, being flanked by the sea and mountains, is the perfect spot for stashing bodies out of sight. 'The possible grave sites are endless,' Drennan said. 'If there is a predator out there, he may have a common grave site. But finding that is so difficult.'

A more plausible scenario, however, would involve a person, like Chicago killer John Wayne Gacy, stashing the bodies in a basement of their home. Even grimmer is the possibility of someone dumping the corpses in the open sea. 'I think it's a combination,' said Elaine Allan. 'There's so many women missing it's almost ridiculous to think it's one person doing it.'

John Lowman, a criminology professor at Simon Fraser University, believes several factors could explain the mystery. Since 1985, at least sixty prostitutes in British Columbia have been killed by johns, drug dealers and pimps. 'It suggests that these missing women may well have met the same fate,' Lowman said.

It is not unusual for women who sell sex in the street and are addicted to drugs to disappear. They check in for rehab. They leave the streets. They move to another city. They overdose. They commit suicide. They are committed to hospitals. In the past, police say, women reported missing usually reappear within a year or two, dead or alive. 'All of sudden that wasn't happening anymore,' Drennan said. 'They just stayed missing. That's what became most frightening.' And though all circumstantial evidence indicates foul play, investigators cannot confirm that any of the disappearances are even related.

Police have sent missing-persons reports to psychiatric hospitals, morgues and welfare offices across Canada and the US hoping to close some of the case files. Of the original 31 women reported missing, only two of them were located, both found dead. One, Karen Anne Smith, died on 13 February 1999, from heart problems related to Hepatitis C, in an Edmonton hospital. She was last seen on the streets of Vancouver in 1994. The other, Linda Jean Coombes, died of a heroin overdose in an east Vancouver bowling alley on 15 February 1994.

To keep track of the prostitutes, two law-enforcement agencies have asked the women to record personal data into registries that would give police clues if they were to disappear. The registries, which have been signed by sixty prostitutes, include questions about previous bad dates, stalkers, or anything or anyone they were concerned about. It also records who would most likely know if they were missing. Police have been given special telephone codes to the street women and asked them to call in occasionally to let authorities know they are still alive. 'A lot of them are being more cautious now, working by day or with somebody else,' said Deb Mearns, who co-ordinates safety programs for prostitutes. Mearns has also organized self-defense classes for the women and meetings with detectives handling the investigation.

By inputting all information gathered about the cases into a new vice squad computer program, the Deter and Identify Sex-trade Consumers (DISC) database, investigators hope to identify more suspects. The program allows officers to index every piece of information they gather about johns, pimps and prostitutes into a searchable database. The information includes regulars in the red-light districts, their nicknames, physical and vehicular descriptions, and even states if they have any specific perversions or tattoos. Like in the Green River Killer and the Spokane Killer investigations, detectives believe the solution to the case lies in the data already collected. By computerizing the data detectives hope to extract relevant information that could give a new 'linkage perspective' to the case.

Former District Commander for the Downtown Eastside, Gary Greer, said he believes the street women make the perfect target for a serial killer. They readily get into cars with strangers, not many people notice their disappearance, and fewer still would report them missing. 'With a prostitute who goes by a street name, who's picked up by a john, and then another john, whose intention is to be unseen, to be anonymous – for a predator, that's perfect,' Greer said.

Constable Dave Dickson, a twenty-year Downtown Eastside veteran who was the first policeman to notice the disappearances, believes prostitutes still working the streets are upset by the mystery, but not enough to change their lifestyles. 'If they're heavily addicted and need money, they're probably going to jump in the car with a guy no matter what anyone tells them . . . They come from such horrible backgrounds, they've been sexually abused their whole lives. They're not afraid of anything.'

The Downtown Eastside Youth Activity Society (DEYAS) compiled a list of bad johns – like in Spokane – from information obtained from the task force, social workers and sex-trade workers, which they distribute every week to prostitutes and police. The list – called the Creep List – already has fifty potential suspects. 'There are a lot of bad dates out there,' Dickson said. 'Where do you start when you've got a thousand guys capable of doing something like this? Some of them don't come down here for sex. They come down to beat on the girls.'

Allan says the streets around the Downtown Eastside are dark and isolated, making the women 'vulnerable to men who want to get off being violent. They might not be serial killers, but they are still very dangerous customers.' At the WISH Drop-In Center, Allan says all the women she sees 'have been beaten up by creeps and face it every night when they go out.'

Alarmingly, most prostitutes are unable to get away from their lifestyle because of their lack of basic human needs like shelter, job training, health care, counseling and treatment for drug addiction and alcoholism. After a lifetime of being treated like trash and being paid to be raped, one cannot expect these damaged human beings to change. Unlike the fairytale Hollywood portrayal of prostitutes walking away from 'the life', these women cannot leave the streets without some sort of institutional support and government assistance that is presently non-existent. Ironically, Joel Rifkin – a serial killer in jail – in an attempt to make amends for a lifetime killing women, has addressed this need for shelters to help prostitutes break away from their chains.

In an article for *Newsday*, Andrew Smith describes how Rifkin has developed blueprints for a shelter that would offer counseling, drug treatment, medical help, and job training for prostitutes. The Oholah House – named after a biblical prostitute who was killed by her clients – is an impressive proposal, though a strange one coming from a man who in 1993 was charged with killing seventeen prostitutes in the New York area. The East Meadow native was caught by police while driving his pick-up truck with no license plates and a three-day old corpse sitting next to him. Sentenced to 203 2/3 years to life in Attica Correctional Facility, Rifkin has been confined to his cell 23 hours a day, where he's been working on his concept. 'My view of what I did – you can't pardon it. I don't see forgiveness coming my way. It's a way of paying back a debt, I guess,' Rifkin said.

'A lot of the feelings you get with girls is total worthlessness,' Rifkin said. 'They see themselves as being incapable of being loved. Their only experiences with men are abusive.'

The Oholah House would give these women the tools and the confidence they need to leave behind their highly dysfunctional lives. Residents get psychological counseling, job training, substance abuse treatment, medical care, parenting skills training, and money management classes.

'It's obviously well thought out,' said Sidney-Anne Ford, executive director of the You Are Never Alone Project, a nonresidential treatment center for prostitutes in Baltimore. 'This is a great thing he's working on. It's a pretty compassionate model for service.'

Like in the serial killer cases in Spokane, New Orleans, Los Angeles, Chicago, Vancouver, and Rifkin's in New York, the victims come from the most vulnerable and damaged segment of society. 'More than 90 percent of them were abused as kids. A smaller percentage started doing drugs, got into the life and couldn't get out.' Allan believes all her clients are suffering from some sort of Post-Traumatic Stress Disorder, a disorder more commonly associated with battle-shocked veterans and torture survivors. 'Incest abuse victims, if they were in treatment with a psychiatrist, would be getting anti-depressants, anti-anxiety medication, sleeping pills. But these women who are not in treatment, they self-medicate. That's what the heroin is all about. That's why we're here. That's why all these women are here.' Concurring with studies by psychiatrists Melissa Farley and Norma Hotaling, mentioned in the Spokane chapter, Allan believes that most prostitutes she sees suffer from acute Post-Traumatic Stress Disorder.

Vancouver police have been talking to officers in Spokane and Portland, comparing notes about their recent cluster killings. But with no crime scenes, corpses or any other tangible evidence, Vancouver authorities have few notes to compare. Local officers have also spoken to King County detective Tom Jensen, who is the only investigator left working on the Green River Killer case. Being just 117 miles north of Seattle, there is the possibility that a serial killer could be simultaneously working on both sides of the border. Authorities have also sought advice from Detective Lieutenant William Siegrist, of Poughkeepsie, New York, who investigated the case of Kendall Francois.

On 3 September 1998, authorities in white jumpsuits and surgical facemasks started pulling bodies out of the family home of the then 27-year-old Francois. A total of eight bodies of Poughkeepsie prostitutes in various states of decay were found tucked away in the attic, basement and crawl spaces of the home. Incredibly, other family members were not aware of the household grave. 'It's not the cleanest house in the world,' a police spokesperson said, explaining how the family lived with the smell of rotting flesh. In the usual post-arrest serial killer media blitz, neighbors said Francois, a former school helper known to the children as 'Stinky', was 'mild-mannered' and 'friendly'. Others described him as an obese, foul-smelling, unemployed slob who reminded them of the cartoon character 'Fat Albert'. His pants were always undone, his belly hung out and he constantly had 'stuff' caked on his lips.

In both the Vancouver and Poughkeepsie cases, prostitutes with close ties to the community, who were in contact with their families on a regular basis, vanished without a trace. In the Poughkeepsie cases Siegrist reported that Francois had sex with more than fifty prostitutes and was well-known on the street. Francois also had a history of committing acts of violence against the women. He was arrested after authorities were led to his home when a woman contacted them claiming to have escaped from him after being abducted at knifepoint. The missing women all had histories of prostitution and drug use. They had been disappearing from the same gritty Poughkeepsie neighborhood since October 1996. With the exception of one black woman, all the missing women were white and petite. Francois had been jailed for fifteen days in February 1999 for sexual misconduct and assault involving a prostitute. At the time the assault caught the attention of FBI profilers working on the case. Authorities said Francois had been interviewed previously by police in connection with the missing prostitutes.

Not unlike Poughkeepsie's red-light district, Vancouver's Downtown Eastside is a neighborhood of junkies, pawn shops, saloons and run-down rooming houses. Known world-wide for its high HIV rate and a 1993 heroin overdose epidemic, the Downtown Eastside – which is steps away from the city's trendy Hastings Street – is the perfect place for a person to 'evaporate'. Whereas in 1998 only eighteen people were murdered in Vancouver, 193 died from overdoses of heroin, cocaine or illicitly bought methadone. It is estimated that more than a quarter of the local junkies and 80 percent of Eastside prostitutes have tested positive for HIV. The local needle-exchange center at the DEYAS hand out about 2.4 million needles a year, more than any other center in North America. Due partly to Vancouver's mild winters, the area is a magnet for runaways, drifters, impoverished Indians and mentally ill people, many of whom end up living on the streets, doing drugs and turning tricks. 'We don't have a lot of success stories,' said Allan, whose drop-in center is used by nearly every prostitute in the Downtown Eastside, especially the ones that are whacked out on drugs.

Allan knew several of the women who disappeared. 'It was tragic,' Allan recalled when she found out her friend Jacquilene McDonell went missing. 'She was young, was articulate, she was nice, she was 21 years old, had a son and was kind of tripping on her drugs. She was too good for this place.' Like the others, Jackie's existence on earth was surrounded by tragedy since she was young. 'Their forearms are solidly scarred with cigarette burns and deep cut marks,' Allan says of the women she mothers at her center. 'There are signs of being extremely abused from a young age. They have to self-mutilate because the pain in their head is so bad; those are the ones that are going missing.'

'I really hope it is a serial killer,' said the Reverend Ruth Wright of Vancouver's First United Church, a community pillar for 114 years which houses the WISH drop-in center for sex-trade workers. The alternative, according to the reverend, 'would mean there are 29 separate killers out there and that much evil would be too much.' Wright, a veteran of the ravaged Downtown Eastside, has survived the neighborhood's ballooning AIDS epidemic and the effects of a 1993 lethal batch of heroin that killed 300 junkies. However, this new scourge is what she finds most horrifying.

Allan believes the 29 missing prostitutes could have been killed at sea. Prostitutes are often lured onto ships at the

Vancouver harbor with promises of free heroin and eager johns, but end up as sex-slaves in a heroin daze until they are thrown overboard. Authorities see this as a possibility.

'Whether the boats could be involved is one of the possibilities we're looking into,' said Constable Drennan to the *Calgary Sun*.

Allan knows, from conversations with prostitutes at the Safe House, that the ships play a pivotal role in their lives. 'Many of the women I've talked to have been on the boats,' she said. 'Many of these sex-trade workers are heavily into heroin addiction, desperate for their next fix. Also remember, something like 95 percent of all the heroin coming into Canada hits the shore first right here in Vancouver.' By and large, sailors make up a large percentage of the prostitute's clientele. Consequently, it's not uncommon for prostitutes to go on a boat. Once on board the women are kept captive as the ship's sex-toys. Some escape, others . . . who knows?

Allan says that usually the younger women, whose drug habits are raging out of control, are the ones that end up in the ships. 'The lure of the drugs,' she says, 'the lure of being able to do more dates', gets the women to work the port. Many of those who go on the boats try to have someone 'keep their six' – a street expression meaning to watch their back. In a story related to Allan at the drop-in center, one woman was locked in a cabin in a Filipino freighter with a big block of heroin. She was only let out after her friend – a Russian sailor – 'keeping her six' threatened to go to the police with pictures of her getting on board.

'It would be very easy to hide someone on a boat,' said Allan. 'When you get to open sea and you're on night watch it would be very easy to toss someone overboard.' Women working the streets near the docks told the *Calgary Sun* they believe the sea slaughter is a feasible explanation for the disappearances. Dumped from freighters and international commercial ships far out in the Pacific Ocean, the bodies would vanish for ever. If several men were involved, one would expect someone eventually to talk. Plausibly, it could be a foreign crew coming into town periodically and having little contact with people on shore.

On Portside Park, overlooking the harbor, a memorial stone dedicated to all the Downtown Eastside murder victims has been unofficially made into an altar in honor of the missing women. There, Wayne Leng told the *Calgary Sun* how he remembers with sadness his friend, 29-year-old heroin-addict, Sarah DeVries. Leng, a 50-year-old automotive technician, was the last person to see DeVries alive in Vancouver. She disappeared in 1998. Consumed with finding her, Leng has done everything from plastering posters all over Downtown Eastside to making a website dedicated to the missing prostitutes.

The disappearance of Black Sarah – as she was known on the street – was a particularly hard blow for everyone. Warm and friendly, Sarah was known and liked by everyone in the area. Unlike other victims, Sarah came from an upper middle-class family who have put in the time and energy to bring to attention the enfolding tragedy. DeVries's sister Maggie, who has been openly critical about the authorities' attitude, has put a grieving face to the endless cavalcade of unsolved cases. Together with Wayne Leng they have turned Black Sarah into the symbol for the missing. DeVries, like the 28 other women, was a street junkie and prostitute. Like the others, she was shooting up to $1,000 worth of drugs a day. She had HIV and hepatitis.

But unlike the others, Sarah had a restless mind that she revealed in a journal full of poems, thoughts and drawings. In a strange twist of fate, she appeared in a TV documentary where she appears talking to the camera and shooting-up. 'When you need your next fix, you're sick, puking, it's like having the flu, a cold, arthritis, all at the same time, only multiplied a hundred times,' she said to the camera. Sarah said there are only three ways off the streets: 'You go to jail, you end up dead, or you do a life sentence here.'

Here is one of her poems, reflecting her tragic struggles with drugs and life on the streets:

Woman's body found beaten beyond recognition.
You sip your coffee,
Taking a drag of your smoke,
Turning the page,

Taking a bite of your toast.
Just another day, just another death,
Just one more thing for you to forget,
You and your soft sheltered life,
Just go on and on,
For nobody special from your world is gone.
Just another Hastings Street whore
Sentenced to death.
No judge, no jury, no trial, no mercy.
The judge's gavel already fallen,
Sentence already passed.

Sadly, Sarah's poems will remain as the only voice for these 29 victims who have lived and died on the margins of society. Hers is but another lost life cut short by someone preying on the weak and vulnerable – someone who sees no value in life.

VANCOUVER UPDATE

Since the case of the missing prostitutes was made public in 1999, the original VPD task force dwindled to three officers and the investigation was eventually taken over by the RCMP cold case squad. To date, police have found four of the 31 missing women. Two of them were dead, one from heart problems, the other from a drug overdose. Two were found alive, but police have not released details about them. However, four more missing women have been added to the list. First, Brenda Ann Wolfe, 32, who disappeared in February 1999, and was reported missing the following April. Then, Jennie Lynn Furminger, who was reported missing in March 2000. Finally Dawn Teresa Crey, 42, and Debra Lynne Jones, 43, were both reported missing in December. 'I guess it does say that the problem still exists,' said VPD Sergeant Geramy Field. 'For a while there – for the majority of 1999 – we felt that we didn't have any [more missing] and that either somebody was in custody or the perpetrator had died or moved on, perhaps because of the media pressure.'

In June 2001, Kim Rossmo, 46, a geographic profiler in the VPD, sued the department for wrongful dismissal. Rossmo, who at the time was Canada's first police officer with a Ph.D., developed a ground-breaking computerized crime investigation tool for geographic profiling, making him a fast-rising star in the department. Rossmo was quickly promoted from constable to detective-inspector and was allowed to set up a geographic profiling unit, which went on to win the department international acclaim and awards, but jealousy and the department's 'old boy's network' kept undermining his work.

In 1998, when Rossmo said that there was a strong possibility of an active serial killer being in Vancouver, others n the department, perhaps out of spite, quickly rejected his claim. In his suit Rossmo, who now works in Washington D.C., specifically accuses Deputy Chief John Unger and major crime police Inspector Fred Biddlecombe of freezing him out of the missing women investigation. According to court documents Biddlecombe 'threw a small temper tantrum' when Rossmo suggested that police should tell the media of the possibility of a serial killer at work on the Downtown Eastside. Rossmo equated the experience to being on a 747 jetliner when someone tells the pilot there's smoke in the cabin. 'If the captain says, "Prove to me there's a fire," you know he's either a fool or incompetent.'

Remarkably, this was not the first time Rossmo had warned fellow officers about a serial killer on the loose, and it was not the first time he found himself being stonewalled by his colleagues. In 1994, after analyzing three sets of remains discovered outside Saskatoon, Rossmo suggested they were the work of a serial killer. Police dismissed his claims, even though they had a convicted rapist – John Martin Crawford – under surveillance. Crawford turned out to have murdered at least four native women and is suspected of killing three others.

According to Warren Goulding, author of *Just Another Indian – A Serial Killer and Canada's Indifference*, Crawford was able to elude authorities and kill repeatedly because his victims were native women. Goulding believes that there are as many as 450 aboriginal women missing from western Canada and no one seem to care. Not surprisingly, a large number of the missing Downtown Eastside women are also of aboriginal descent.

Since 1999, Wayne Leng, the friend of Sarah DeVries, has been keeping track of the investigation of the missing women on his web site, *www.missingpeople.net*. Though he started the web site as an online memorial for his friend Sarah, the site has grown into the nerve-center for keeping track of all the disappearing women. With the help of his web site a small but vocal contingent of family and friends of the missing have kept the police investigators from completely dismissing the case. Leng and the others are now talking about filing a class action lawsuit against the VPD, for incompetence and neglect in their handling of the missing women file.

Recently, Vancouver city police finally dropped their guard and now publicly acknowledge the strong possibility that one or more serial killers are abducting women from the Downtown Eastside. In fact, a new joint force of city police and Mounties has been formed to look into at least 60 solved and unsolved homicides of women working in the sex trade or living a similar lifestyle in the past two decades. Vancouver police Sergeant Geramy Field said the task force has been in the works for some time and wasn't prompted by the recent disappearances. Field added her department has assigned two homicide detectives to the task force, which will be focusing on the known murders of women in the sex trade as well as the files on missing women. Investigators will be trying to see if any patterns emerge or if there is useful evidence in solved or unsolved murder files from across Western Canada that can provide clues on Vancouver's missing women cases.

One can only hope the renewed interest in the case will yield answers on the fate of the missing women. 'Historically, that's where a lot of these have been solved in the past: A policeman stumbling upon something or stopping somebody and being able to follow up on something that's fresh – being vigilant out there with our street checks,' said Sergeant Field at a press conference announcing the new joint task force. 'I don't think somebody's going to walk in [with the answer]. But somewhere in this body of evidence is the man or the men, and we just have to find them.'

4. GETTING AWAY WITH MURDER IN THE BIG EASY

There is a possible serial killer, or serial killers, roaming the streets of New Orleans with 26 kills under his belt. The victims are mostly black women and transsexuals with histories of drug abuse and prostitution. Most were strangled, or died of drug overdoses. All but one was found, totally nude, dumped in swamps, remote roadsides and bayous on the outskirts of New Orleans, Jefferson Parish and further west of the city. The killings started in 1991. The last known victim was discovered in April 1996. Authorities said the first six victims, including a seventeen-year-old, were abducted from Algiers, a part of the city on the west bank of the Mississippi River. The rest came from the Treme area, a poor neighborhood next to the historic French Quarter.

Police have one credible suspect, Russell Ellwood, in custody serving a life sentence for one killing. He is suspected of seventeen other homicides. Still, authorities believe that more than one person is responsible for the string of slayings. Although New Orleans police suspected a connection between some of the murders as early as 1992, the task force wasn't formed until May 1995. Four years later, following the conviction of Ellwood, the task force was dissolved and the different sheriff's departments involved announced they would re-examine any of the cases only if new information was uncovered. No more arrests or charges have been made, and as of this writing, someone in the Big Easy has got away with murder.

As with other cases involving prostitutes and drug addicts, the official response, at least initially, was sluggish. Family members of the victims complained that the deaths of their loved ones were being overlooked. 'It was like the Police Department went into denial,' said Tony Radosti, assistant managing director of the Metropolitan Crime Commission, a civic watchdog group in New Orleans.

'A few short years ago, people were saying that police did not care about the victims because they were poor, black, and had questionable reputations,' said St Charles Parish Sheriff Greg Champagne. 'As shown by hundreds of thousands of dollars . . . and thousands and thousands of investigator man-hours, we do care.'

In 1993, police began suspecting something was amiss when two naked women were found over a two-day period in close proximity to each other in a ditch alongside a two-lane road in the rural swampland of St Charles Parish just outside New Orleans. The first body, a 30-year-old strangled female clad in nothing but pink socks, was discovered by two crawfishermen on 21 February. She had been dead for several days. The next morning, another strangled, naked female body was discovered 700 feet away. 'The second body had been there less than twelve hours,' said Angela Champagne of the St Charles Parish Sheriff's Office. 'They were both known prostitutes. We linked it to a murder from September. Then we discovered New Orleans has ten or so similar cases. It looks like the work of a serial killer.' In fact police found that six women of similar lifestyles were found strangled outside the city in 1991, five more in 1992, and the above-mentioned two in 1993. Things picked up afterwards with seven strangulation murders in 1994, seven more in 1995, and one final one on 8 April 1996.

Because the victims were what police call 'strays' – people who don't get reported missing and don't have others pushing to find their killers – it took more than a dozen murders for police to recognize the emerging pattern. 'We haven't linked all these murders to one suspect,' said the then Sergeant Sam Fradella of the New Orleans police. 'The murders are similar; the victims are similar. But we can't call this a serial killing. We're handling each one as an independent murder.' After 26 similar victims, killed in similar fashion, and dumped in similar areas, however, it became increasingly hard to call it anything other than the work of one or more serial killers.

The first man who was publicly linked to the string of killings was Victor Gant, a New Orleans police officer. Gant, an eighteen-year police force veteran, was identified as a suspect in only two slayings, even though both were attributed to the suspected serial killer. One of the victims, his girlfriend, a 28-year-old coin changer named Sharon Robinson, was reportedly spotted leaving Harrah's Casino with Gant shortly before her death. Her body and that of her friend, Karen Ivester, 30, were found on 30 April 1995, floating in a swamp near Interstate 55 northwest of the city.

After four years of investigation, no charges were brought against Gant. His attorney, John Reed, told the *New Orleans Times Picayune* that police officials' careful statements showed there was no evidence against his client. 'If they had any clear reason to believe Victor Gant is involved they would arrest him. They haven't,' he said. After being named as a suspect Gant remained in the force in a desk job. Although he was never charged with murder, the department fired him a year later, charging him with departmental violations, including carrying a revolver when restricted to desk duty and showing up late for a police-sanctioned boxing match.

Once Russell Ellwood became the focus of the task force investigation, Gant's name was not mentioned again as a suspect. Gant filed an invasion of privacy and defamation suit against New Orleans Police Chief Richard Pennington. The suit claimed that Pennington named him as a suspect even though the 'paucity or lack of evidence linking [Mr Gant] to these crimes was well-known by [Chief Pennington]'. Gant's lawyers also fought the city to win back his job in the Police Department. In March 1999 a Civil Service Commission ruling reduced his penalty to a 30-day suspension, claiming the dismissal had been 'far too severe'. The following November, without much fanfare, Gant was let back on the force and was assigned to tagging and warehousing evidence in the basement of the Police Department.

On 2 March 1998, taxi driver and longtime suspect Russell Ellwood, 47, was charged with second degree murder for the deaths of Cheryl Lewis, 30, and Delores Mack, 40. Lewis, a mother of four, worked as a nurse and was not believed to be a prostitute. She was last seen leaving her house on foot on her way to a convenience store. 'We have been miserable without her,' her oldest son Dorrean Lewis told the *Times Picayune*. 'My brothers have had to grow up without a mom.' Mack was a transsexual known as Benjamin who was born in Charleston, South Carolina; she lived in the neighborhood of Metairie at the time of her death. Lewis was asphyxiated and drowned while under the influence of cocaine and amphetamines. Her body was found on 20 February 1993, in a canal off a road in a swamp in Hahnville, just west of New Orleans. A day later and one-fifth of a mile away, Delores Mack was found strangled and suffocated in the canal. Toxicology tests revealed large quantities of cocaine in her blood-stream.

A year later Ellwood became a suspect when he was spotted in the middle of the night by two off-duty officers near the two crime scenes. A well-known characteristic of serial killers is that they tend to return to their crime scenes to re-live the killings. When Ellwood was questioned by the police officers he told them he was changing his car's oil and didn't want the Department of Environmental Quality to catch him illegally dumping the old oil in the canal. After their encounter with Ellwood, authorities added his name to the suspect list. Ellwood, who was 47 at the time of his arrest, is considered a viable suspect in eight to sixteen more killings.

Police interviewed Ellwood in 1995 while he was incarcerated in Sebring, Florida, where he was serving time for cocaine possession. Strangely, Ellwood told them he had dreamed that the serial killer task force would be paying him a visit. Once he was released from the Florida jail he went to Ohio to stay with relatives. There he was questioned again by police and allegedly told task force leader Lieutenant Sue Rushing and a former detective from the Cincinnati police force that he had dumped two bodies in the Hahnville swamp. In a statement released by authorities Ellwood was quoted as saying he would confess to two killings if he was returned to Louisiana. 'I'm willing to say I met a black female, I put her in the back seat, that's where all my fares went, and that I took her out in St Charles, and I put her body in water; I'm willing to give you that. I'm willing to go back to Louisiana for those two overdose cases, I had a black prostitute in the back of my car and I IV'd them; I can't incriminate myself any more than I've already done.' In

January 1998, Ellwood agreed to return to Louisiana to, in his own words, 'clear his name', and help solve the cases. Once he entered the state, he was welcomed by Sheriff Greg Champagne at the New Orleans International Airport in Jefferson Parish, and was promptly arrested on an outstanding traffic warrant.

Later, Ellwood, in a telephone interview with Associated Press from the St Charles Parish jail, denied he ever admitted killing the two women and added that anything he told police in Ohio was so they would fly him to New Orleans to meet with his longtime lawyer, Ross Scaccia. 'My only thought was that if I can get to Mr Scaccia, everything would be all right,' Ellwood said. 'I told the task force anything, almost anything, to get to Scaccia.' The suspect, who had a long record of drug and parole violation arrests, had been a regular in Scaccia's office for over thirty years. Ellwood was first represented by Scaccia in the mid-sixties when he was charged with possession of marijuana. Following Ellwood's latest arrest, Scaccia told the *Times Picayune* that his client was charged with murder based on unsatisfactory evidence and statements he made during 21 hours of intense interrogation without his attorney present. 'They're attempting to convict him on statements taken completely out of context. It's infuriating.'

Precipitating the crumbling of the case against Ellwood, allegations of investigative improprieties by the task force surfaced, prompting the FBI to investigate the work of task force Lead Detective Sue Rushing. An officer of the Jefferson Parish Sheriff's Department, Rushing was accused of losing or destroying evidence that would have helped exonerate the suspect in at least one of the two murders he was charged with. In November 1998, Rushing failed a lie-detector test asking if she destroyed or lost receipts that placed Ellwood in Canton, Ohio, when the murders of the two women occurred. The test also indicated that Rushing was 'not telling the truth' when she denied coaching a witness who claimed Ellwood showed her two bodies in a canal twenty miles west of New Orleans.

Ellwood, a meticulous record keeper, had receipts detailing his activities throughout his life. But the 1993 receipts seized by police had an uncharacteristic two-week gap in

February that would have included receipts placing Ellwood in Ohio at the time of the murders. Ellwood filed a federal civil rights lawsuit against the task force asserting that police had destroyed evidence and lied when they said he confessed under interrogation. 'It's clear they have deprived him of his right to a fair trial,' said Maria Chaisson, Ellwood's court-appointed attorney.

'These receipts were allegedly destroyed in the presence of the secretary to the task force, and in the presence of a co-worker, Officer Phil Ramone, who worked with Lieutenant Rushing,' Scaccia said. 'It was Phil Ramone who blew the whistle on Lieutenant Rushing.'

After vehemently denying that she had tampered with any evidence, Rushing admitted to throwing away an envelope with a Texas postmark that could have contained receipts contradicting the task force's assertions that Ellwood was in New Orleans at the time of the killings. At the time of the controversy Rushing was briefly hospitalized for exhaustion. 'After she failed the tests, she all of a sudden remembered – well, maybe there was an envelope that she had thrown away,' Chaisson said. 'I think the envelope was filled with receipts. They track him for years and years, almost on a daily basis with these receipts, and then strangely there's this two-week gap surrounding the murders that he's charged with.'

Prosecutors admitted they have no physical evidence placing Ellwood where the bodies of Lewis and Mack were found other than when the officers found him dumping car oil. But they say Ellwood's own contradictory statements and other evidence pointed to him as the killer of the two said victims and perhaps many others. Sheriff Champagne said that there was no single piece of evidence tying Ellwood to the killings. Instead investigators correlated a 'general pattern' of behavior that pointed to him as a viable suspect. During interrogation, Ellwood, while not naming any specific victims or locations, talked about 'homicides I've committed' and 'black women I've killed'.

Ellwood allegedly told his cellmate in Sebring, Florida, that he liked to have sex with men and women who were drugged into insensibility. According to the cellmate, the suspect injected his partners with drugs and 'enjoyed the fun of having sex with people who were not in control of their bodies. He said if they were high on cocaine or heroin, the heroin would put them in a state of mind as if they were paralyzed and he could take advantage.' Ellwood also allegedly told the inmate that he sold drugs from his cab and he would help the buyers inject. Then he 'got off watching their eyes roll to the back of their head.' In court, the cellmate testified that Ellwood also told him about killing several women in Louisiana and a prostitute in Florida. Local officers in Sebring said that the details furnished by the prisoner closely matched an unsolved murder in the area. From jail in Louisiana Ellwood dismissed the statements from the 'flunkies' he was locked up with in Florida, categorizing them as lies said for their own self-interest.

Ellwood, a serial loser, grew up in Massillon, Ohio, and moved to New Orleans after finishing high school, thirty years before his arrest as a suspected serial killer. Scaccia described him as a '60s hippie, 'a little far-out', fairly introverted, and 'humorous about his oddity and his lifestyle'. In the Big Easy he worked as a freelance photographer, then became a cab driver. According to his lawyer, Ellwood never had a girlfriend and constantly planned get-rich-quick schemes that never worked. Once he inherited $15,000 from his mother but quickly lost it all investing in penny stocks. Soon after, he was sleeping in his cab because he couldn't afford a boarding house. He was a man of few friends who had a history of intravenous drug abuse, but said he stopped injecting drugs before 1988. Ellwood also claimed he was close to the streets, admitting that he regularly used prostitutes and dated several black women. 'I fit a profile, and they used me to justify a fruitless investigation in order to obtain further grant money,' he told the *New Orleans Times Picayune*.

'Lieutenant Rushing recognized that here was a guy who fit the profile of somebody who could be responsible for these terrible offenses,' said Defence Lawyer Chaisson. 'He's a loner, he's never been married, he dated some black prostitutes while he was down there, so I think she pursued it and pursued it until she made her case.'

According to Scaccia, Ellwood helped police because he enjoyed the attention from detectives who were hanging on his every word. 'He's just an unswift, lonely man who's always trying to be a success and has never succeeded at anything,' Scaccia said.

According to Scaccia, Lieutenant Rushing – in an attempt to seal the case against the suspect – persuaded Sharon Jones, the key witness in the trial, to say that in 1993 Ellwood took her to a canal to smoke crack and see a 'surprise'. Jones, with whom Ellwood had been romantically involved, said she went with him in his car to get high; he showed her two bodies in the canal, one with an arm and hand showing and another that was almost submerged. Then Ellwood, according to a police affidavit, became very angry and told her: 'You know what I do to bitches like you? I kill them.' Ellwood denied ever taking Jones to see any bodies and claimed that during most of February he wasn't even in Louisiana. Both lawyers representing Ellwood believe their client was the victim of an overzealous investigation.

'They wanted to get a conviction,' Chaisson said. 'But whoever did this is certainly still out there.'

Chaisson said that Jones had five interviews with police detectives and never mentioned the fact that Ellwood had shown her two bodies. 'She told some wild stories about Russell being involved in drugs and that he had killed somebody and she went into all kind of detail about it. They determined that half of the stories she was telling were not true, but despite that they kept interviewing her. Ultimately, she indicated in about the seventh interview that Ellwood had shown her two bodies in St Charles Parish.'

Jones's story, according to the lawyer, was consistently inconsistent. 'Sometimes she said they were in water, sometimes she said they're on the bank; she changes her story quite often. She's changed the location of the bodies on several occasions. She had originally pointed to locations in St John Parish, which is quite a distance away from where these bodies were actually discovered. And that's where the allegations of witness coaching come in. It's our position that she was coached by certain investigators to change her story so that it would fit a certain crime scene.' Challenging Jones's assertions, Chaisson said Lewis had been dead at least a week before she was discovered and Mack died at most 24 hours before, which would make it impossible for both corpses to be in the swamp at the same time.

Scaccia said the prosecution had no evidence, other than the testimony of jailhouse snitches and a prostitute, linking his client to any of the killings. 'There is no other evidence,' he said. 'They have no one who places him in the company of the people who died, they have no forensics, they have no blood tests, they have no hair samples, they have nothing found in the cab that would indicate that he had anything to do with any murders; they don't have anything physical.' On 24 February 1999, authorities announced they dropped one of two murder charges against Ellwood, saying he could not have committed the crime because he was out of Louisiana at the time of the killing.

With one murder charge dismissed Chaisson told the court that the key prosecution witness Sharon Jones could not be put on the stand now that the Mack charge was dropped because, 'it would be illegal to put perjurious testimony on the stand.'

Amid charges of corruption and mismanagement, the four-year-long, $700,000 task force investigation came to a quiet end on 17 August 1999, when the District Judge Kirk Granier handed Ellwood a life sentence for the murder of Cheryl Lewis. No other charges or arrests have been made involving any of the other murder cases. The task force itself was dissolved following the conviction, even though 25 cases of murder remain unsolved. Because of the possibility of violence against him from other inmates, Ellwood is now in solitary confinement in the St Charles Parish jail. He said his routine consists of eating, sleeping and reading the Bible. Only one person, other than members of his lawyers, has visited him since his arrest. Asked by APB Online who he thought was responsible for the murders in New Orleans, he answered, 'There's somebody real sick running around out there. It has to be an abnormal person.'

Ellwood still believes that he'll be acquitted. 'No F. Lee Bailey, no Johnny Cochran, no judge or jury is capable,' Ellwood said. 'It's all in the hands of my judge and jury, God.'

As the investigation into the death of the 26 women wended to a close, a new serial pattern in the area emerged. This time though, the victims were young black men. To date, there is a cluster of at least eight murders that could be related. Although no hard evidence connects the murders together, circumstantial evidence points to the possibility of one sole perpetrator. All the victims have been young men from poor areas with histories of drug arrests. Some were selling drugs, mainly coke, while others were merely users. Most were killed in one place, then dumped in or near garbage containers in Parishes outside the city. Three of the victims knew each other. Seven were found shoeless. All victims were strangled, which is a highly unusual way to kill men.

Strangulation is favored by many serial killers murdering women and children because it is a very 'intimate' way of killing. According to Tom Petee, director of criminology and criminal justice at Auburn University, at least 25 percent of serial killers strangle their victims. 'It's kind of an intimate form of killing, hands on, and it's a control type of killing.' But if the victim is a capable young man, it would be difficult to overpower him. Authorities believe the perpetrator removed the shoes of the victims intentionally, perhaps because he lured them inside his home. Another theory postulates that the killer might have kept the shoes as trophies, to remember and re-live the killings. The victims, police believe, may have known the killer or might have been in a drug-induced stupor at the time of their deaths, explaining how the killer was able to get close enough to strangle them.

The most prominent murder cluster is in the city of Kenner in Jefferson Parish, where the bodies of three young men were found between October 1998 and June 1999. All of them were dumped within a one-mile radius of the New Orleans International Airport. All three were asphyxiated, all had drug connections, all were missing their shoes, and two knew each other. The first victim, found on October 20, was sixteen-year-old Joseph Brown. He was wearing only gym shorts and had cocaine in his blood. Forensics determined that he had been struck repeatedly on the head with a blunt object but died of asphyxiation. A bloody plastic bag was found next to him. Investigators believe this could have been used to suffocate him or to keep his blood from staining the perpetrator's car as the corpse was driven to the dumpsite.

The second victim, Manuel Reed, was found on 30 May. He was left in a dumpster about a mile from the Brown crime scene. He, too, was suffocated, had coke in his system, and was shirtless and shoeless. When the third victim, 21-year-old Angel Mejia was found near a garbage container seven blocks away, Kenner Police Chief Nick Congemi suggested the three murders were related. Mejia, found on 20 June, was strangled and had ligature marks on his legs. Like the other two Mejia had a history of drug-related arrest. Both Mejia and Brown, who were acquaintances, knew a fourth victim, twenty-year-old Gary Pierre, who was found murdered nearly a year before. All three – Pierre, Brown and Mejia – lived within walking distance of each other, near the Boutte housing projects, which is about ten miles from the Kenner dumpsites. Coincidentally, both Pierre and Mejia had been previously arrested in the same drug deal. According to friends and family, Pierre was not involved in drugs. Pierre was found on 14 December 1997 on the shoulder of a remote road in nearby St Charles Parish. He too was found asphyxiated, but he was fully dressed and there were no drugs in his system.

The other recent killings that could be related to the Kenner cluster are as follows: Murray Ranson, who was found on 31 July 1998, beaten and asphyxiated, in the St Charles town of Hahnville; Oliver Le Banks, 26, found in Jefferson Parish on 5 October 1998, three miles from the Brown-Mejia-Reed dumpsites; and eighteen-year-old Bruce Williams, who turned up in a ditch in Metairie, Jefferson Parish on 27 November 1998, a month after the Le Banks murder. Williams' body was about eight miles from the Kenner victims. The latest victim, Mitchell Johnson, was found on 1 September 1999, a few feet from the Le Banks' dumpsite. Johnson was nude, died of asphyxiation, and had cocaine and methadone in his system. Given the similar lifestyles of the victims and the proximity between the bodies, investigators in Jefferson Parish, Kenner and St Charles Parish acknowledged the possible relationship between the killings. Presently they are trying to determine whether all the cases are the work of one individual or merely a series of unfortunate coincidences. As of this writing there has been no official pronouncement about any forensic evidence tying the murders together, and no new task force has been formed.

5. THE SPOTSYLVANIA CHILD KILLER

Someone is snatching children from the small-town refuge of Spotsylvania, an affluent community in the lush Virginia countryside where once Robert E. Lee battled Ulysses S. Grant. In the summer of 1997 authorities announced the shocking reality that the killings of three local girls could be the work of a serial killer. All three girls disappeared from their homes after school, leaving behind no sign of struggle, indicating that they probably knew their killer. All had dark hair and slim, athletic builds. They lived within a ten-mile radius of each other. All three corpses were found partly submerged in water. All three were fully clothed, except two had their bras missing. The same two girls also had their pubic area shaved.

The first disappearance happened on 9 September 1996, when sixteen-year-old Sofia Silva vanished from her front porch where she was doing homework after school. After a five-week search authorities found her decomposing body wrapped in a blanket in a swamp in King George County, Virginia, about twenty miles away. Seven months later, two sisters, Kristin and Kati Lisk, disappeared without a trace after arriving at home from school in separate buses. Within five days, their bodies were found thirty miles away in the South Anna River, in Hanover County, Virginia. A thirty-to-fifty-person task force – culled from nine law enforcement agencies, including the Virginia State Police and the FBI – was created to hunt for the killer.

Nearly five years later, after countless hours of police work and posting a $150,000 reward for information, authorities have no viable suspects in custody or even under investigation. Stumped, officials admit they have absolutely no leads that could point them in the right direction. With more than one hundred people questioned in connection with the case as well as fifty search warrants served – including several DNA searches – investigators are hoping for a much-needed lucky break. Until now, someone has got away with murder in Spotsylvania and there is no doubt he will eventually try to do it again.

An hour's drive from Washington DC, Spotsylvania is a rapidly growing middle-class enclave of 80,000 residents. Since 1980, its population has more than doubled, with many retired FBI and other government agents moving in. Considered a haven for those wanting to get away from the urban chaos, Spotsylvania was like a storybook community in which to raise kids. Children played in their front yards, doors were left unlocked, and neighbors trusted each other. It was a picture-perfect setting, the ideal community to live out the American dream. But all that changed on 9 September between 4.30 and 5 p.m., when someone, somehow, took sixteen-year-old Sofia from her home; she was never to be seen alive again. 'This has changed the fabric of our community,' said Leslie Sorkhe, who co-ordinates local safety programs throughout the county. 'Growing up in Spotsylvania is forever changed.'

Now, parents dread leaving their children unsupervised. 'I don't have freedom any more,' complained Veronica Cartwright, fifteen, to a reporter of *USA Today*. 'I have a parent or another adult with me everywhere I go.' Families and neighbors have developed strict schedules to keep a watchful eye over the children with elaborate phone chains to track their every movement. Vigilant parents trail school buses scribbling down the license plate numbers of passing strangers. Children have been instructed to stay in the buses if they don't see their parents at their stop.

'We're living under the fear of another snatching. Everyone is suspicious of everyone else, and people give each other dirty looks,' said Belinda Richards, 38, a mother of four.

'It's devastating to no longer be safe,' said William Neely, the county prosecutor.

Sofia Silva, the first child to disappear, was five feet five inches tall and weighed one hundred pounds. She had long, dark-brown hair, wore braces and was a few days into her junior year in high school when she was snatched. No one noticed her disappearance until her mother, Phyllis, couldn't find her as the family sat for dinner. By night, after searching for her at all her friends' homes, a group of neighbors dispersed throughout the county looking for the spunky teenager and distributing missing person flyers. The next day, state and local authorities joined the search with tracking dogs and helicopters. Police detectives quickly determined that Sofia, an eager and involved student, was not likely to be a runaway. However, they were perplexed by how she vanished, leaving no evidence of a struggle, as if into thin air. Authorities theorize that the lack of a struggle points towards the perpetrator being an acquaintance or someone posing as a law-enforcement officer.

Five weeks later a nursery worker, investigating beaver damage in a wooded swamp sixty miles away, found her decomposing remains. She was partly submerged in water, her jewelry and clothing intact, except for her bra, which was missing. An oral pathologist made a definitive identification of Sofia using her dental records. Forensics determined she was killed no more than three days after her abduction. Autopsy reports revealed that her pubic hair had been entirely shaved by the suspected killer. The medical examiner was unable to determine the exact cause of death, but suggested it was strangulation or asphyxiation.

Weeks after Sofia's body was found, police arrested Karl Michael Roush, an itinerant house painter and neighbor of the Silvas. Fibers found in Roush's van were linked to those found on Sofia's body. Though he proclaimed his innocence, Roush was immediately indicted by the community. Typically, according to Clint Van Zandt, a retired head of an FBI serial killer unit, child abductors tend to live in the vicinity of their victims – which Roush did, making him the obvious guilty party. As circumstantial evidence against him mounted, some detectives started doubting they had the right man. Nonetheless friends and neighbors instantly indicted him saying his behavior changed following the disappearance of Sofia. He switched to harder liquor. He packed up and moved out of his basement apartment. While in jail for another felony, he allegedly boasted to cellmates about killing the girl. Meanwhile, Roush's defense lawyers called into question the reliability of the forensic evidence against him.

Seven months after Sofia's remains were identified – and with Roush still in prison – the killer struck again. This time Kristin Lisk, fifteen, and her sister, Kati, twelve, disappeared from their home on 1 May 1997, after returning from school in separate buses. Both girls arrived home at 3.00 p.m. At about 3.10, Ron Lisk, their father, phoned to check on his daughters. By then they were already gone. 'Every community in America has children that stay home from 3.15 to 5 o'clock, waiting on the parents,' said Charles Pickett, a case manager at the Arlington, Virginia-based National Center for Missing and Exploited Children. In an interview with *USA Today* he pointed out that the Lisk family was 'doing everything right' and still they were victimized by the killer.

Following the abductions of the Lisk girls an army of five hundred volunteers immediately fanned out around Spotsylvania. Officers, bloodhounds, and helicopters with special heat-seeking detection equipment searched the heavily wooded area behind the Lisk home. A two-mile radius from the girls' home was searched door-by-door by police and federal agents, twice. Special agents from the FBI's child abduction and serial killer unit were called in to help with the investigation. Five days after the two sisters disappeared, State highway workers found their bodies floating in the South Anna River, about forty miles away. Both were fully dressed, except that Kristy's bra was missing. And her pubic area was partially shaved.

Coincidentally, Spotsylvania is the home for many active and retired FBI agents. One agent, William Hagmaier, chief of the FBI's Child Abduction and Serial Killer Unit, lives within a few miles of the homes of the Silvas and Lisks. 'I couldn't sleep, but then I never sleep much anyway,' Hagmaier told *People* magazine. The father of two, Hagmaier could not stop thinking about the abductions in his neighborhood. 'Lots of people were suspicious that these cases were related, and it bothered me.' As details of the three murders surfaced, obvious links emerged indicating that the same individual was responsible for the three killings. All three girls disappeared from their homes after school leaving behind no sign of a struggle. All lived within a ten-mile radius of each other. All had dark hair and slim, athletic builds. All were found clothed and partly submerged in water. Two of them had their bras removed. The same two had their pubic hair shaved.

Following a hunch, Hagmaier phoned the director of the state forensics lab and asked him to take another look at the forensic evidence of the Silva case. The re-examination of the evidence at the Virginia State Crime Lab showed that the fiber tests linking Roush to the Silva case had been flawed and the lab technician had committed a mistake. Embarrassed prosecutors quietly dropped charges against Roush and the investigation focused on looking for someone else responsible for the three killings.

Once police announced they were searching for a serial killer all convicted sex offenders in the area were interviewed. Investigators were especially intrigued by reports of a man in a white van or pick-up seen cruising the Lisk neighborhood before the children disappeared. Police did an extensive search of all white vans and pick-up trucks in the area but found nothing. A year after the Lisk sisters' slaying, the Spotsylvania County Sheriff Ronald T. Knight announced the task force was looking for a small or mid-size red car that may have been in the vicinity at the time of the Lisk abductions. Knight added that the task force believed the killer took a watch – with an imitation leather strap and a Tweety-bird face that plays a thirteen-second sample of the Warner Brothers' cartoon theme song – that Kristin had been wearing the day she was snatched. Like many other serial killers the suspect might have taken the watch as a memento of the murder so as to re-live the act of killing.

In what appeared to be a solid lead, police announced on 20 October 1999, that a local carpet cleaner had become a 'person of interest' in their investigation. Task Force Lead Investigator Major Howard D. Smith of the Spotsylvania County Sheriff's Office, said Melvin Hogan, 32, had approached a local girl at her home, inquired about her sexual experiences and asked her for a hug. Hogan, who drives a white 1987 Ford van, was first questioned days after the abduction of the Lisk sisters, when police learned that he had been working on a job about a half mile from their home. His was one of several white vans police were looking into. Investigators found nothing particularly suspicious about Hogan, even though he declined to give a DNA-sample, and was never questioned again – until, that is, two and a half years later following his provocative 11 October conversation with a fifteen-year-old.

According to the affidavits filed to obtain search warrants in Stafford and Prince William circuit courts, Hogan knocked on the door of a home and asked the fifteen-year-old who answered to point out a neighbor's house where he was supposed to do work. After Hogan and his co-worker cleaned the neighbor's rugs, he returned alone to the girl's house. On his second visit he asked the girl if her parents were home, then asked to go into her house and use the phone. 'He made several comments concerning her looks, whether she was sexually active and requested hugs and other contact,' Detective Mark A. Lane wrote in the affidavit.

Frightened by the stranger at the door, the young girl called her father, who then called the police, rushed home and blocked Hogan's van in the driveway. When a sheriff's deputy arrived Hogan gave a false name, birth date and address. That night Hogan called the police station to give his real name and address saying that he had lied because he had been one of the people questioned about the Silva and Lisk killings and did not want to become a suspect in the serial killer case. 'This individual has drawn a lot of suspicion to himself,' said Investigator Smith. 'You act that way, you're going to receive a knock on the door from the task force.'

Police obtained search warrants for Hogan's home, workplace and van, where they collected fingerprints, carpet and hair samples, receipts and business records. Hogan also submitted a DNA-sample that ultimately exonerated him of any wrong. Hogan's wife, Concetta, told the *Washington Post* that police were 'grasping at straws', and had enough evidence to prove her husband's innocence. 'They want to hold someone responsible because they don't have a clue who it could be,' she added.

'The average guy who flirts around doesn't get put through this,' Hogan said, adding that he was guilty only of showing poor judgment and of 'disrespecting' his wife. 'I have not and would not ever take the life of another human being,' he added. 'I do have children of my own that I love very dearly. The thought of being accused of taking the life of another child is painfully insulting to me and my family.'

'My husband may have been wrong by flirting and a bad judge of character on age, but he's no killer,' Concetta said. 'It's as if our lives are being taken from us, and I know that we're not going to be able to get our dignity back.' Hogan and his wife both said they were at a Ford dealership in Orange County on 9 September 1996, when Sofia Silva disappeared from her home. They went to replace the engine of their van and had given police receipts proving it. The day the Lisk sisters disappeared Hogan spent the morning on the job in Spotsylvania, picking up rugs, and later went to Fredericksburg, where he was cleaning carpets with a co-worker. Once the DNA evidence collected came back negative Hogan reiterated that he had been unfairly targeted by law enforcement in their desperate attempt to find the killer.

'The only relief I have is that everyone will know that my DNA came back negative, and I'm not the guilty party,' Hogan said. 'I have no feeling of vindication . . . I'm very angry.'

Hogan, who was suspended from his job with Squeaky Clean Cleaning Service when his name surfaced in news reports, said he has not heard from his employer and is unsure whether he will be allowed to return to work. 'My innocence was proven before and has been proven once again, but at the expense of my family's privacy, dignity and loss of employment,' Hogan said in a prepared statement. 'To my wife and employers, I will never make a mistake like this again if given another chance; this has been the ultimate wake-up call.'

Since the investigation into the three killings began, authorities have chased close to ten thousand tips, conducted thousands of interviews and dedicated more than fifty thousand work hours to finding the killer. There are still twenty people working full-time on the Silva–Lisk investigation, and FBI spokeswoman Mary Johlie said the bureau is still fully committed to the case. But they still have no clue to who is responsible for the three killings. And they don't doubt that the perpetrator, unless he is dead or in prison for an unrelated offense, will sooner or later strike again.

6. DEATH WALKS THE STREETS OF CHICAGO

In July 1999, Chicago authorities issued a citywide warning about four separate predators stalking the windy city's South Side, specifically the crack and heroin ravaged neighborhoods of Englewood and New City. All victims were crack-addicted prostitutes who were found strangled and/or beaten to death inside abandoned buildings. Once the four distinct patterns were identified a fifty-member task force – including local homicide detectives and agents of the FBI – was assembled to solve the cases. The FBI has posted a $20,000 reward for information that will lead to the arrest of the killers involved.

'We are now dealing with four distinct patterns. We have four individuals involved in thirteen homicides, and in three criminal sexual assaults,' says Wentworth Area Detective Commander Frank Trigg, of the Chicago Police Department.

'It's the place, the time and the opportunity – you have all that here,' said police Commander Maurice Ford. 'This couldn't happen on the North Side. You don't have the abandoned buildings there, you don't have the chronic use of narcotics, and you don't have the prostitution problem.'

In fact, serial killing is nothing new for Chicago's tough South Side. Over the past eight years seven men have been responsible for the deaths of at least three dozen women and six men around the neighborhoods of Englewood and New City. To date four multiple killers have been arrested and charged with 29 murders, and at least three more still remain active and at large. This recent string of killings in the South Side has challenged one of the most pervasive myths about serial killers: that they are white, middle-aged men. This misconception, still prevalent among a number of investigators, has slowed law enforcement's efforts to identify these minority killers.

The victims have all been African-American women between nineteen and 49, who lead 'high-risk' lifestyles in which they sold sex for drugs, specifically crack cocaine.

Police believe the women were lured into abandoned buildings with the promise of drugs or money for sex. Once inside
they were raped, then strangled and/or bludgeoned to death.
To keep track of the victims and suspects, detectives have
categorized the cases by the first four letters of the alphabet.

The most perplexing case has involved Suspect A, who
detectives say is responsible for seven slayings and one rape.
Suspect B is responsible for one homicide and two rapes.
Suspect C has been linked to two homicides, and Suspect D
to three. Adding to the logistical nightmare both suspects C
and D have murdered one victim in the same abandoned
building, opening the possibility that the two men might
know each other. Frustrating the efforts to apprehend the
killers, the three women who have survived attacks have not
been too co-operative with the police. Obviously, being
prostitutes and crackheads, the last person they would want
to speak to would be a homicide detective.

The first break for detectives investigating the killings
came on 20 September 1999, when police arrested three
alleged gang members in connection with one murder
attributed to Suspect C. Robert Jarrette, 24, of Glen Ellyn,
Michael Mallet, 21, of Galesburg, and Eugene Rivers, 28, of
Chicago, were charged with the March 1998 rape, robbery
and slaying of LaCreesha Avery, 27, whose body was found
in a derelict building in the Englewood area. Though DNA
evidence linked the Avery slaying to one other Englewood
victim, police said the suspects in custody were not involved
in any of the other killings. The second murder attributed to
Suspect C – that of Juanita Butler, 27, whose body was found
in the 4600 block of South Wabash Avenue in May – remains
unsolved.

Less than a month later, in what police qualified as a
major breakthrough, Ronald Macon was linked through
genetic evidence to Suspect D. Macon, 35, was re-arrested on
11 October in Cook County Jail where he was serving time
for an unrelated rape charge. Confronted with the evidence,
the now suspected serial killer confessed on videotape to
strangling three women on the South Side after buying crack
cocaine for them and having sex. Macon killed all his three

victims in 1999. The first one, Angelnetta Peeples, 43, was found on 20 February in the basement stairwell of the same abandoned building where LaCreesha Avery was killed. Peeples was strangled, then hit on the head with a brick. Friends said she was last seen with a man named 'Ron'. His second victim, Linda Soloman, 36, was found on 14 April in the stairwell of an empty building. She was also strangled and hit on the head. His last known victim, Rosezina Williams, 50, was found strangled in a dumpster near a derelict building on 21 June.

Englewood detectives don't understand why Macon's DNA was not contained in the computerized DNA-databank designed to help track sex criminals. DNA-samples from suspects charged with sex crimes are supposed to be taken from them and stored in the Combined DNA Index System, or CODIS, where they can be matched with DNA-samples taken from unresolved crime scenes. Macon was, after all, sitting in the Cook County Jail since 9 August on charges that he raped his 65-year-old former baby-sitter. It took homicide detectives nearly two months to match his DNA to that gathered at the murder scenes of his three South Side victims.

With two of the DNA patterns partly solved, police focused their attention on capturing the still-at-large suspects A and B. Suspect B, who raped one South Side woman and killed another in 1995, didn't resurface until October 1998 when he raped a woman on the city's North Side. Authorities believe the killer could be traveling from somewhere else to Chicago, or could be dead or in prison for an unrelated offense. In any case he hasn't resurfaced since the end of 1998.

These new forensic tools have given Chicago police the ability to locate crime patterns around the city in a way that would be unimaginable in the past. 'Without DNA evidence, we might not have linked the North Side crime to the others,' says Sergeant Brian Murphy.

Homicide expert James Alan Fox believes the cases in Chicago are a powerful lesson in how DNA-testing can make police work both simpler and more complicated. 'In the old days, we could implicate one suspect in many murders just because the crimes fit a pattern. Now DNA forces us to grapple with the truth.'

And the truth is that the prime suspect left, Suspect A, is also the deadliest. With eight kills under his belt authorities believe he is good at what he does and that's why they fear him most. Furthermore, they have no reason to believe he will not try to kill again. Some think the recent publicity on the South Side killings could have driven the killer out of Chicago to continue with his deadly forays.

Suspect A, according to investigators, appears to have been scouting the abandoned buildings by day, then taking his victims there at night. Case in point is where Constance 'Tiny' Bailey, his seventh victim, was discovered. Bailey's body was found in a hard-to-reach attic of a three-floor abandoned tire-shop that was only accessible through a trap door above a stairwell. It's not the type of place one locates casually. Chicago Police Commander Thomas Cronin believes Suspect A lives in the neighborhood because of his familiarity with the empty buildings. He also believes he is a great 'con man', and could know his victims, because he's able to persuade street-smart prostitutes to accompany him to dark, isolated places.

The first victim attributed to Suspect A, Patricia Dunns, was found on 21 September 1993. The second, Shanteen Angel, was found nearly a year and a half later, on 3 April 1995. Then, on 13 August 1998 two women – Nichole Townsend and Evandre Harris – were found dead in separate places. His last three victims, Bailey, Sheryl Johnson and Cheryl Cross, were found within a mile of each other. Johnson was found first in December 1998. Two months later Cross was found two blocks away. Bailey was found in April 1999 in an abandoned building a quarter-mile away. Since Suspect A started killing, three other serial killers have been arrested in the South Side. Having four independent killers active in the same general area is not unprecedented, especially if the area is a hotbed of prostitution and drugs. What is unprecedented is four separate murderous rampages genetically identified in such proximity.

Noting that the killings stopped abruptly in 1999, Peter Smerick, a retired FBI investigator who now works with The

Academy Group in Manassas, VA, a private behavioral science consulting firm, remarked that the absence of new crimes rarely means the person has stopped committing crimes. 'With serial killers, there's a cooling-off period of weeks to months, sometimes years,' Smerick said. 'Sometimes a person has left the area, but they're still going to have those urges.'

In an attempt to widen the scope of their investigation Chicago authorities contacted law-enforcement agencies in ten states to inquire about pattern slayings similar to those that mysteriously stopped in Chicago when the investigation was made public. On 24 January 2000, Chicago officials announced they talked with authorities in Wisconsin, Indiana, Ohio, Iowa, Minnesota, Michigan, Arkansas, Missouri, Tennessee and Colorado. Police are searching for similar cases involving African-American women who may have been arrested on drug or prostitution charges, who have been found strangled in abandoned buildings. Police feel Suspect A probably moved elsewhere after the investigation was made public. A recent rash of murders of crack-addicted prostitutes in nearby Flint, Michigan, might point towards the killer's relocation.

Police and FBI agents in Flint have formed another task force to investigate the killings. Like the Chicago women the victims have been black, involved in drugs and/or prostitution, and were found in or near abandoned houses. 'The victims have been female, African-American, late twenties to late thirties, and all have a history of drug use and/or prostitution,' police said in a news release. The first victim, Helene Fails, 38, was found on 15 February 1999, in an abandoned house. The second, Brenda Millender, 27, was found by police on 22 August in another abandoned house. The third, Hermetta Harris, 33, was found on 29 September by a man walking his dog in a park. The latest victim, 31-year-old Lisa Marie Price, was found by a passerby on 8 October.

No foreigner to multiple murders, the Flint Police Department already has another task force investigating yet another separate set of possible serial killings. Police believe the killings of three prostitutes between September 1993 and June

1994 in Flint, Genesee Township and Saginaw County's Thomas Township area could also be the work of a single individual. The three murders in question are as follows: Angela Tate, 39, who was found on 14 September 1993, in the Flint River; Dawn M. Hendon, 30, who was found on 20 March 1994, by children playing outside the Richfield Bowl in Genesee Township; and Pamela S. Newton, 35, of Flint who was found the following June in a creek in Thomas Township. A Grand Blanc Township man convicted of kidnap and rape is listed as the primary suspect in these cases, but no charges have been brought against him. Police indicated in no uncertain terms that these murders and the recent cluster of killings are completely unrelated.

And like Flint, Chicago has had more than its share of serial killers at work. At least thirty women have been found sexually assaulted and murdered in abandoned buildings in the city's South Side since 1991. At one point in 1995, three separate killers worked within a twelve-block area. Two of these killers are now in custody; one has been sentenced to death for killing six women; the other is awaiting trial on fourteen murder counts. In 1997 Hubert Geralds Jr was sentenced to death for killing six women in Englewood between 1994 and 1995. Though he was not charged, authorities believe he is responsible for one more killing. Gregory Clepper, who was arrested in 1996, confessed to killing fourteen women in the area between 1991 and 1996.

In 1995, Englewood residents complained to police that a serial killer was active in their neighbourhood, strangling women and leaving their corpses in alleys and trash containers. Police dismissed their complaints until thirty-year-old Hubert Geralds, a mentally retarded drug addict, was turned in to police by his sister after he killed a woman who lived at his home. Described as a 'child in a man's body' by his lawyer during his trial, Geralds suffered from an array of mental disorders. At the time of the murders, Geralds, who for most of his life had been in and out of jail on drug and burglary charges, was working in a neighbourhood store as a stock clerk.

His first known victim, 25-year-old Rhonda King, was found strangled in the attic of an abandoned building on 21

December 1994. She was a prostitute who worked around an area in Englewood known as 'The Stroll'. The next day police found his second known victim, Dorthea Withers, 37. Geralds told police he strangled her after she tried to steal his cocaine. In March 1995 two more women were found strangled in Englewood: Alonda Tart, 23, on 14 March, and Joyce Wilson, 28, on 26 March. In custody Geralds told police he killed Tart after she tried to grab his stash of cocaine and run from the basement of a derelict building. He strangled Wilson after quarreling with her over smoking too much from his crack pipe. Geralds himself led police to her body. He strangled her inside a delivery truck parked in a vacant lot. At the time police did not suspect his involvement in the crime and found no evidence associating him with the killing.

His next victim, Millicent 'Peanut' Jones, 25, was found on 12 June. She vanished from Garfield Boulevard when her boyfriend went to buy a cigarette lighter. Geralds said that she approached him and they went to a nearby building where, when she began taking off her clothes, he 'flipped out and strangled her'. Shortly after the Jones killing, Jacqueline Kelly, who was visiting her sister next door to his home, heard him brag about killing several women. At the time, Kelly testified, she thought he was kidding. When she dismissed his claims, he insisted that he was the feared 'Englewood Strangler' and that he 'was too smart for police'.

His last victim, Mary Blackman, 42, lived-in with him and his sister at their home. Police said he strangled her on 14 June 1995, while the two were smoking crack in the basement of the house. Geralds was arrested when his sister, Angela, turned him in after finding Blackman's body in a trash dumpster near their home. Geralds told police he and Blackman were smoking crack in the basement when his sister called down in a suspicious tone. He said he put his hand over Blackman's mouth to prevent her from saying anything and when he took his hand away, she was dead.

Geralds's defense attorney Allen Sincox claimed his client had an IQ ranging from as low as 59 to as high as 73. He also had frontal-lobe brain damage – which is a common trait in serial killers – that was probably caused by a childhood head injury. In court Dr Frederick Berlin, a Johns Hopkins University psychiatrist, testified that Geralds suffered from a paraphilia – in this case a sexual compulsion to have sex with women who are asleep or unconscious. 'Hubert Geralds is a man with a man's urges,' attorney Susan Smith said. 'But Hubert Geralds has the mental capacity of an eight-year-old. He has the urges, but not the brakes, the controls that you and I have.'

Family members testified that Geralds acted strangely as a child, lying down on the street in front of cars, using his head to bash through storm doors and jumping from second-story windows while proclaiming he could fly. The Geralds case raised serious questions about the efficacy of Chicago's vaunted community policing program. Five serial killers later, the program itself obviously does not work. A year after Geralds's arrest, Gregory Clepper – a 28-year-old crack addict – was arrested and charged with murdering fourteen South Side women.

Like Geralds, Clepper's victims were mostly black, crack-addicted prostitutes whom he strangled, then dumped in alleys and garbage containers around the South Side. Clepper allegedly killed his victims when they objected to his refusal to pay them for sex. The slayings began in 1991 and continued until his arrest in 1996. At the time of his arrest, again police did not realize they had a serial killer in the area. Clepper's arrest came after he boasted to an acquaintance about killing thirty-year-old Patricia Scott. On 24 April Scott was found raped and strangled in a trash dumpster behind a South Side high school. Clepper confessed to killing Scott at the home he shared with his mother and stashing her body in the closet. But then he kept confessing to the tune of thirteen more killings. Until his confession, police had not linked any of the killings together and were unaware of having another serial killer at work.

His mother Gladys Clepper, 46, was charged with con-cealing the Scott murder and helping her son dispose of the victim's body. A neighbor, Eric Henderson, 30, was also charged with witnessing one murder and helping conceal two. Clepper, who according to neighbors could not have been a nicer person, was arrested at an aunt's house. Chicago police said Clepper had been co-operative and had helped investigators find the bodies of the victims. While in custody Clepper boasted of killing up to 40 women. If found guilty of the fourteen killings he's been charged with, Clepper will become Chicago's most lethal serial killer since John Wayne Gacy slaughtered 33 boys and buried them in the crawlspace under his home.

During these earlier killing sprees, community leaders accused police of paying no attention to the crimes. But with the new set of thirteen cluster killings, explained police, the same civic leaders – together with local clergy and activists – have taken to the streets, blanketing the area with leaflets, leading meetings and marches, trying to get the residents involved. 'This time around, the community has gotten more involved and gotten more information,' said Josephine Robinson, area director for the Chicago Commons Mary McDowell Settlement House, a local community agency.

Relations between the community and the police department became strained in 1998 when charges were filed against two boys, seven and eight, accused of the brutal murder of Ryan Harris. The body of the eleven-year-old honor roll student was found half dressed, her mouth stuffed with her underpants, behind an apartment building, three blocks from her godmother's house. She had been hit on the head, suffocated and sexually molested. Charges against the two pre-adolescent boys were dropped a month later when the children were unable to produce semen samples that investigators wanted to match with semen recovered on the victim's dress.

Community members became even more enraged when it was disclosed that the officer who extracted the murder confessions from the two little boys had coaxed a similar admission from an eleven-year-old four years earlier. The community was shocked by the willingness of white officers to believe that two black children would commit such a horrifying deed. Charges of racism flooded the Chicago media. 'There was an uproar about the whole situation,' said a neighbor who lives across the street from where Ryan's body was found. 'They wanted to find who did it. Then they come up with these two little kids. They're just railroading those little kids. It's wrong.' Eventually the suspected killer was identified as serial rapist, Floyd Durr.

However, tensions between the community and the force prevailed. Many felt police were never doing enough to track the area's decade-long series of serial killers because the dead women were black and poor. At one of the crime scenes, residents complained that police showed a total lack of respect for the neighborhood when they left the naked corpse of a victim uncovered for more than half an hour, even though several children were nearby. Englewood and its residents are not unaccustomed to violence. As well as rampant prostitution and drug use, murder and violent crime are part of life. In 1998, the Englewood police district – which is barely four square miles – reported 55 murders; that is three murders less than in the entire city of Minneapolis.

Police say the neighborhood is close to being the perfect hunting ground for a lust killer. Because of a growing number of halfway houses and shelters in the area, Englewood has over 190 registered sex offenders – more than any other part of the city. According to police records, eight registered sex offenders live on one block alone. Alderwoman Shirley Coleman, the district representative and the first public official to show concern for the victims, said the only growth industries in her district are halfway houses and sex-offender rehab institutes, which leaves little hope for the rest of the constituents in the area.

'People are overwhelmed by their struggle for survival. They don't have the time to pay attention to what is happening in their community,' said Josephine Robinson, area director of the Chicago Commons Mary McDowell Settlement House. Some of the victims had sought drug counseling at Mary McDowell House. Others just came to the soup kitchen. Frieda Holley, who runs its women's help program, said one day she realized she knew every one of the women who turned up dead: 'That's when I started getting scared,' she said.

One of the reasons why the Englewood serial killers and their victims have not received much attention lies both in the nature of the victims and the crimes themselves. The victims, drug-addicted prostitutes, tend to lead lives that make investigating their deaths next to impossible. Complicating matters, some view the victims as people whose lifestyle and behavior may have brought their fate upon themselves. 'If white middle-class college students are targeted, then it becomes a national case,' says Jack Levin, director of the Brudnick Center on Violence at Northeastern University in Boston. 'If it's black prostitutes, you're talking about marginalized people. It doesn't even get the attention locally.'

According to Eric Hickey, a criminologist who teaches at California State University in Fresno, it is factually untrue that most serial killers are white. In his study of 399 serial killers, Hickey found that about 22 percent of the killers were black, indicating that there is a larger percentage of black serial killers than the percentage of blacks in the population of the US. A considerable number of cases mentioned in this book – Chicago, Flint, Los Angeles, South Africa and Belize – involve suspects who are believed to be black. Though all research done on serial murder has been on white killers, experts have no idea if the behavior of black serial killers is any different from the general profile. Asked if the number of black serial killers was on the rise Hickey said: 'We have had black serial killers for many years but they have not made the press much, except for Wayne Williams. I suspect that the percentage is really not changing much, it is just that we are finally hearing more about them.'

Ironically, DeKalb County Sheriff Sidney Dorsey and Fulton County Police Chief Louis Graham, both Atlanta police homicide investigators at the time of the rash of Atlanta child murders, believe that Williams, who was convicted in 1981 of killing two black men, was probably not responsible for the bulk of the killings. Instead, they believe, a cadre of white supremacists killed most of the children. Lynn Whatley, Williams's lawyer, has been pushing for DNA-testing of the evidence to exonerate her client. John Douglas, the former FBI agent whose serial killer profile led to Williams's arrest, believes that he was probably one of four killers who, at the time, were active in the area.

Undoubtedly many readers are familiar with Jeffrey Dahmer, John Wayne Gacy, Ted Bundy, Fred West and Andrew Cunanan. But the same cannot be said of Carlton Gary, Craig Price and Vaughn Greenwood. Other black serial killers have recently been arrested in Norfolk, Virginia, Detroit, Michigan, and Charlotte, North Carolina.

Known as the 'Stocking Strangler', Carlton Gary was sentenced to death for the strangulation murders of three older women in Columbus, Georgia. Between 1977 and 1978 Gary – one of the few black serial killers of the seventies – was suspected of killing at least seven women within Columbus's Wynnton neighborhood. All victims were wealthy white women between 59 and 89 years of age. In most cases the victims were raped, strangled with their own stockings, and left covered with bedclothes. Gary was said to be highly intelligent and to have a phenomenal memory. He was arrested on 3 May 1984 – six years after the killings – in Albany, Georgia, after police traced a stolen pistol from one of the 'Strangler' killings to him.

Craig Price was only thirteen when he committed his first murder. Known as the 'Warwick Slasher' for a four-victim murder rampage in Rhode Island in the late 1980s, Craig, a fifteen-year-old black youth when he was arrested, was, according to the FBI, the youngest serial killer in American history. Because he was arrested as a minor, Price was scheduled to be released in 1998. Not having been a model prisoner he still faces an additional twenty years in prison for crimes committed while incarcerated. The FBI and local authorities believe that once he is released, it's only a matter of time before he starts killing again.

In 1974–75 LAPD found six derelicts in Downtown Los Angeles with their throats slashed and their bodies bearing signs of ritualistic abuse. They had cups of blood next to them, salt sprinkled around the outlines of their heads and cryptic marks scribbled around the slash wounds. When the cops announced that the killer, known as the 'Skid Row Slasher', was probably 'a blond, sexually impotent and cowardly homosexual', Vaughn Greenwood, a black man, was obviously not at the top of their suspect list. Eventually

Greenwood was arrested and charged with eleven murders after he axed someone next to actor Burt Reynolds's house.

Elton M. Jackson, suspected of being the 'Hampton Roads Killer', is believed to be responsible for twelve homicides in and around Norfolk, Virginia. Nearly all his victims were drifters or transients. Their bodies were found around the Chesapeake Bay. Most were last seen near gay bars in the Norfolk and Portsmouth areas. On 5 March 1998, Chesapeake Police Chief Richard A. Justice identified Jackson, a black man, as their main suspect. Though he was only charged with one murder, authorities believe Jackson is responsible for all twelve homicides. Not surprisingly there have been no other similar slayings since his arrest. Coincidentally, Jackson's arrest came right when the saturation coverage of the Andrew Cunanan manhunt was getting under way.

Benjamin Atkins, a black, homeless crack addict, was reportedly the fastest serial killer in American history. He raped and strangled eleven women over a nine-month period between 1991 and 1992 in and around Detroit, Michigan. 'I killed all eleven of them so I didn't have to worry about them pressing charges,' Atkins, 24 at the time, told investigators after his arrest. He was sentenced to life in prison, where he died of AIDS in 1997.

In Charlotte, Henry Louis Wallace confessed to raping and killing ten black women. Police started suspecting there was an active serial killer in the area in March 1994 after a burst of four slayings in three weeks. Once again authorities had to deny any charges of racism because of their reluctance to find any links between the crimes. Eventually police tried to exonerate themselves for their lack of interest by claiming that Wallace, who is black, did not fit the general serial killer profile. Uncharacteristically he preyed on acquaintances, a very rare trait in serial killing and, according to serial killer expert Robert Ressler, Wallace did things in his pre- and post-offense behavior that didn't make any sense. 'If he elected to become a serial killer, he was going about it in the wrong way,' testified Ressler in his trial. 'Mr Wallace always seemed to take one step forward and two steps back. He would take items and put them in the stove to destroy them by burning them and then forget to turn the stove on.'

After the closing of Chicago's stockyards in the 1970s, many of the middle-class families living in the Englewood area moved out, leaving the neighborhoods to wither with neglect. With time the once thriving community sank deeper into desperation culminating with this decade-long serial killer hell. Presently the area is full of garbage-strewn vacant lots, crumbling single-family homes, and, unfortunately, abandoned buildings. Adding to the misery, at least one-third of the area's residents are believed to be unemployed.

Critics charge that the area has largely been forgotten by City Hall which, they contend, has focused its development might on the Loop and white neighborhoods in the northern part of the city. Because of race, politics and money, the area has been passed over by the wave of economic development that has swept over Chicago. Instead, the derelict structures that cover the district serve as intravenous shooting galleries, crack houses, and convenient spots for prostitutes to turn tricks and for tricks to kill them.

In fact the district is packed with more than six hundred empty buildings, with three to four per block in some areas. While some have been demolished, officials are frustrated by the time it takes to identify the owners and make them fix up or tear down the building. 'You have to go right after the landlord or absentee landlords,' said Mayor Richard M. Daley. 'Many of the women have been killed – dragged into abandoned buildings – and you have to eliminate those immediately.'

City officials, the police department and Alderwoman Coleman organized a special force to catalogue the abandoned buildings in Englewood and other vulnerable neighborhoods and search out the mortgage companies and absentee land-lords who own them. Officials believe the demolishing of these buildings would cut down on crime. According to the city's Building Department, 58 structures in the Englewood Police District are slated for 'fast-track' demolition. The fast-track program, started in 1993, is designed to streamline the procedures to demolish buildings. Complicating matters, the identities of the owners of many of these buildings are hidden behind bank trusts, making the legality of the demolition process more difficult. Still, the buildings alone are not responsible for the bloodshed.

On 31 January 2000, to the delight of Alderwoman Coleman and Chicago's 50-member Police Task Force, authorities announced the arrest of 37-year-old Andre Crawford. Crawford, who was genetically linked to seven murders and eight rapes, was arrested on 28 January after police received several tips about him while interviewing the friends of the victims. With his arrest police have solved the most worrisome cluster of slayings in the Englewood and New City areas. Known previously as DNA Pattern A, Crawford confessed on videotape to the seven murders he was linked to genetically as well as to three others authorities had not considered to be related to the case. The extra three killings also involved drug-addicted prostitutes and occurred between 23 July 1997 and 2 February 1999.

In all he was charged with ten counts of first-degree murder, eleven counts of aggravated criminal sexual assault and one count of attempted murder. With Crawford's arrest the Chicago Police Department solved eleven of the thirteen murders originally under investigation with three of the four DNA-Patterned-suspects under arrest.

An elated Chicago Police Superintendent Terry Hillard, while flanked by dozens of police and FBI agents, said, 'These men and women worked night and day tracking leads, knocking on doors, and on stakeouts, and searching dozens of abandoned buildings. Because of their efforts, and particularly because of the efforts of the residents in Englewood and New City, who never gave up the faith to solve these crimes, the residents of the community and the entire city can rest easier.'

Following the news of his arrest, Alderwoman Shirley Coleman said, 'I'm breathing a sigh of relief tonight and the entire community is breathing a sigh of relief.' Then she added that, '[The arrest] tells the city of Chicago that when police and people in the community work together they can solve crimes.'

Prosecutors said Crawford's videotaped confession took three days. In it he said he killed the women he lured from the streets to exchange drugs for sex. 'When women would resist having the sexual favors before the delivery of the cocaine, he would then strangle them,' said Assistant State Attorney Thomas Epach. In at least one case, the prosecutor added, Crawford had sex with a victim after she was murdered. Then he moved her to another building where he would return to have sex again.

Crawford was well-known in the New City and Englewood areas. According to residents he was the type of person who would offer to do small chores for cash. 'You'd never expect it,' said Englewood resident Quincy Ray. 'This is a man who'd ask if he could shovel your snow.'

Another neighbor said Crawford often voiced his hatred of prostitutes. 'He said they shouldn't be out there, they should get a job and do something better with their lives.' Though at the time of his arrest he was unemployed, he worked for thirteen years as a newspaper delivery-truck driver for the *Chicago Sun-Times*.

Just as the police profilers had warned, Crawford lived in the community and traveled in the same circles as his victims. 'I was glad I was caught, because I was like a shark in a pool,' Crawford told his interrogators. Crawford grew up in the area and lived in several vacant buildings that, not coincidentally, were close to the murder scenes. In the summer of 1999 he moved away from the Englewood area, 'because there was too much heat'. Relocating to Chicago's West Side he found over there that the 'women were tougher,' he confessed.

Katrina Martin, 34, who describes herself as a recovering drug addict, was one of three people who passed Crawford's name to the police. In an interview with the *Chicago Tribune* she said she had known Crawford since 1992, when she was making a living swapping sex for drugs. At the time she lived with a man who allowed crack users to get high in his apartment. Crawford was a regular there, and so were Patricia Dunns, Tommie Dennis, Sonja Brandon, Constance Bailey, Sheryl Johnson and Shaquanta 'Pumpkin' Langley – six of the ten women Crawford allegedly murdered. She started suspecting Crawford was one of the South Side killers in December 1999 when he sat behind her on a bus and told her that the victims deserved to die. '[They] need to be strangled and have their heads beaten in,' she remembered him saying.

To track the investigation into his crimes, Crawford – who had a police record dating back to 1985 – went to community meetings where police and residents discussed the progress of the serial-killer probe. 'I found out this man was attending my meetings, clapping when I walked in,' Wentworth Area Detective Trigg said at a Chicago Commons Mary McDowell Settlement House meeting following the arrest.

Crawford also participated in Operation Safe Passage, in which men escort children through tough South Side neighborhoods as they walk to school. 'It's scary that this man was able to be among a community and society for as long as he was, to be a part of the very effort that was supposed to protect us from him,' Coleman said.

Adding complexity and confusion to the streak of serial killings in the South Side, on 11 February authorities announced that one of the new killings confessed to by suspect Andre Crawford had already been pinned on convicted serial killer Hubert Geralds. Both Crawford and Geralds confessed to killing 24-year-old Rhonda King. Geralds said after his arrest in 1995 that he killed King when she tried to steal his cocaine. Detectives, who believe Crawford's confession to the murder was more detailed and compelling, have chosen to pin the killing on the new suspect.

Because the case against Geralds consolidated the six murders and tried them before one jury, Chicago authorities have been forced to throw out his 1997 conviction and retry him for the remaining five murder charges. Of the five other murders, police have DNA evidence linking him to four. Though Geralds allegedly confessed to the six killings, there was no DNA evidence at the King crime scene and another crime scene. The change of suspect also brings into question how police obtained Geralds's confession. Geralds, who is mildly retarded, was described by his former lawyer as someone having the mind of an eight-year-old. 'This was a man of extremely low intelligence. They could have gotten him to go along with anything,' said Assistant Public Defender Allen Sincox about his former client. 'This certainly throws Geralds's statements into question.'

Residents have no illusions that the arrests of Crawford and the others will signal the end of their troubles. 'The people in the neighborhood have just been so bombarded,' community activist Dee D. Smith Simmons told the Associated Press. 'When you're with crime everywhere, you develop almost an insensitivity to it. That's the horrible crime of letting crime go undetected.' In addition to the two unsolved killings and the two unsolved rapes, crime is still rampant in the area and police mistrust still commonplace. But at least, for now, residents of Chicago's South Side have one less creep to worry about.

CHICAGO UPDATE
Adding a new degree of uncertainty into the serial killer investigations in Chicago's South Side, authorities announced they were dropping all but one of the murder charges against Gregory Clepper. DNA testing excluded Clepper as a suspect in some of the twelve cases, while investigators uncovered scientific and other evidence pointing to other suspects in the others.

On 21 March 2001, in a plea agreement with prosecutors Clepper, who once bragged about being Chicago's most prolific serial killer, was sentenced to 80 years in prison for the 1996 murder of Patricia Scott. Assistant State's Attorney William O'Brien said Clepper would still remain a suspect in fifteen murders and could be charged if evidence pointed to him as the culprit. The plea agreement allows prosecutors to file new charges against Clepper in the twelve cases that were dropped if DNA tests implicated him. However, Clepper would not be eligible for the death penalty in any future judgement against him.

The Clepper case began crumbling in 1999 after the Chicago police Cold Case Homicide Unit turned up evidence implicating another suspect in the 1994 murder of a still-unidentified black woman. Following a tip, the case was reinvestigated by the unit's Detective Brian Killacky, who turned up DNA evidence pointing to another suspect, Earl Mack Jr, as the real killer.

With the Mack fiasco fresh in their mind, the cold case unit and state's attorney's investigators began re-examining all remaining Clepper cases, leading to the dismissal of twelve of thirteen pending murder charges. Prosecutors noted, as if excusing their negligence, that DNA evidence from the victims was hard to interpret because the women were prostitutes and most had several sexual partners before they were murdered.

The unraveling of the Clepper charges called into question the behavior of both police and prosecutors in the investigation. Police said Clepper confessed to the murders and gave specific details of the crimes. However Cook County prosecutors obtained their 1996 indictment against him without waiting for a complete laboratory analysis of the evidence. 'It's not a fine piece of investigative work,' said a police official who did not want to be identified.

7. *LUSTMORD* IN LOS ANGELES

In the greater Los Angeles metropolitan area there are at least two suspected killers on the loose acting separately in different sections of the city. One killer, known as the 'Southside Slayer', has claimed up to fifteen victims. The second, known as the 'Pomona Strangler', is believed to be responsible for at least seven deaths. Though unrelated, both killers are hunting the same type of women: drug-addicted, black prostitutes. Profiles point at both killers being black. As of this writing, neither killer has been active since 1995. Though two men have been convicted for five killings related to the Southside Slayer, all the other murders remain unsolved with no suspects under investigation or in custody.

In 1985, shortly after the arrest of serial killer Richard Ramirez put an end to his 'Night Stalker' rampage through the city, officers in the predominantly black neighborhood of South-Central announced the existence of another serial killer. The new killer, dubbed the Southside Slayer, was targeting 'strawberries', the street term for crack-addicted black prostitutes. The killings started in September 1983. The last victim was found in May 1987. At first the killer was credited with nineteen deaths, but then his body count was revised to thirteen after three men were separately charged and convicted of six murders.

In 1988 Louis Craine, an unemployed construction worker with an IQ of 69, confessed to three of the Slayer killings. Though he later recanted, Craine was charged with five murders, two of which were not on the 'official' Slayer list. Daniel Lee Siebert, a convicted killer imprisoned in Alabama, was also charged in 1988 with two of the killings. In 1986 a third man, Charles Mosley, was convicted of one more Slayer killing.

All the Southside victims had a history of drug and prostitution arrests. Their ages ranged from 22 to 34. All had been strangled and nearly all were also stabbed. Many of the corpses showed a pattern of 'overkill'. Forensic evidence suggested the women were first tortured with superficial cuts, then strangled and/or stabbed to death. Their bodies were dumped in residential streets, alleys, parks and schoolyards within the city limits of Los Angeles and neighboring incorporated areas.

In 1985, with nine murders already under his belt, the Slayer attracted hardly any press attention. However, that was not the case with the Night Stalker killings. During the mid-eighties city-wide warnings had been posted about the growing Stalker menace. Ramirez, who was eventually convicted for the serial slayings, had literally set siege on Los Angeles. His characteristically brutal home invasion rampages of rape, mutilation and murder in predominantly middle-class neighborhoods around the LA basin had captured the attention of residents, police and press. The seemingly random attacks were only related by the facts that the intruder entered through unlocked doors and/or windows and left all those inside either maimed or dead. Survivors fearfully described the killer's piercing eyes and rotting teeth. The crime scenes spoke of unthinkable savagery. With a flair for the theatrical, the killer sprayed satanic slogans throughout the homes, mutilated and/or took the eyes of some of the victims and carved pentagrams on the bodies of others.

Newspapers ran sensationalized accounts of the Stalker exploits, TV stations tapped into the primal fear of a random killer running amok in the safety of the very homes of the victims. On 30 August 1985, Richard Ramirez – a Texan drifter, drug addict, petty thief and heavy metal Satanist – was identified as the serial killer. The next day, with his face plastered all over the morning papers, Ramirez was apprehended in Boyle Heights, a predominantly Latino neighborhood, by an angry mob who beat him to a pulp after he attempted a carjacking. In 1989 Ramirez was sentenced to death for thirteen rape–murders. With one more murder charge pending in San Francisco, Ramirez now lives in Death Row in San Quentin Prison where he is married to a groupie and enjoys answering fan mail.

The consummate rock-and-roll-type killer, Ramirez played every photo opportunity like a star amassing a legion of groupies and adoring fans. During a pre-trial hearing, Ramirez, in his distinctive manner, drew a pentagram on the palm of his hand and flashed it at the press cameras while mouthing: 'Hail Satan'. After receiving the death penalty he turned his venom onto the court: 'You don't understand me. You are not expected to. You are not capable of it. I am beyond your experience. I am beyond good and evil. I don't believe in the hypocritical, moralistic dogma of this so-called civilized society. I need not look beyond this courtroom to see all the liars, the haters, the killers, the crooks, the paranoid cowards – truly trematodes of the Earth, each one in his own legal profession. You maggots make me sick! Hypocrites one and all.'

Then, in more ominous tones, he concluded: 'I don't need to hear all of society's rationalizations. I've heard them all before and the fact remains that what is, is. Legions of the night – night breed – repeat not the errors of the Night Prowler and show no mercy. I will be avenged.' As he was led out of court, he was asked by reporters what he thought of his death penalty. 'No big deal,' he answered, 'death comes with the territory. See you in Disneyland!' In jail Ramirez fixed his teeth and fell in love. On 3 October 1996, Doreen Lioy, then 41, married Ramirez in a simple and tasteful ceremony in San Quentin's waiting room. The now Mrs Ramirez, who is rumored to have a bachelor's degree in English literature and an IQ of 152, said she was first attracted to the convicted serial killer in 1985 when she saw a picture of him in the paper. A truly devoted lover, Lioy wrote 75 letters to Ramirez before she was allowed to visit. The couple got engaged in 1988, but prison regulations delayed the wedding until 1996.

Strikingly different has been the reaction of the public, the media and the police to the Southside Slayer killings. In fact, it was as if no one really cared. No one feared they could be next. No one even knew about the killings. That is, except for the other street women who felt they could be next. 'Our guys have told every hooker they can find about this case,' said Lieutenant Cooke. 'Prostitution may be illegal, but as far as I know, it doesn't yet carry the death penalty.' Margaret

Prescod, a community organizer and leader of the Black Coalition Fighting Black Serial Murders, said police were less than aggressive in the case because most of the victims were black prostitutes. 'If this was another community in which these murders had happened, you wouldn't have the lackadaisical attitude that you see on the part of the police,' she told the *Los Angeles Times*.

Unlike the Stalker victims, who were mostly from middle-class families, the Slayer victims were strawberries. They were seen as mere refuse of the mean streets of LA, women who had surrendered their lives to the evils of prostitution and drugs and were on the fast track to oblivion. Perhaps that's why Ramirez is on Death Row and the Southside Slayer is still on the loose.

At first police were uncertain that the killings were the work of the same person. 'Killing a prostitute is not a terribly unusual crime,' said Lieutenant Dan Cooke, spokesman for the Los Angeles Police Department. 'But now we've concluded that this one leaves a unique signature. A number of things indicate that there is a pattern and a single killer or team of killers.' Police would not elaborate on what the pattern was.

The first woman to be officially included in the Southside Slayer victim list was Loletha Prevot. She was found in Los Angeles on 4 September 1983. Next came Patricia Coleman, found in Inglewood, on 1 January of the next year. Ten months later, on 18 November, the mutilated body of Sheila Burton was discovered inside city limits. In 1985 the killer claimed twelve lives: Frankie Bell on 1 January; Patricia Dennis on 11 February; Sheily Wilson on 29 March; Lillian Stoval on 23 March; Patsy Webb on 15 April; Cathy Gustavsonon on 28 July; Gail Ficklin on 15 August; Gayle Rouselle, in the suburb of Gardena, on 6 November; Myrtle Collier, back in Los Angeles, the next day; Nesia McElrath on 18 December; Elizabeth Landcraft four days later; and Gidget Castro, in the City of Industry, on 26 December. One of the women escaped alive from an encounter with the suspected killer by jumping out of a moving car on 6 August.

The killer kept his deadly schedule with four reported murders in 1986. On 5 January Tammy Scretchings was the first to fall to the Slasher's wrath. Then came Lorna Reed, found in San Dimas on 11 February. On 26 May Verna Williams was found in the stairwell of a Los Angeles elementary school. Next, Tina Chaney was found dead in Watts on 3 November. Three more murders in 1986 have remained unsolved and are believed to be related to the Slayer killings. In January 1988 police added Carolynh Barney, murdered on 29 May 1987, to the official Southside Slayer list.

Another prostitute and a friend also survived a potentially lethal encounter with the suspected killer. Both sets of survivors described the killer as a large dark-complexioned black man with muscular arms and chest, 30 to 35 years old, between five feet ten inches and six feet tall, with black hair, brown eyes, a small mustache, white teeth and wearing a baseball cap. However, the descriptions of the killer's car were markedly different. One witness said the suspect was driving a 1984 or 1985 dark-colored Buick Regal with a baby seat in the back. The other reported seeing a 1960 to 1969 Ford pick-up truck with gray primer paint.

In 1988 LAPD officials, convinced they had multiple killers working in the same area, changed their official body count noting that one defendant was found guilty of one of the 1986 killings. Five other cases – Barney, Burton, Castro, Ficklin and McElrath – were solved with the arrests of Louis Craine and Daniel Siebert. In 1989 authorities made another arrest in connection with the series of prostitute killings. The suspect, in a lurid twist, turned out to be an eighteen-year veteran of the sheriff's department working as a narcotics investigator. Rickey Ross, then 40, was stopped by officers for driving erratically and found to be in the company of a known prostitute. The prostitute was carrying drug paraphernalia and said they had been smoking crack. When officers found a loaded 9-millimeter Beretta pistol in the trunk of his car, Ross was put under arrest.

Following his arrest, LAPD ballistics experts matched the gun to three 1989 strawberry killings. For the next 82 days Ross was in jail in a special section called by inmates 'Death Row', in a cell next to Richard Ramirez. Guards harassed Ross by calling him and Ramirez the 'Double-R Murderers'.

Prisoners spat on him and threatened him on the way to the shower. Finally investigators, realizing they had made a mistake in the forensics of the weapon, released Ross and cleared him of any wrongdoing. 'I was treated like an animal . . . almost destroyed for a crime I didn't commit.' At first he was relieved, but then, he said: 'A great, sweltering anger came over me. I had been totally ruined.'

In a 1994 interview with the *Los Angeles Times* Ross said that on the night of his arrest he was on his way home from the airport, searching for a gasoline station that would accept his county gas vouchers. While he was at a light, a woman knocked on his window, saying she was stranded and needed a ride. 'She was not dressed like a prostitute; I was not looking for prostitutes,' he said. 'There was never any cocaine smoking . . . In fact, there were absolutely no drugs found in my system that night.'

Until his arrest, Ross, who was raised in South-Central, had an enviable career in the Sheriff's Department. In four years of service he had become an undercover narcotics investigator. 'He was a hell of an investigator,' J.C. Reiff, a retired sheriff's detective, told the *Los Angeles Times*. 'He turned seven or eight murder cases because he had such great rapport with people on the street.'

After being cleared of the three murder charges, the sheriff's department prodded him to resign. His life in tatters, Ross filed a civil rights lawsuit against the Los Angeles Police Department and then against Chief Daryl Gates and several prosecutors. As he found himself broke and his home near foreclosure, Ross was re-arrested with former Los Angeles Dodger baseball player Derrel Thomas for trying to buy cocaine from a Drug Enforcement Administration informant in a McDonald's parking lot near Los Angeles International Airport. Investigators contend that Ross went into the inform-ant's white van to test the quality of the cocaine. David Herriford, his lawyer, contended that his client never got into the van. Eight years and three mistrials later, Ross was acquitted of all drug and conspiracy charges.

'The Judge said [that] there comes a time when all these cases have to end,' said Herriford, who represented Ross through all three trials. 'It's kind of numbing now because it's hard to believe it's over,' he added. 'It's like a nightmare, really. My feeling is this case could be tried ten, fifteen times and it would still come out the same.' According to Herriford the prosecution's relentless pursuit of the case was motivated by Ross's pending civil rights lawsuit against the city and the LAPD. 'There are a lot of people [in the district attorney's office] who still think that he's guilty of murders, and that he was never brought to justice for that,' the lawyer said. 'And because he's a [former deputy] ... they think they should come down a little bit harder.'

In 1987 the police–sheriff task force created to catch the Slayer was drastically reduced as leads to the case dried up. At its peak the task force had fifty members working in the investigation. The task force, over the two years of its existence, logged more than 4,800 tips and solved dozens of non-related felony investigations. As interest in the investigation dwindled authorities cited that they thought the slayings were the unrelated work of perhaps up to four separate killers. As of this writing, no new reports have appeared about the status of the Southside Slayer investigation or Ross's civil rights trial. With three men behind bars and a quarter of the case files closed, officers are no longer actively working on the investigation. The hope of finding the killer or killers of these thirteen prostitutes – bringing a sense of justice to their unjustly shortened lives – is all but forgotten.

Less than an hour's drive away from South-Central, authorities in the suburb of Pomona have been reluctant to confirm the existence of a serial killer hunting black prostitutes in their own community and the neighboring towns of Claremont and Rosemead. In the last two months of 1993 five women who frequented West Holt Avenue, Pomona's prostitute strip, have been discovered bound and strangled to death. Another prostitute was similarly discovered in 1995. Because of similarities in the method of killing and the victims' profiles, investigators, and many Holt Avenue regulars, believe the killings could be the work of the same individual.

The five victims were abducted at night from the same Holt Avenue prostitute area and found dead around the eastern edge of Los Angeles County. A sixth one disappeared in 1995. The victims, who were alleged drug-addicted prostitutes, were all found strangled and with their hands tied behind their backs. The first one to be discovered was Betty S. Harris, 37, of Pomona. She was found on 1 November in the nearby community of Diamond Bar. Next came Roxanne Bates, of Montclair, who was found in Chino on 5 November. On 14 November, Helen R. Hill, 36, of Pomona, was found strangled in the City of Industry, one mile from the Harris crime scene. Two days later, Donna L. Goldsmith, 35, of Pomona, was found dead inside the Pomona city limits. The last victim of 1993 was Cheryl Sayers, 34, whose clothed body was found on 30 December, also within city limits. There is no information available on the 1995 victim.

'We have no suspects in custody, and we are still investigating it,' said Lieutenant Leon Sakamoto of the Pomona Police Department.

'We think they were killed by the same guy. It appears he is working the eastern edge of Los Angeles County,' said a Pomona police officer speaking to the *Precinct Reporter* newspaper on condition of anonymity. 'The manner in which they were killed was done so specifically, we are pretty sure they were all killed by the same person.'

'The cases have some similarities we are looking into. All are being considered, all are being investigated,' said Pomona Detective Birtch Holtzburger. 'We are in contact with the Chino Police Department and Los Angeles Sheriff's department. Basically, what we have found is all the victims were black females, people who all knew each other from contacts on the street. All of them seem to have had drug problems and it appears that they were all prostitutes.'

Community members, though, believe police are not doing enough to solve the killings. At a public rally in honor of the slain women, resident Albert Midgette told the *Precint Reporter*: 'Perhaps they see these cases as not important because the victims were black, or because some of them had police records . . . All [five] were human beings.'

After five murders in less than two months the street women in the area grew angry and terrified. 'Just because we are out here working, trying to make a living, they think we are nothing,' said a Holt Avenue prostitute named Chocolate. 'We wouldn't be out here if people weren't buying. Just because we do what we do does not make us worthless, does not mean it is OK to kill us.'

In March 1994 Pomona Valley NAACP President Stanford Fox accused the police department of inactivity in the serial slaying case. 'They are just doing what the Pomona Police Department does with murders – not solving them,' said Fox. 'I truly believe that is because most of the victims were black and Hispanic.' According to Fox, only six of 41 murders committed in the city in 1993 were solved. Of all 41 murder victims two were white, and one of those cases was solved. Pomona Police Captain Ron Hargett, who is in charge of the serial slaying case, disputed Fox's figures and denied that the victims' race played a factor in the investigation.

According to Hargett, the department's efforts to capture the killer have been hampered by a lack of witnesses and a lack of co-operation from the victim's associates. 'We are doing all that we can. We have four detectives and two officers who continue to be assigned to attempt to solve these homicides,' said Hargett. 'We are also in daily contact, in person or by phone, with the Los Angeles Sheriff's homicide department, and detectives from the Ontario, Chino and Montclair police departments.'

'We can't be tactful anymore because life is not a tactful or fair thing,' said Fox. 'I find it unusual that most of the unsolved murders were of blacks and Hispanics. To not call it prejudice would be a lie.' Fox compared the current investigation with other cases of serial killings, noting that those involving white victims were allotted more resources and manpower. 'When the Hillside Strangler was killing white women, they had a dragnet out; they kept going until they got their man,' said Fox. 'Six African-American females are dead, and their deaths are not noticed because of the chance that they were prostitutes. So what if they were. They were women.'

Like other cases in this book, race seems to have played a factor in both investigations in Los Angeles, as has the uncertainty as to whether there is a serial killer involved, or if the killings are just horrifyingly similar. In any case, the murders of 21 mostly black, drug-addicted women have gone unpunished throughout Los Angeles and the guilty parties remain on the loose. With the case files barely active it appears that at least two multiple killers have got away with murder in sunny LA.

THE ORIGINAL NIGHT STALKER

On 3 October 2000, investigators announced that through DNA testing they had uncovered the existence of an undetected Southern Californian serial killer. Dubbed 'The Original Night Stalker' the killer – who was active between 1979 and 1984 – is believed to be responsible for at least ten deaths in six separate attacks spanning three counties. The victims were mostly couples in upscale communities in Orange, Santa Barbara and Ventura counties.

In 1984, the suspected killer disappeared, leading authorities to believe he may have died, been incapacitated, or been incarcerated for an unrelated crime. 'It's very doubtful that he would have just stopped,' Orange County Sheriff's Detective Larry Pool said. 'Serial killers don't just stop.' The mystery began to take shape four years ago when scientists at the Orange County Sheriff's Department's DNA lab started applying new technology to old murder cases, and started finding a genetic thread tying together the six murder scenes.

Further DNA testing linked the killer to a series of rapes in Northern California. Known as the 'East Area rapist' at the time, the suspect was responsible for at least 44 rapes spanning from Sacramento to San Ramon during a three-year period in the 1970s. 'Unfortunately it's still a faceless person,' said Jim Amormino, a spokesman for the Orange County Sheriff's Department. 'Now more and more information is going to come out. There is lots of work to do.' Now investigators have 44 new cases to search for clues that could lead to the killer's apprehension.

According to an FBI-trained profiler, at the time of the killings the suspect is believed to have been in his early 20s, of medium build, with a broad, muscular chest. He is also believed to have brought his German shepherd to several of the crime scenes. Based on the nature of his crimes, Pool said, investigators have concluded that the killer harbored a murderous rage towards women, probably because he perceived some sense of wrong from 'a girlfriend, a mother, a stepmother'.

His first known attack in Southern California was in 1979, when he broke into the home of Jennifer Horinek and her boyfriend Abraham Himmel in Goleta, Santa Barbara County. The lucky couple managed to escape when the man started rubbing himself over his pants. Several weeks later, the same man – accompanied by a dog – broke into the Goleta home of Alexandra Manning, a clinical psychologist, and Dr Robert Offerman. There, he caught the couple sleeping and bludgeoned them to death. As in all other cases, he used an object he picked up in the home as the murder weapon.

The next attack came more than a year and a half later. This time the victims were Cheri Domingo, 35, and Gregory Sanchez, her 27-year-old lover. Domingo was bound and her head smashed with a blunt object. Sanchez was first shot, then beaten to death.

By 1980, authorities say, the killer moved south to Ventura County, where he killed Charlene Smith, 33, and her husband, Lyman Smith. The Smiths were clubbed to death in their home with a log from the fireplace. A short time later, the killer surfaced in Orange County, south of Los Angeles, where he bludgeoned to death Keith Harrington, 24, and his bride, Patrice, in their Laguna Niguel home. A year later, authorities say, Manuela Witthuhn was raped and killed in her Irvine home. His last known victim, eighteen-year-old Janelle Cruz, was found in 1986, raped and killed in her Irvine home.

No new information has been made available about the 'Original Night Stalker' case. With the renewed interest in the investigation, the families of the victims have posted a $100,000 reward for any information leading to an arrest. Still, after fifteen years of inactivity, it's unlikely the suspect is still alive unless he relocated somewhere else in the country, where he continued killing.

8. OPERATION ENIGMA

In order to find out whether or not there were any undetected serial killers in the UK, British authorities launched an investigative operation codenamed Enigma. The operation, which was announced on 26 May 1996, reopened 207 'cold cases' involving unsolved murders of 'vulnerable women', a euphemism for prostitutes. The investigation looked mostly into young, drug-addicted women murdered between 1986 and 1996, found dumped along the country's highways. FBI agents from Quantico, Virginia, and agents from the Royal Canadian Mounted Police would help British detectives acquaint themselves with the latest crime-fighting computer data-shifting techniques, DNA-profiling and the vast knowledge they have gained investigating and profiling numerous serial murderers.

Enigma, which has been classified as Britain's biggest-ever murder investigation, was set up in response to a spate of seemingly related killings of women in the Midlands between late 1993 and 1994. The potential serial killer, dubbed the 'Midlands Ripper', was first uncovered when a series of six prostitutes who worked the rest stop areas off the M1 and M6 appeared dead near highway exits. All victims were strangled but not raped. Their bodies were found naked or partly dressed with the killer or killers hardly making any effort to cover them. Authorities theorized that the suspected killer could be a trucker, like the feared 'Lisbon Ripper', or someone whose employment required that he regularly drive across the nation.

Once the Midlands Ripper theory emerged, investigators reopened several older cases that fitted the victim profile, upping the victim count to eight. The oldest case investigated was the January 1987 murder of 27-year-old prostitute and heroin addict Marina Monti who was found partially clothed on waste ground near Wormwood Scrubs prison in west London. She had been strangled and beaten. Next, in

February 1991, the body of prostitute Janine Downes, 22, was found half-naked in a hedge near the Wolverhampton to Telford road. She, too, had been severely beaten and then strangled. Like the six 1994 victims, both Marina Monti and Janine Downes were not raped.

The first 1994 victim found was twenty-year-old Samo Paull. Her badly decomposed body was discovered on New Year's Day in a lane in nearby Swinford. She had been strangled and was discovered half-naked. The youngster, who left behind a one-year-old daughter, was said to be missing her underwear and shoes. Like the subsequent victims, there was no evidence of a sexual assault. Her family reported her missing early in December. Paull, from Rowley Regis, West Midlands, was a prostitute who worked in the red-light district of Balsall Heath in Birmingham.

The second victim, Tracy Turner, was last seen alive at a service station on the M6 in Staffordshire in March 1994. Shortly after, she was found naked and strangled in a remote Leicestershire lane, just four miles from where Samo Paull was found dead. The 32-year-old Stafford resident worked as a prostitute and was known to regularly pick up customers at highway service stations in the Midlands.

In May two more suspected prostitutes appeared dead. The first was eighteen-year-old Emma Merry, from Tividale, near Dudley, in the West Midlands. She had been strangled and stripped, then dumped at the Sneyd Hill industrial estate, in Burslem, Staffordshire. She was last seen the previous evening outside a local pub. The other woman, nineteen-year-old prostitute Dawn Shields, was found naked and strangled in a shallow grave covered by stones at Mam Tor in the Peak District of Derbyshire.

In August 1994, the naked body of Julie Finley, 23, was found dumped in a field by a lovers' lane near Skelmersdale, Lancashire. Finley was a known drug addict who was thought to occasionally turn tricks. Like the others, she was strangled. Injuries to her upper body and arms suggested she put up a fight against her attacker. The last suspected victim, 21-year-old Sharon Harper, from Grantham, Lincolnshire, had no convictions for prostitution. She had a steady partner and a regular job as a barmaid in a pub. A post-mortem examination of her body revealed she had sexual intercourse with someone other than her boyfriend shortly before her death. Her body was discovered on 3 July 1994, in an ornamental shrubbery in a parking lot in Grantham, located half a mile from home and just over a mile from the Market Cross pub where she worked. She was last seen alive leaving the pub a little after midnight on the night she was murdered.

In November 1995 senior officers from four police forces met to discuss whether indeed there was a Midlands Ripper killing prostitutes in parts of the Midlands and northern England. At the meeting officers mentioned the high-profile murder case of nineteen-year-old French student Celine Figard as perhaps another victim of the Ripper. However, Stuart Morgan, a 37-year-old truck driver, confessed to raping and killing the nineteen-year-old student after she hitched a ride with him at a highway service station in Hampshire. Detectives said Morgan carried her body in his truck for over nine days during Christmas. He even stopped at his home to celebrate the holiday with his wife and son, with the dead girl laid in the bunkbed of his cabin. He then burned her clothing and dumped her body in a lay-by near Worcester. Although the murder was in many ways similar to Midlands Ripper attacks, Morgan was ruled out as a suspect after DNA-tests exonerated him of any of the other killings.

Eventually authorities concluded the highway killings were unrelated and the feared Midlands Ripper was merely a figment of the imagination of some overeager investigators and the press. However, in light of the escalating body-count of prostitute-related deaths the Crime Committee of the Association of Chief Police Officers (ACPO) decided to set up Operation Enigma. The new investigative operation was co-ordinated by experts at the National Crime Faculty of the Police Staff College in Bramshill, Hampshire, and headed by the Assistant Chief Constable of Essex, James Dickenson. Officers from the National Crime Faculty, the National Criminal Intelligence Service, the Forensic Science Service, and the Home Office's Police Research Group made up the investigating team.

In the 207 Enigma case re-examinations investigators analyzed factors such as geography, dumpsites, methods of murder and medical details of sexual assaults. Computer analysis was used extensively to provide psychological profiles of the killers as well as their probable *modus operandi*. 'Operation Enigma will collate and analyze relevant information regarding the victim, the crime and any suspects from a limited number of detected and undetected murders where the victim is female,' said Chief Constable Dickenson at the onset of the operation. 'The research will determine whether and how the service provided to officers investigating such crimes can be improved. For some years there have been arrangements to assist senior investigating officers in conducting comparative case analysis of major crimes. Work is currently being undertaken with a view to enhancing existing arrangements. This will take account of experiences within the UK and advances in other countries.'

In 1997, as a result of Operation Enigma, Scotland Yard created a 26-strong Serious Crime Bureau to examine unsolved gay murders, missing people cases, and serious sex crimes. Detective Chief Superintendent Doug Smith, head of the bureau, said: 'We will be looking at all sexually orientated murders, including children, stranger rapes, offences of abduction where there is a sexual involvement, and unsolved murders of gay men. We will eventually look at all murders.'

Unlike in the US, British police have recently discovered the advantages of cross-referencing between different police departments and different cases. Following the Green River Investigation the FBI developed the VICAP (Violent Criminal Apprehension Program) system to track all violent crime in the US in one main database. The system can correlate cases in different counties or even different states and link emerging serial patterns that would be impossible to detect without access to the database. The newly formed Serious Crime Bureau is expected to build a VICAP-like database to identify suspected multiple killers and serial attackers at an early stage. The importance of having more cross-referencing between forces became evident in the UK following the Yorkshire Ripper inquiry, in which Peter Sutcliffe was

Sketch of suspect in a 1995 unsolved murder in Kitsap County. Though authorities think it is unlikely that he is the Spokane Killer, in 1998 they distributed copies of the sketch around the East Sprague area to generate tips in their investigation.
© Spokane Sheriff's Department

Longtime Green River suspect William Jay Stevens II was arrested by Spokane police at his parents' house in January 1989, following a series of phone tips.
© Robert Stevens

An avid police paraphernalia collector, Stevens had a fully equipped Washington State motorcycle, an ambulance, and a police cruiser. The cruiser, pictured above, was customised with a police radio, a radar unit, and a blue emergency grill light. © Robert Stevens

Believed to be the most accurate composite picture of the Green River
Killer, this image was drawn from a description furnished by a fifteen-
year-old Portland prostitute who miraculously survived an encounter
with the possible killer on 6 September 1985.
© From the author's private collection

The mean streets of South Central LA where the Southside Slayer
claimed at least fourteen lives between September 1983 and May 1987.
Most of the victims were black strawberries – crack-addicted prostitutes.
© Jose Perez de Lama

A protest march through Vancouver's ravaged Downtown Eastside from where 29 women have disappeared.
© Steve Bosch/Vancouver Sun

Left Andre Crawford

Below Ronald Macon

Police mugshots of
two of the Chicago
killers.
© From the author's
private collection

A Ciudad Juárez bus. In 1999 a group of Juárez bus drivers was arrested and charged with several murders. The gang is believed to have been acting under the payroll of Sharif Sharif. © Jose Perez de Lama

Border crossing between El Paso and Ciudad Juárez. Authorities speculate that there could be one or more serial killers crossing from the United States to kill Mexican women. © Jose Perez de Lama

Patricia Prieto, 36

Mariela Jimenez, 27

Veronica Andrea Chavez, 25

Maria del Carmen, 25

Victims of Argentina's Highway Maniac. © Clarín Agea SA

Above Costa Rican OIJ agents recovering the bodies of two lovers, Ileana Alvarez, 23 and Mauricio Cordero, 24, who were brutally murdered by the feared Psychopath in the Triangle of Death area of San Jose. © Rodrigo Montenegro, La Nación, Costa Rica

Left The funeral of two women and five girls who were massacred by the Psychopath. The killings, which marked the first known attack by the Psychopath, are considered Costa Rica's most heinous crime. © La Nación, Costa Rica

interviewed nine times by different agencies before being identified as the key suspect.

Operation Enigma was instrumental in the creation of a new crime database developed at the National Crime Faculty under the auspices of ACPO. Detectives re-examining the cases filled in questionnaires covering every aspect of both the crime and victim, which were fed into a computer database for comparison. As the Enigma investigation reached its conclusion, the database created was absorbed by the National Crime Faculty at the Police Staff College. Since then officers have started adding new details of more recent rapes and abductions to try to establish patterns and enhance the database.

Forensic scientists working on Enigma, using new methods to extract DNA fingerprints from tiny traces of genetic material, have tried to 'upgrade' evidence found at the various crime scenes to form a better picture of the suspects. 'It is highly possible that the use of new techniques may establish further links between the murders,' said Dave Barclay, a senior forensic scientist of the National Crime Faculty. 'The forensic science service worked hard to upgrade existing evidence. We will now be working with individual forces to obtain new physical evidence.'

On 15 February 1999, Barclay alluded to a technological breakthrough in forensic science which allows investigators to produce DNA-profiles of criminals from a single blood cell, a sperm or a fleck of dandruff. 'The new procedure is cutting edge. We have only started using it during the past couple of weeks. It's based on the idea of taking DNA from smaller and smaller pieces of evidence . . . a speck of blood so small it is invisible to the naked eye.' Within a decade, Barclay believes, scientists will be able to produce a full genetic profile of a suspect's weight, height, facial characteristics, hair and eye color from a single cell or a drop of blood. 'We are trying to ally new techniques such as DNA to new ways of looking at crime scenes so that we can reinterpret circumstances and try and discover in more detail exactly what happened.'

In 1998, after two years, Operation Enigma reached its conclusion. At a press conference officers acknowledged that of the 207 murders originally investigated, 135 of them were found to be random and 72 needed 'further analysis'. Of these 72 cases, detectives identified 21 potential 'clusters' of connected activity. Kent Chief Constable David Phillips said there were 'strong grounds for some sort of potential link' between the cases. The 72 murders involved 21 clusters in 26 different police districts across the country. Chief Constable Phillips, who chairs the crime committee of the Association of Chief Police Officers, said the Enigma squad, after concluding its investigation, would pass on their findings to the forces that originally investigated the cases. The respective departments would then analyze the data and decide whether the cases should be re-opened.

The 72 case files singled out by Enigma were eventually narrowed down to 14 linked cases in four distinct clusters. Authorities concluded that there were four potential serial killers stalking Britain and, since 1990, fourteen women may have died at their hands. None of the clusters, though, showed obvious 'signatures' such as a distinctive way of mutilating their victims, which would strongly suggest the work of an individual. However, investigators correlated several murders through characteristics of the dumpsites, evidence found at the crime scenes and similarities in the victim profiles. 'This has therefore been a very painstaking process and involves reconstructing the minutiae of many different offenses, crime scenes and victims,' said Chief Constable Phillips.

One cluster appears to be centered around Lincolnshire where at least three women have been strangled and sexually assaulted in similar circumstances. Two of the cases on the Lincolnshire cluster, the murders of Sharon Harper (who was originally considered a Midlands Ripper victim) and Julie Pacey, occurred within a four-month period. Harper was never seen alive again after leaving the Grantham pub where she worked. Four months later Julie Pacey, 38, was strangled and sexually assaulted at her Grantham home after she returned from visiting her father. She was found on the bathroom floor by her 14-year-old daughter. Chris Cook, Detective Superintendent at Lincolnshire police force, said

Enigma provided his officers with a detailed analysis of both murders, pointing out several similarities that had been previously overlooked.

Another of the cluster involves the murders of four prostitutes in the West Midlands and Leicestershire. Contradicting the 1995 assertion that there was no Midlands Ripper at work, the Enigma findings seem to indicate that, in fact, there is. Of the four suspected victims in the cluster – Samo Paull, Tracy Turner, Gail Whitehouse and Janine Downes – three of them were listed as possible Midlands Ripper victims. In May 1998 police charged a 33-year-old Leicester man with the Turner murder. No information is available on the name and status of the suspect. Police are also looking for connections between the four West Midlands murders and the death of Natalie Pearman, a 16-year-old prostitute who was found strangled in Norwich in November 1992.

The third cluster identified involves the murder of four women. One of the killings is the July 1992 frenzied knife attack of Rachel Nickell on Wimbledon Common, southwest London. Nickell was stabbed 49 times as she was walking her dog with her 2-year-old son, Alex. The case drew national attention when an undercover detective became intimately involved with Colin Stagg, the prime suspect in the case, in a controversial 'honey-trap' operation. The trap involved a 33-year-old married detective constable who, under the name 'Lizzie', befriended the suspect in an attempt to get information to incriminate him in the brutal killing. The officer, posing as a disturbed woman looking for a partner to indulge in violent sexual fantasies, developed a relationship with Stagg in which he allegedly told her about sexual acts involving knives and bondage. His lawyers said he was enticed to do so by the licentious policewoman.

The operation was so secret that the officer was ordered not to tell her husband, who was also a police officer. In September 1994, a judge threw the case against Stagg out of court and severely criticized the operation's director for attempting 'to incriminate a suspect by positive and deceptive conduct of the grossest kind'. Four years after the failed operation the detective formerly known as Lizzie sued

Scotland Yard for emotional distress resulting from the investigation. In the suit the detective alleged she was not offered a leave or professional support following her 'traumatic' role in the investigation, and that led to her accepting an early retirement from the force.

The Nickell case was linked with the January 1993 stabbing to death of Claire Tiltman, a sixteen-year-old schoolgirl from Greenhithe, Kent. Tiltman was stabbed more than fifty times in an alley near her home. Her murder occurred six months after Nickell's death. Kent Police were unable to comment on whether her death was included in one of the Enigma clusters. Scotland Yard also said that the Nickell inquiry team had examined possible links to two other killings, but had not found evidence of a serial killer. A spokesman for the Yard would not say whether the Enigma cluster represented new uncovered relations or previously examined cases.

Unfortunately researching the Enigma and the four resulting investigations has been more than arduous because of the lack of information released by authorities. In essence, investigators have been less than forthcoming about clarifying the situation. Enigma investigators have not even clearly identified the locations and characteristics of the four suspected serial clusters. However, at least three of the clusters seem to be centred around the Midlands and involve cases originally attributed to the suspected Midland Ripper.

One set of cases that has been seemingly ignored by Operation Enigma is a string of prostitute murders in Glasgow. Scotland's leading industrial centre, Glasgow rebounded from a depressed economy in the early 80s to what is now a lively cultural metropolis. With its newfound prosperity this sixth-century city with a population of more than 650,000 has also experienced a rising wave of violent sex murders. Since 1991 seven women from the city's red light district have been brutally murdered, raising the fear among the city's 1,000 prostitutes that someone is out there hunting for them.

Glasgow police, who initially ignored the growing body count, were forced to take steps to help the street walkers by giving them alarms as well as having specially-trained police officers teach them self-defence. The change in attitude came after the March 1998 discovery of Margo Lafferty. Lafferty, 27, was found battered to death in a doorway next to a cobbled street where she lay undetected for sixteen hours. Strathclyde's Assistant Chief Constable George Macdonald said the new safety measures were part of their ongoing commitment to the safety of all women. 'Margo Lifetree's death serves to underpin further the need for organizations such as ourselves to continually look at the ways in which we deal with issues such as prostitution and how we can best offer protection to those women.'

All seven prostitutes killed in Glasgow were drug addicts. Diane McInally was the first to die. The 23-year-old was found on 15 October 1999, in Pollok Estate, home of the Burrell Collection, Glasgow's most famous art gallery. Two men – drug dealers to whom she allegedly owed money – were arrested for her murder, but never charged.

Then Karen McGregor, 26, was found dead in April 1993 at the Scottish Exhibition Centre. She had been brutally beaten on the head and face with a hard object, she had been throttled and an object had been forcibly inserted into her vagina. Her husband, Charles McGregor, was charged with the murder. In court, their friends gave evidence that Karen was fed up with having to support his raging drug habit. In court he was found not guilty after two witnesses who said they saw him beating her to death withdrew their statements. After his release, McGregor died of a drug overdose.

In 1995 both Leona McGovern and Marjorie Roberts were murdered. Leona was stabbed seventeen times with a screwdriver in broad daylight. She too apparently owed money to her drug dealer. Jackie Gallagher was murdered in 1996. Then Tracey Wylde, a 21-year-old single mother, was murdered in November 1997.

The last victim was Lafferty. Detectives are trying to establish links between her murder and the murders of Gallagher and Wylde. However, differences between all the MOs and the various crime scenes suggest that rather than one serial killer on the loose, the carnage is coming from several individual murderers.

According to Sophia Young, project leader of Turnaround, a group that offers support to female drug-takers and women who work the streets, 93 per cent of Glasgow's prostitutes are addicted to drugs. But what she finds most disturbing is the poverty they live in and the level of violence exercised against them. 'The number of rapes, attempted murders, kidnaps and assaults against them is almost unbelievable,' said Young. 'The west of Scotland has a real problem with violence against working women, which seems to be because more of them are visible and work on the streets.'

Despite the rash of brutal killings, many of Glasgow's prostitutes, like their counterparts in Spokane, Vancouver and Chicago, have continued working to feed their veins. Roseann Coutts, a worker at the city's Base 75 support center, said: 'The women are terrified. Some have stopped working because they were so frightened. But most of the street workers are drug users and they need the money to feed their habit – most are on heroin. They just don't see any other option.'

As of this writing, police have caught and convicted 21-year-old Brian Donnelly for the murder of Margo Lafferty. Authorities claim to know the identities of the killers of Jackie Gallagher, Dianne McInally, Karen McGregor, Leona McGovern, Marjorie Roberts and Tracey Wylde, but have been unable to bring their suspects to justice for lack of evidence. No new links have been uncovered bolstering the theory of a serial killer at large on the streets of Glasgow, but street women remain fearful of the violence that might await them with their next score or their next trick.

ENIGMA UPDATE

Marking the first arrest resulting from Operation Enigma, on 15 August 1999, police charged 35-year-old Alun Kyte with the murders of Birmingham prostitutes Samo Paull and Tracy Turner. Kyte, who could end up being the discredited Midland Ripper, was arrested in December 1997 for an unrelated rape and sentenced by the Bristol Crown Court to eight years in jail. In March 1998, a routine DNA test 'blind' matched him with residue found on the body of Turner. In prison, while describing the murder of Paull, Kyte said she had laughed at his sexual prowess so he had choked her until she stopped laughing. He also allegedly bragged to a fellow convict that he had killed up to ten women, saying: 'They were sluts and deserved everything they got.'

Kyte, a truck driver and confirmed misogynist, led an itinerant lifestyle that covered a great part of the UK. According to lead Detective Superintendent Mick Creedon, of Leicestershire Police, Kyte, who seems to enjoy his newfound celebrity as a star killer, 'wants to be elevated to Ripper status. Such was his mobility, his name can be discounted from nothing unless it can be shown he was in some other place on the day of an attack.'

Police believe Kyte could be linked to as many as 20 murders spanning nearly two decades. Several cases stand out to be re-examined in light of his arrest. One is the August 1994 murder of 23-year-old Julie Finlay. Since 1995 her death was linked to Paull's and Turner's and the Midlands Ripper investigation, because the women were all prostitutes working highway service stops within the same area. Police are also looking into the 1997 murder of Glasgow prostitute Tracey Wylde, the 1992 murder of Natalie Pearman, and the 1984 murder of 28-year-old Yvonne Coley.

Police believe the March 1993 murder of 32-year-old Carol Clark and the 1994 death of nineteen-year-old Dawn Shields could also fit in the Alun Kyte victim list. Both women were killed in one location and transported more than 40 miles before being dumped next to the highway. Both had underwear and jewelry removed. Adding to the linkage, at the time of Clark's murder, Kyte was living in Weston-super-Mare, less than 20 miles from her home in Bristol.

Hoping to build a more inclusive case against Kyte, police have released information on 21 locations where he spent time and details of the seven cars he drove. They also distributed his photograph and a tape recording of his voice in the hope that women whom he may have raped or who escaped his attacks will recognize him and step forward.

Another development marginally related to the Enigma investigation is the arrest and conviction of truck driver, woman hater, martial arts expert and overall dangerous individual David Smith. Smith, nicknamed 'Lurch' by his coworkers because of his giant size and slurred speech, was convicted for the April 1999 mutilation-murder of 21-year-old prostitute Amanda Walker. During his sentencing the judge described him as being 'extremely dangerous to women and likely to remain so'.

Six weeks after her disappearance, Amanda Walker's body was found in a shallow grave near the Royal Horticultural Society gardens at Wisley. Weeks earlier, her clothing and handbag were discovered near Hampton, Middlesex, a mile from Smith's home. Fingerprints and blood stains on the bag were matched to Smith, 43, who had already served a stint in jail on a rape conviction.

In custody, Smith told a fellow inmate that he killed Amanda Walker as well as several other women. According to his cellmate, Smith boasted of wrapping Amanda in polythene and mutilating her 'downstairs' before and after having sex with her. Then he crushed her throat and choked her to death. Not surprisingly, Walker's murder was not the first one to which he had been linked. In 1993 Smith was cleared by a jury of the murder of another call girl, Sarah Crump, because police allegedly suppressed evidence during his trial. Investigators are now creating a timeline of his whereabouts over the last decade, looking for instances where he was in the vicinity of unsolved prostitute murders, some of which are Enigma cases.

A third developing investigation in the periphery of Enigma is centered in the West Midlands area, where detectives have arrested 35-year-old Philip John Smith of Sparkbrook, Birmingham, and charged him with the murders of Jodie Hyde, Rosemary Corcoran and Carol Jordan. The three women were brutally attacked and mutilated over a 48-hour period in November 2000. The first victim to be discovered was 21-year-old Jodie Hyde, whose smoldering body was found by two police officers on 9 November in an adventure play area in Birmingham. Three days later the battered body of 25-year-old Rosemary Corcoran was discovered by a man walking his dog on the side of a road in

Rashwood, Worcestershire. That same day the body of 39-year-old Carol Jordan was discovered in a park less than two miles from where Hyde was murdered.

The three women were mutilated almost beyong recognition. Jordan and Corcoran were beaten to death, while Hyde was strangled and set afire. Blood samples on his pants, steel toe boots and his Volvo linked Smith to the murders of Jodie Hyde and Rosemary Corcoran. A broken indicator light from his car matched a similar item found at the Jordan murder scene. As of this writing Smith has been convicted for the three murders and is being investigated in relation to 40 more unsolved cases.

Investigators have even traveled to Co Meath, Ireland, to exhume the body of 47-year-old Patricia Lynott, who was found dead in her flat in Birmingham in October 2000. The inquiry into Lynott's death – who was at first believed to have died from natural causes – was sparked by the investigation into the three previously mentioned murders. One West Midlands detective said: 'We are continuing our inquiries into the three murders and we are re-examining between 14 and 40 murders of women which have taken place in the past ten years.' However, no link has yet been established between Smith and the Enigma operation.

9. THE SOUTH DUBLIN KILLER

Irish Gardai have called in the FBI to help track down a suspected serial killer believed to be responsible for the disappearances of at least six young women. The Garda hopes to use the bureau's expertise in psychological profiling to try to achieve a breakthrough in the string of disappearances that began in 1993. Four of the 'Missing Six', all aged between seventeen and 26, have vanished within a thirty-mile area of the Wicklow and Dublin mountains, south of the capital. To date, there is no conclusive evidence pointing to a serial killer at work. Gardai, in fact, doubt they are dealing with one individual killer. Still, circumstantial linkage suggests the probable existence of a multiple murderer.

Police, in spite of basic similarities in the victim profiles, originally dismissed suggestions that the 'Missing Six' were connected. But after the 19 July 1998 disappearance in broad daylight of Deirdre Jacob, officers had to face what locals have been fearing for years: that there is a serial killer in their midst. Assistant Commissioner Tony Hickey, who is acting as lead officer in the case, said that the only links between the women are that all six were attractive, young and disappeared without a trace. 'We cannot be one hundred percent sure that there is not a serial killer; there is a very slim chance,' he said. According to locals, those who support the suspicions about a serial killer at work in the area have a mounting body count and a solid foundation of facts. Since 1979 more than six other women have disappeared or been murdered in the same general area that has become known by locals as the Vanishing Triangle.

'We cannot confirm they are dead because we haven't got their bodies. There is nothing to say one of them won't walk back in the door. But realistically we are looking for bodies. We know that none of these women planned to disappear,' said Garda Superintendent Jerry O'Connell. None of the girls took their passports or packed their belongings. Police have closely monitored their bank accounts and recorded no transactions since they were reported missing.

'We have no bodies, which means that we have no crime scene and that in itself is a tremendous disadvantage,' said Garda Commissioner Pat Byrne. 'They all have that common characteristic. We want to find out if they were enticed or if they were forced from where they were last seen.'

After reviewing the evidence, retired FBI profiler Bob Ressler said there were probably two serial killers working together in the hills of South Dublin. Ressler theorized that the six abductions were most probably planned out in detail and meticulously executed. Ressler, who has written extensively about serial killers, believes the killer acts like a typical 'organized killer': carefully planning his attacks, keeping the crime scene under control, and remaining calm and collected during his pre- and post-offense behavior. 'Before he launches his first attack,' the former FBI agent added, 'he [the killer] is likely to have methodically reconnoitered the locale – his way in and way out.'

The former Fed profiled the killer as a local man, who is perhaps single or separated, living in the southern edge of Dublin or north Wicklow, near the Vanishing Triangle area. 'Once decided on the type of person he intends to kill, he will probably stake out a specific locale: a shopping precinct, a singles bar, a lonely bus stop – or even a busy main road.' Because some of the abductions happened during the day, the killer may be self-employed or work as a driver. And like the subjects of many other serial investigations in this book, the killer has probably talked to investigators and his name is perhaps already in police records.

The first woman to disappear was Annie McCarrick, 26, an Irish-American literature student in Dublin. McCarrick had come to Dublin some years earlier and fallen in love with the city. An enthusiastic hiker, Annie vanished after leaving her apartment in Sandymount for a trip to Glencullen Mountains on 26 March 1993. Her disappearance prompted one of the largest missing person's searches in Irish history, with US ambassador Jean Kennedy Smith and Vice-President Al Gore lobbying the Irish Government on behalf of the missing girl and her family. Her father, John McCarrick, a former NYPD officer – who was hypercritical of the shoddy policework demonstrated throughout the investigation – offered a $150,000 reward for any information leading to the solving of his daughter's case. Believing his Irish counterparts were merely incompetent, McCarrick hired a private detective to help unravel the mystery. Sadly, after five frustrating years, Annie, his only child, remains missing and McCarrick has been left with a broken marriage, in bad health, and his bank account in tatters.

Following Annie's suspected abduction, Josephine 'Jo Jo' Dullard was next to disappear. The 21-year-old beautician vanished on 9 November 1995, at a telephone booth at Moone, County Kildare, while hitching home from Dublin after missing her bus. Dullard was talking to her best friend when she hung up, saying she had just got a ride. It is believed she hitched a ride as far as Castledermot, but never made it home to the village of Moone.

Jo Jo's sister, 46-year-old Mary Phelan, turned her personal battle to find her sister into a national crusade for the search of missing people. Along with her husband Martin, Mary – who raised her little sister after their parents' death – has built in her kitchen a shrine/nerve-center dedicated to the latest news clippings and fliers concerning the disappearances. 'I knew in my heart the moment Jo went missing that that was it. It was totally out of character for her to disappear,' Mary said of her sister. Police refused to listen, she added critically, and vital investigating time was lost right after she was reported missing. Like Annie McCarrick's father, the Phelans are skeptical of the Garda's less-than-thorough policework.

Fiona Pender was the next to go. A hairdresser and part-time model, Fiona, who was seven months pregnant, disappeared the evening of 23 August 1996. The 25-year-old was last seen leaving the apartment where she lived with her boyfriend in Tullamore, County Offaly. Police believe they know the man responsible for her death but have no evidence to charge him with her abduction or murder. As of this writing the suspect is under surveillance. He's been quoted by the local press as saying the Garda will never get him because they are too stupid.

Six months after Fiona's disappearance Ciara Breen, seventeen, slipped out of her home in Dundalk, County Louth, and was never seen again. Though a bit of a wild child, no one believes Ciara, the night of her disappearance, was planning to run away. She took no possessions and, at the time was undergoing protracted orthodontic procedure to replace her front teeth. Nearly a year later, Fiona Sinnott, of Lady's Island, vanished the night of 8 February 1998. The nineteen-year-old single mother was last seen by friends leaving a pub in Broadway, Rosslare, County Wexford.

Five months after, on 19 July, Deirdre Jacob, an eighteen-year-old student teacher, disappeared in broad daylight. Deirdre had returned to Ireland for the summer from Strawberry Hill College in West London. She spent the afternoon she went missing in her hometown of Newbridge, in the southwest of Dublin. First she had lunch at her grandmother's shop. Then she was picked up by the security cameras at the Allied Irish Bank sending a £180 bank draft for her share of the rent on her apartment in London. Ten minutes later she went to the post office and chatted with a friend on the street before turning into the tree-lined country road where she was last seen 300 yards from her parents' front door.

Nothing about the missing eighteen-year-old indicated that she planned to run away. On the contrary, everything about her pointed at a sweet and personable young woman with a great future ahead of her. A neat freak, Deirdre had all her college files cleanly laid out and her personal papers bundled up and neatly tied with pieces of ribbon or string. Her parents described their daughter as a bubbly, methodical, conscientious person. 'Neither of us are that organized, but Deirdre was,' said her mother, Bernadette. 'She would plan everything, making lists and ticking things off.'

No one ever heard from these six women after they vanished. Dublin, being a city of more than one million people, does have big city crime problems. But people just don't disappear. And not all disappear from the same general area. Most murders in the area are the result of domestic violence and drunken brawls so the guilty party is always easily identifiable. But not in the disappearances.

Several suspects, linked to individual victims, hang in the fringes of investigation, leading Gardai to believe that they are not dealing with one exclusive killer. One young patient at an Irish mental hospital told the Garda he knew where the bodies of three of the missing women were buried, but a search of the area he mentioned proved that he was lying. Another man, serving a life sentence for a 1996 murder of a Dublin woman, was questioned about the McCarrick and Dullard cases after it was discovered he was, like Annie, an avid hiker and drank in the same pub as Jo Jo. Other local murderers are being investigated for possible linkage with any of the victims. In 1996 a Dublin man, Michael Bambrick, was convicted of murdering two women who had been missing for three years. The Garda originally had not linked the cases until Bambrick's arrest. In the same year two Englishmen, John Shaw and Geoffrey Evans, were charged with kidnapping and murdering two young women. They too are being looked at for any possible connection with the missing women.

Two months after Deirdre Jacob disappeared the Garda launched Operation Trace to re-examine all the cases and look for 'linkage' and 'common threads'. Operation Trace, which stands for Tracing, Reviewing and Collating Evidence, recruited six officers not involved in initial investigations to re-examine the evidence and uncover possible new data patterns. Similar re-investigations of 'cold cases' (pending, unresolved cases with no leads) are common in the US and recommended by the FBI. Fresh eyes, according to the FBI, can always uncover something that, until then, was obvious but remained undetected. In three of the cases Operation Trace is analyzing – Fiona Pender, Fiona Sinnott and Ciara Breen – investigators believe the victim knew the killer. In the three others, they have no clue.

Operation Trace said it would also look into six other murders and disappearances in the same general Wicklow Mountains area that occurred within the last twenty years. 'It's painstaking, old-fashioned police work,' said Assistant Commissioner Hickey, emphasizing that the change of investigators would bring 'fresh ideas, fresh minds, and fresh eyes' to the case files. The first murder being re-examined, from 1979, is eerily similar to the Deirdre Jacob situation. Nearly twenty years before Deirdre was seemingly abducted, Phyllis Murphy, 23, was found raped, strangled and partially hidden in bushes in the Wicklow Mountains. Like Deirdre she was taken off a main road while making her way home in broad daylight. Phyllis was believed to have hitched a ride from someone as she left her grandmother's house in Newbridge en route to her home in Kildare.

When family members discovered she was missing the Garda launched a massive search of the surrounding countryside with no results. Four weeks after her disappearance, officers familiar with the mountains searched the Wicklow Gap above Hollywood and found Phyllis Murphy's naked body partially hidden among trees near Ballinagee Bridge. She had been raped and died from a form of strangulation known as vagal inhibition in which the killer cuts off the blood supply to the brain.

As well as the Phyllis Murphy case, Operation Trace is looking into the still-unsolved case of Patricia Furlong. The twenty-year-old was found raped and murdered on 24 July 1982, in a field at Glencullen. She was last seen the previous evening at the Fraughan Beer Festival in Glencullen. Also attending the dance was Vincent Connell, who in May 1990 was arrested and charged with murdering her after an alleged verbal admission of the crime to detectives. The case against Connell, who emphatically protested his innocence, was later thrown out on appeal. Shortly after, the suspect, who had a history of violence towards women, died of a heart attack.

On 3 April 1988, the decomposed body of Antoinette Smith, 27, a mother of two from Clondalkin, was found in a boggy, shallow grave in the Dublin Mountains at Glendoo, Kilakee. She was last seen in downtown Dublin the previous July leaving a David Bowie concert at Slane Castle. It is believed she, too, was raped and strangled. No suspect ever emerged in the case. On 14 September 1989, Deirdre

Mulcahy, nineteen, was found raped and strangled in Midleton, County Cork. A 25-year-old Cork man was charged and convicted with her murder then acquitted four years later. Her murder is presently unsolved.

Marie Kilmartin, 36, disappeared from Portlaoise on 16 December 1993. Her body was found six months later in a remote bog at Pims Road, half-a-mile off the Mountmellick–Portarlington road. She had been submerged in a bog hole by a concrete slab placed on her chest. One other woman, Patricia Doherty, a prison officer and the mother of two, was found on 23 June 1992, in a collapsed peat bank about two miles from the Antoinette Smith dumpsite. She was last seen alive two days before Christmas 1991 when she left her home in Allentown, Tallaght, for last-minute shopping.

In 1999, in a strange transcontinental twist, Canadian serial killer Clifford Robert Olson contacted Dublin authorities and told them he had knowledge of the disappearances. Olson, considered Canada's deadliest serial killer, claimed to have letters and photographs from an accomplice in Dublin who had murdered five women. A Vancouver native, Olson had a long career as a criminal logging in 94 arrests for robbery and sexual assault before 1981. In prison he was known as a homosexual rapist and informer.

His reign of terror began in November 1980 with the abduction and slaughter of a twelve-year-old girl. From then until August 1981 Olson managed to kill at least ten more young hitchhikers he abducted while around Vancouver in his van. He was arrested while police had him under surveillance after picking up two female hitchhikers. A search of his van produced his phone book with the name of one of the victims. Once he was charged with murder, the conniving serial killer somehow struck a deal with prosecutors in which authorities would pay his wife and child $10,000 per body he recovered. By confessing to eleven kills, Olson assured his family a nice chunk of change. On 11 January 1982, Olson pleaded guilty to eleven counts of murder and was sentenced to life imprisonment.

While in jail, anything-for-a-buck-Olson announced through his lawyer that he had registered with the Canadian copyright office a video series he planned to produce offering psychological insights into serial killing. The busy killer said he wanted to call the video, 'Motivational Sexual Homicide Patterns of Serial Child Killer Clifford Robert Olson.' No further information is available on Olson's coming video productions. After talking to FBI and Canadian police, Gardai realized Olson had 'a history of contacting law-enforcement agencies with such stories,' said Assistant Commissioner Hickey. After Olson's initial flourish of messages, the Canadian killer severed all contact with the Garda and refused to acknowledge his previous claim. Most investigators believe Olson was just stirring trouble or perhaps looking for a trip to Ireland.

Hopefully the Garda will unravel the mystery surrounding the disappearances of the Missing Six and the families will be able to put an end to their grief. And hopefully the killer or killers responsible for one or all the deaths will be brought to justice for ending these six beautiful lives.

10. THE BUTCHER OF MONS

Since 1997, Belgian authorities have been searching for an elusive serial killer who has been dismembering women and leaving their remains neatly packed in garbage bags in and around Mons, a historic town of about one hundred thousand residents located fifty miles south of Brussels. To date authorities have found fifteen garbage bags containing thirty severed body parts of at least four, and possibly eight, victims. The Butcher of Mons, as he has been dubbed by the media, has orchestrated a bold game of cat and mouse with police by provocatively linking the monstrosity of his crimes with the chillingly evocative names of the streets and landmarks surrounding the chosen dump-sites.

The grim saga began on 22 March when a mounted policeman patrolling the nearby suburb of Cuesmes saw a hand protruding from a black plastic bag in a ditch near the River Trouille (meaning, 'Jitters'). In all, that day, nine trash bags with body parts were found around the canal separating Mons and the neighboring Cuesmes. Perhaps coincidentally, a wall next to where the bags were found had the words '*La Morte*' spray-painted on it in bright red. Two days later a driver, whose car broke down, discovered the mutilated torso of a transsexual with both breasts removed on the banks of the River Haine (Hate) near the Chemin de l'Inquietude (the Path of Worry). A little more than a week later, on 12 April, police discovered a severed head on Rue du Depot (Dump Street).

The following weekend a thigh, an arm, a forearm and a hand were found in three bags by workers cleaning drains in Rue St Symphorien, a street named after a third-century French saint who was decapitated and whose relics are displayed in a church nearby. 'The locations all have a special name, so it is important to know whether there is some message, some sign,' said Mons prosecutor Didier Van Reusel. Police also established, through forensic evidence linking the cut marks, that a floating torso found in 1996 in the Haine was also the work of the same macabre killer.

All the remains found in March and April were transferred to the Liege University Hospital where forensic pathologists faced the mind-boggling task of completing the anatomical jigsaw of unmatched limbs and torsos presented by the killer. According to Mr Van Reusel, none of the bodies were complete, leading police to believe the killer was saving the extra body parts to use later. Laboratory analysis of samples of soil and insect life around the bags indicated they had been dumped at different intervals since the beginning of winter. The remains inside the bags were found to be between one week and two years old, suggesting that the killer had access to a large refrigeration unit in which to store his victims.

Chief investigating magistrate Pierre Honore remarked that all victims were dismembered with 'remarkable precision', leading authorities to believe the killer was a surgeon or a butcher. However, this initial supposition was disproved as officials determined that the killer dismembered the women mechanically using a wood-chopping machine with circular blades placed at twelve-inch intervals.

'There are not that many places you can carry out that operation, with the blood and the smell,' said Mr Van Reusel. 'And there are not that many people who own a machine like that.'

A Belgian specialist trained at the FBI's Behavioral Science Unit in Quantico profiled the killer to be an intelligent, calculating, methodical and obsessive man, whose pleasure is derived from the ritualistic dismemberment and disposal of his victims. In general, murderers who derive satisfaction from 'displaying' their victims publicly are a particularly dangerous breed of psychopathic killer. A police spokesman said: 'This is clearly the work of a highly intelligent, ritual psychopath, as you can see from the way the body parts are cut, the way they are wrapped and the places in which they are deposited.'

A fastidious and anal-retentive individual, the killer bundled up and knotted all the bags in precisely the same fashion. Each body part was wrapped in its own white plastic bag, which was tied tightly at the top. These white bags were then placed inside larger grey-colored bags. Each grey bag was knotted very tightly in the same fashion, and the top of the knot was then snipped off with scissors. 'Very neatly, very precisely, the work of an obsessive,' says Mr Van Reusel. On 3 June 1997, investigators stated that they were looking into a religious motive, perhaps even Satanism, as a factor behind the killings. 'The treatment of the bodies is very methodical, which is often the case with Satanic practices involved in ritualistic killings,' said Mr Van Reusel. Other evidence, like the killer leaving body parts in places that have already been searched by police, suggests he is merely playing a morbid game with authorities in which, up to now, he's been winning.

Historically the medieval city of Mons has been a pretty grim place. Throughout the ages Mons has been a town associated with many saints involved in decapitation. One of the more famous local sites in the medieval part of the city is a stone head of St John the Baptist, which is mounted over the door of the town's oldest inn. Located on the Rue de la Clef (Road of the Key), the inn was built by a member of the Catholic Brotherhood of St John the Beheaded, an order originated in the Middle Ages to escort condemned men to the gallows. In a sense it is fitting that Mons' only serial killer has dismembered and beheaded his victims in such a way.

Authorities believe the killer chose his victims from a loosely connected group of people with social problems who congregate around a string of cheap bars opposite the Mons train station. To date, only three victims have been positively identified, Martine Bohn, Nathalie Godart, and Jacqueline Leclercq. Bohn, 43, was a French transsexual and retired prostitute who worked the bars near the train station. She disappeared on Sunday 21 July. Her mutilated torso was the one found in the Haine.

The second positive identification was that of Nathalie Godart, 21. At the time of her disappearance she had lost custody of her child and was living alone. The staff at the Intercity, the Metropole and the Café de la Gare – the bars she frequented opposite the train station – knew her well. 'She was promiscuous, but not a prostitute,' said her landlady. Sadly, no one reported her missing. The third presumed victim is Jacqueline Leclercq, 33, who disappeared on 23 January 1997. A mother of four, Leclercq drifted into the station scene after losing custody of her children. She was identified as one of the victims by the scarred remnants of a tattoo with the name of her former husband on her left forearm. Apparently the killer – or perhaps Leclercq herself – had tried to obliterate the tattoo with a knife.

On 25 April 1997, police announced that they had arrested a man in connection with the killings. Officials said they kept the arrest secret in the best interest of the investigation. The suspect, whose name was not released, was described as a Belgian male who knew Nathalie Godart, the first victim identified. The man was subsequently released because of lack of evidence. He has now left Mons, and it appears that he is no longer considered a suspect.

Mr Van Reusel believes the killer has a regular nine-to-five job because two of the known disappearances occurred on weekends. Not coincidentally, several of the bags with body parts were also discovered on weekends. Van Reusel said the fact that the killer has not been caught has spread fear through the community with people staying home during weekends and at night. 'The ill-feeling is palpable in the town and the surrounding area,' he told the London *Guardian*. 'The locals are struggling to take it in, and are scared.'

Furthering the scope of the investigation, Belgian prosecutors have been in contact with French counterparts in Valenciennes, to find out if there was any link between the Mons killer and a still-unidentified woman's pelvis found at Chateau l'Abbaye in January 1996. On 21 May 1998, a year after the first dismembered remains were discovered, authorities believe the killer might have resurfaced in the city of Ranst where police found five human heads, and skeletal remains of what could be seven bodies, in a container.

Other cases of dismemberment throughout Europe are being looked at for possible links to the Mons killings. One intriguing serial pattern emerging in Germany involves 40-year-old Olaf Weinert, who confessed to killing and dismembering a 59-year-old woman. The victim, Ruth Buchelt, who had been decapitated, skinned and dismembered, was found in several bags thrown in a channel near Hannover. Starting in 1976, when Weinert was merely sixteen, police have linked him to at least eleven killings. If he is convicted of all killings Weinert will be Germany's most prolific serial killer since 1976 when Joaquim Kroll was arrested for killing and cannibalizing fourteen people.

Police are particularly interested in his activities, starting in 1994 with the decapitation murder of Ludwig Schinkel. Also he is suspected of strangling and dismembering Yasmin Stiehler, a Hannover-area teenager, in 1996. Her remains were found in several bags. Her arms and hands were never recovered. In 1997 he is believed to have skinned, dismembered and dissolved in hydrochloric acid the body of an unidentified woman in the Dutch city of Tiel. Allegedly, the body had been frozen for a short time before she was mutilated. Another set of unidentified body parts found in 1999 in three suitcases near the city of Oberhausen was linked to Weinert by an old girlfriend who told authorities she remembered seeing a similar suitcase in his possession.

Also, on 5 November, 1994, the dismembered remains of Sabrina Graf were found in a trashcan in a rest stop near Hamburg. Police said the frozen head, heart, lungs, kidney and liver of the young woman were found wrapped in plastic bags. The organs, according to German authorities, still held the shape of a container where they had been frozen. Police determined that the Graf murder was actually not related to the Weinert killings. There is no indication that Belgian authorities have tried to link any of these crimes to the ones in Mons. Other mutilation murders in Europe are being considered by Interpol as the work of the 'Lisbon Ripper', another sadistic killer featured in this book.

Belgium, a historically peaceful nation, has been stricken since the mid-1990s by a series of monstrous crimes that have shaken the very foundations of its society. The serial butchery in Mons has only increased the prevailing climate of civic anxiety, Belgium having been yanked out of its placid existence by a string of child sex killings committed by Marc

Dutroux and his international ring of pedophiles. The horrifying discoveries in Mons followed the botched investigation into the pedophile killings as well as another breaking scandal involving Belgian troops in Somalia. The Belgian Ministry of Defence announced that an elite paratrooper battalion would be disbanded after photographic evidence was disclosed of atrocities committed against Somali civilians during the 1992 UN peacekeeping operation. The evidence given to a newspaper included a photograph of a paratrooper urinating on the corpse of a Somali, and another showing a child being 'roasted' over a brazier by two grinning soldiers.

The Dutroux scandal burst into public consciousness on 13 August 1996, when Marc Dutroux, a 39-year-old unemployed electrician, was arrested in his home near Charleroi for abducting two girls. Thus began one of the most horrifying episodes in Belgian history. The two girls – Laetitia Delheze and Sabine Dardeene, aged fourteen and twelve respectively – were found in a concrete dungeon under the house. Both girls were near-starved, drugged and showed signs of repeated sexual abuse. Four days later police discovered the remains of two eight-year-old girls, Julie Lejeune and Melissa Russo, and a man, Bernard Weinstein, buried under a tile patio garden in the back of yet another of Dutroux's six properties. The two girls allegedly died of starvation when Dutroux was arrested and incarcerated for an unrelated violation. In a fit of rage Dutroux killed his accomplice after his release from prison when he discovered Weinstein had failed to feed the two prisoners.

By 3 September two more bodies – An Marchal, seventeen, and Eefje Lambreks, nineteen, who were abducted in 1995 while on holiday in Ostend – were unearthed under his home in Jumet. Though Dutroux confessed to six murders, he is a suspect in a half-dozen more missing children cases. To this day, it is not known how many victims the pedophile ring he ran with his wife and five associates may have claimed. Waves of outrage swept through the nation when leaked police documents showed that authorities had been receiving tip-offs about Dutroux's activities since 1993, and no official action was taken. Some suspect the wily pedophile enjoyed high-level protection by procuring drugs and young children for ranking public and law-enforcement officials. Others blame the scandal on sheer incompetence on the part of the investigators.

On one occasion, while Dutroux was holding two eight-year-old girls in a cell under his house, police officers searching for the missing girls had heard children whimpering nearby. Although they knew that Dutroux was a convicted pedophile, the two officers accepted his explanation that they were his own children and moved on. More surprising – and more incriminating for Belgium's Justice Minister, Stephane de Clerck – was the discovery that Dutroux served only three years of a thirteen-year sentence for abducting five girls in 1983. Even King Albert II of Belgium entered the controversy, expressing his shock over the shortcomings of the national judicial system that freed such a dangerous individual.

Dutroux's unchecked criminality literally devastated Belgium's socio-political framework with many civic and political figures allegedly linked with his child-pornography, drug-dealing and car-theft rings. Even in prison, Dutroux has enjoyed manipulating authorities into digging up half of Belgium – and borrowing ground radar equipment from Scotland Yard – in a vain attempt at finding more bodies. Belgian journalists covering the Mons serial killings say authorities are determined to avoid the jurisdictional 'turf wars' that hampered the Dutroux investigation. A parliamentary inquiry studying the Dutroux investigation concluded that without the rivalry between police, gendarmerie and judicial officials, and the traditional hostility between police in the Francophone and the Flemish-speaking regions, Dutroux never would have kidnapped and killed so many children.

Hopefully things will fare better for investigators in Mons. As of this writing, there are still no viable suspects in custody for the dismemberment murders, and there have been no new reports associated with the killings. However, serial killers never retire, they just wait for another chance to continue doing their evil. And there is no doubt, unless he is dead, sick or incarcerated for an unrelated offense, that the Butcher of Mons will kill again.

11. THE LISBON RIPPER

A Portuguese serial killer dubbed the 'Lisbon Ripper' has been connected to the murders of five drug-addicted prostitutes in the greater Lisbon area and at least four more in four different European nations. With a 25-man task force in Portugal and Interpol agents throughout Europe investigating the case, authorities have been unable to identify this psychotically brutal killer. And in a mind-boggling twist of intercontinental serial killing, the Ripper is thought to be the Old World incarnation of a New World serial killer who killed eleven women in the US. Because New Bedford, Massachusetts has a large Portuguese population, investigators have tentatively related the 1988 'Highway Killer' rampage to the Lisbon Ripper case. To date the still-unsolved highway murders case remains as one of the most publicized cases in Massachusetts since the 'Boston Strangler' was believed to have killed thirteen women.

The first Portuguese victim was found on 31 July 1992. The victim, Maria Valentina, 22, was strangled to death, then disemboweled with something other than a knife. Her body was discovered by factory workers in a wooden shed in the neighborhood of Odivelas near the southern edge of Lisbon. She was a known drug addict and prostitute who worked primarily in the Politecnico area of Lisbon. In the next eight months two more women were found similarly mutilated in the same general area.

First, on 2 January, Maria Fernanda, 24, was found savagely disemboweled in a shed near a known prostitution area in Lisbon called Entrecampos. Then, on 15 March, Chamayase Maria Joao Santos, 27, was found strangled to death about 50 feet from the Valentina crime scene. Santos, who was known on the street as 'Horse Lady' because of her insatiable appetite for heroin consumption, was said to have worked on the same corner as Valentina a year before. She was found naked behind a wooden shed with her face and body beaten to a pulp. She too was sliced open from her neck to her vagina and disemboweled. Then her body was covered with her coat. Her blood-soaked clothing, except for her blouse, was strewn around the crime scene. Her blouse, in contrast, was neatly folded and placed under her head like a pillow. A bloody shard of glass allegedly used to cut her open was found next to the corpse.

Two other prostitute murders, with different characteristics, happened within the same time period and around the same area of Lisbon. The first victim was a 22-year-old prostitute who was found strangled in November 1992 in the Trafaria neighborhood of Sebutal, just south of Lisbon. She was discovered by a man who pulled off the road to relieve himself. Her body had wounds on her neck and stomach. The other victim, Ana Cristina Santos Machado, 24, was found on 27 February also in Sebutal, near the Tejo River. She was nude, with one side of her face horribly beaten, her teeth broken and the rest of her body covered with cigarette burns. Ligature marks on her wrist suggested she had been tied to a chair and was sadistically tortured before being strangled to death. Afterwards, she was dumped at the crime scene posthumously. Like the others, Ana Cristina was a heavy drug user, a known prostitute and her body was found in an isolated, out-of-the-way area south of the Tejo.

Because the two other murdered prostitutes were not disemboweled, Lisbon's Policia Judiciaria (PJ) have been reluctant to link their deaths to the Ripper killings. However, they do consider the two murders in themselves related because of the unspeakable brutality demonstrated by the attacker. In fact, the five Lisbon victims – all young, drug-addicted prostitutes – were strangled and brutally disfigured by blows to their faces. However, none of them were raped, which is highly unusual for this type of killing.

PJ investigators said they had never before seen crimes of such savagery in the streets of Lisbon. In 1993, though the Ripper killings seemed to have stopped – or merely been interrupted by disease or an unrelated arrest – PJ agents said they would still explore every hypothesis and consider every possibility until they arrested the killer. One theory paints the killer as someone traumatized as a child by his mother, who might have been a prostitute. Authorities believe the brutality the killer demonstrated towards his victims was in fact directed towards prostitution itself. 'Theories range from the killer being a man who became HIV-positive after having sex with a prostitute,' said Lisbon's Sub-Inspector Antonio Amaro, 'to his being a husband who lost his wife to the game and is now seeking revenge.'

Even though there have been no witnesses to the crimes, police have created a profile of the killer by talking to other prostitutes who knew the victims and frequented the same areas in which they worked. The killer is believed to be a white male, between 35 and 40 years old, tall, with a pathological hatred of women. The killer, PJ agents say, 'is certainly a man who kills impulsively'. Like many other killers discussed in this book, the Ripper has demonstrated a certain organized post-offense behavior in which he feels comfortable enough at the crime scene to disembowel the victims without leaving any incriminating evidence.

According to Lisbon's Sub-Inspector Antonio Amaro, officers have had a hard time working with the prostitutes because of the illegal nature of their lifestyles and the traumatic state of shock they live in. 'The prostitute world is a violent and brutal one where many are beaten up regularly,' Amaro told the *Montreal Gazette*. 'Most of the prostitutes are unreliable, mainly due to the world they move in. As a consequence, our investigations have been complicated and forced us to follow leads which go nowhere. I could show them a photo of myself and they would say that was the picture of the killer.'

In March 1993 Lisbon investigators went to New Bedford, Massachusetts to explore any links between the Ripper and the still-unidentified 'Highway Murderer'. The New Bedford killer is believed to be responsible for nine murders and two disappearances of drug-addicted prostitutes or 'semi-pros' from the seedy Weld Square area of New Bedford. All bodies have been found in woody areas within 25 feet of the Interstate 195 and Routes 140 and 88 outside New Bedford. Perhaps being a member of the 40,000 strong Portuguese community in New Bedford, police theorize the killer might have moved back to the homeland when he felt the local heat closing in on his trail. 'We are interested in knowing if in Lisbon they have a suspect list,' said the then Bristol County Attorney Paul Walsh Jr, 'and one of them might have been here in the United States.'

The case of the Highway Killer represents the highest body count by a single suspect in the State of Massachusetts since the dreaded 'Boston Strangler' days. From the summer of 1962 to the early winter of 1964, Boston and its suburbs were terrified of a serial killer who strangled thirteen women in their homes and left their bodies provocatively posed with the strangulating cords tied in ornamental bows around their necks. The terror came to an end when Albert DeSalvo, a handsome, smooth-talking laborer with enormous hands and a voracious sex drive, confessed to the Strangler killings while he was being held at the Center for the Treatment of Sexually Dangerous Persons at Bridgewater on a series of rape charges. Though the authorities were unable to convict him for any of the murders, DeSalvo was sentenced to life in prison for a number of rapes. In November 1973 he was stabbed to death in his cell in Walpole by another inmate.

Some detectives believe that DeSalvo, though a serial rapist, was not a killer. Some said he had too much sexual desire to kill women before raping them, as the strangler often did. In fact many believe George Nassar, DeSalvo's cellmate at Bridgewater, struck a deal with him to take the blame as DeSalvo was already facing a life sentence for his multiple rapes. Notably, when two women who had escaped the hands of the Strangler were brought to MCI-Bridgewater to identify DeSalvo, they pointed to Nassar as their attacker.

On 9 July 1999, Boston Police announced that they will reopen the Strangler case to determine through DNA-technology whether DeSalvo was the dreaded killer. Unfortunately authorities have been unable to find the sperm samples swabbed from some of the Strangler's victims that they wanted to test. Nassar, who is considered Massachusetts' most dangerous living criminal, has offered his DNA to test to exonerate him from the Strangler killings. 'I had nothing to do with it,' Nassar said from his cell. 'I'm convicted under the table, behind the scenes.'

Many officers involved in the Strangler investigation have been supportive of their New Bedford colleagues. State Police Lieutenant Thomas E. Spartichino, who as a Metropolitan Police detective was assigned to the Strangler case, told the Boston Globe that, unlike the Strangler who struck at random, the New Bedford killer stalks his victims and plans his attacks. 'He gets into his automobile and looks for women to kill,' said Spartichino. 'I think he's a psychopath who hates women and is trying to rid the world of bad women.'

'This guy is going after prostitutes and junkies,' said Police Sergeant Fidel Centrella, who investigated one of the Strangler cases in Cambridge. 'He probably figures, who the hell would miss them?'

But they have been missed. 'They were human beings and they deserve the same amount of attention given to the strangling victims or as much as if they were socialites,' said State Police Detective Andrew Tuney. 'They deserve everything you can give them.'

All reported disappearances in New Bedford happened between April and September, 1988. Though the first body was found in July, police did not link the killings until four more bodies were found and the first victim was identified. Because of the advanced state of decomposition of the victims, police could only determine the cause of death – strangulation – for three of them. The cause of death of the others remains unknown. Most of the women had to be identified by their dental charts. Nearly all of the women killed were of Portuguese or Cape Verdian descent, and were regulars at the seedy port-area of the city. At least six knew each other and frequented the same bars.

The first victim was found on 3 July in a wooded area on the side of Route 140 by a motorist who stopped to relieve himself. She was partially naked and had her bra wrapped around her neck. Five months later police identified the body as that of 30-year-old Debra Medeiros who had been reported missing by her family in nearby Fall River on 27 May. On 30 July, a nude and decomposing body was found along the eastbound lanes of the I-195 near the town of Dartmouth, six miles from New Bedford. The victim was later identified as 36-year-old Nancy Pavia from New Bedford. She was last seen on 11 July. Though she was a heroin addict, relatives denied that she worked as a prostitute. Pavia left behind two daughters aged fourteen and seventeen. In a macabre twist her clothes were found near the next victim.

The next victim, 35-year-old Debra DeMello, was found by road crews clearing brush on the side of the road along the westbound lanes of I-195. DeMello, who had spent the previous 21 months in a Rhode Island prison, was last seen alive on 11 July when she walked away from a pre-release center. Her body was found less than fifty feet from the Pavia crime scene. Six weeks later, by the time she was identified, police started suspecting they had a serial killer on their hands. Adding to the linkage, DeMello was found next to clothes and personal items belonging to Nancy Pavia. Also, the three women – Medeiros, DeMello and Pavia – knew each other and frequented the same bars in New Bedford's seedy portside area. Investigators believed the killer switched the victims' clothing either as an attempt to veil the identities of the women or as a sign of the killer's fetishistic relation to objects surrounding the killings.

As police compiled a list of several other missing prostitutes from the area, they realized something was terribly wrong. As far as they could tell a serial predator was dumping bodies along the roads surrounding their city at an alarming pace. Authorities started searching along the highways with specially trained cadaver dogs. On 19 November they found the nude body of 25-year-old Dawn Mendes. She was last seen on 4 September. And on 1 December, they found the skeletal remains of 25-year-old Deborah McConnell. Her body was dumped off the I-140, about two miles from the Debra Medeiros crime scene. McConnell was fully clothed and had a bag of extra clothing next to her. She had been missing since May.

Nine days later the skeletal remains of 26-year-old Rochelle Clifford were discovered by hunters in an abandoned quarry half a mile from the I-195. Clifford was last seen alive with a man who knew Nancy Pavia. Though initially suspected of the two murders, the individual was quickly cleared of both charges. The next victim was found on 28 March, 1989, on the southbound side of the I-140, directly opposite the Madeiros crime scene. She was identified as 28-year-old Robin Rhodes. A single mother, Rhodes was last seen alive in April 1988. According to family and friends Rhodes was not a prostitute, but was addicted to drugs and occasionally turned tricks.

Mary Santos, 26, was found on 31 March off Route 88. A known heroin addict, Santos knew four of the other victims: Clifford, Pavia, Mendes and Rhodes. The last known victim, 24-year-old Sandra Botelho, was found naked on 24 April off the I-195. A drug-addicted prostitute, Botelho was last seen on 11 August. Two more women with similar profiles have been missing and are believed to be victims of the Highway Killer. The two women – Christina Monteiro, twenty, and Marylin Roberts, 34 – were neighbors and disappeared within a month of each other. Facing a multitude of unsolved murder files, authorities turned to the FBI for help. They also talked to San Diego police where a task force was investigating the deaths of as many as 48 prostitutes.

An assortment of suspects were arrested and later released as New Bedford police attempted to solve the case. One suspect, a 35-year-old unemployed trucker and fish cutter named Neil Anderson, was fingered by the local prostitutes as a sexual sadist who enjoyed threatening them with a knife. Arrested on 13 December 1988, Anderson was charged with rape and sexual battery. Although he had a long list of convictions for assault with a deadly weapon, breaking and entering, and a variety of drug and alcohol charges, authorities could not find any evidence connecting him to the killings.

Another prostitute brutalizer, Tony Grazia, was fingered by seventeen prostitutes as a dangerous rapist. After being arrested on 4 May and charged with assault, Grazia was sent to a hospital for psychological testing. Hair, rug and paint samples were taken from him and his home and sent to an FBI lab in Washington for testing. Though he was cleared of the murders, Grazia was genetically linked to several rapes. Released on a $37,500 bond he was re-arrested in 1991 for raping another prostitute. In July 1991, he made bail and was released. A few days later he overdosed on antidepressants in an apparent suicide.

The next person of interest in the investigation was attorney Kenneth Ponte. Described as a cat lover with homosexual tendencies, Ponte was a true Jekyll and Hyde-type character. On the one hand an accomplished lawyer, and on the other a drug addict and sadistic woman hater. By December 1989 the first stories pointing at Ponte as the Highway Killer appeared in the local press. As the investigators focused their attention on Ponte, local prostitutes and drug dealers turned on him, telling stories to authorities about his drug abuse and sexual exploits. One dealer said he once saw a forty-minute pornographic videotape filmed by Ponte that featured several of the murdered prostitutes. Police never recovered such a tape and doubt it ever existed.

On 17 August 1990 Ponte was indicted by a grand jury of first degree murder for the death of Rochelle Clifford, his onetime client. Then, after former District Attorney Ronald Pina was defeated by Paul Walsh, the incoming District Attorney changed the course of the investigation. By 1991 special prosecutor Paul Buckley, who was asked to examine the Ponte case, found grounds to dismiss the murder charge against him. By 1992 Ponte's name was completely cleared from the investigation by forensic analysis performed by the FBI. After Ponte's release New Bedford Police Detective Richard Ferreira said, 'The murderer is still out there. There is no way this person is able to stop what he was doing, which is testified to by the frequency and savagery of the murders. He must be doing this somewhere else.'

Back in Europe, Portuguese police and Interpol agents agreed with Ferreira and recognized the possibility of a linkage between the Ripper killings in Lisbon, New Bedford's Highway killings and five other brutal murders in five different European nations. One theory expounded by Interpol agents at a May 1996 serial killer conference in Holland was that the Ripper may have taken his act on the road, leaving in his wake a trail of death. Between 1992 and 1997 between four and seven savage murders of young, drug-dependent prostitutes throughout the Continent have been eerily, and brutally, reminiscent of the Lisbon killings. These murders in Belgium, the Czech Republic, Denmark, Germany and The Netherlands have shown a consistent pattern that led investigators to think they were committed by the same madman. All women were strangled and mutilated. And none of the killings had any evidence of rape. Police think that the killer may be a truck driver, which could place him regularly in different parts of Europe, enabling him to move in and out of the area undetected before and after each crime.

Czech, German and Portuguese law-enforcement officers met in Prague in July 1996 hoping to link a series of mutilation murders spanning the three nations. 'We are definitely finding similarities,' said Zbynek Teply, Chief Commissioner of Central Bohemia's Bureau of Investigation. In all cases investigators agree the suspect is someone familiar with, at least, the anatomy of mammals, and may work as a butcher. Four of the five cases discussed at the meeting involved the victims being repeatedly hit over the head with a blunt object and having one or several vital organs removed from their bodies.

According to Josef Nedela, head of the Czech Republic special homicide squad, all five women were discovered near important international roads, which ties in nicely with the killer trucker theory. 'It's impossible to tell by the *modus operandi* whether it was one and the same killer, but it can't be ruled out,' Nedela told the *Prague Post*. 'If it's a maniac, he is probably no longer in the Czech Republic, because he would have struck again.' The Czech victim, 21-year-old Dita Hrabankova, was found on 9 June 1992, in the bushes of the Pruhonice Park, a secluded wooded area southeast of Prague. Her chest had been cut open from the neck to the waist and all her organs had been emptied out.

For years, reports throughout Europe of dissected human bodies missing vital organs have fueled speculation of the existence of a thriving illegal organ market. So far, however, there has been no real evidence suggesting that such theories are anything more than gruesome urban legends. Doctors familiar with transplants say that they are extremely complicated procedures involving dozens of professionally trained personnel, strict sanitary conditions and state of the art operating facilities. Stefan Vitko, head of Prague's Transplant-centrum, said he sincerely doubts that Hrabankova was killed for her organs. 'It totally lacks logic to kill somebody for organs,' he told the *Prague Post*. 'You would have to know in advance who the transplant recipient was and carry out a number of tests (to match the donor with the recipient).'

The last victim tentatively linked to the Ripper in his transcontinental rampage has been Alice Kansiime, a 37-year-old African prostitute who was savagely killed in the Danish town of Ringsted. Kansiime was murdered on 4 September 1997. The killer, in a gruesome act of savagery, cut off one of the victim's hands and masturbated over her corpse.

Perhaps the killer in New Bedford, Lisbon and the other European nations is the same individual, or there are several people with similar manias, or maybe even a combination of both. Still, the body count has been rising steadily in seven nations and no one has been held accountable for the mayhem in a court of law. Maybe this butcher, with cunning and mobility, has again outwitted the cops. But such monstrous crimes should never go unpunished and the evil maniac responsible should be locked away before he kills again. It is up to law-enforcement personnel in Portugal, New Bedford and the European Interpol to put an end to this intercontinental rampage before the killer spills more innocent blood.

12. ROME'S GAY SERIAL KILLER

As of August 1997, following the deaths of an art-loving nobleman in Florence and an American lecturer in Rome, Italian authorities announced there may be a serial killer on the loose targeting influential homosexual men. A third related death, the murder of Enrico Sini Luzi, a reputed gay aristocrat and gentleman-in-waiting to the Pope, confirmed for many the fact that someone was indeed targeting Italy's gay elite. When a chaplain from Milan and an art-restorer from Umbria were similarly killed, police realized they had a serious problem on their hands.

In fact twenty gay men have been killed in Rome under similar circumstances since 1990. Most of the victims were middle-aged, mild-mannered, cultivated, and highly respectable semi-public figures. They were found mostly bludgeoned and strangled to death in their homes in a naked or half-naked state. In most cases the victim had apparently invited the murderer inside. Evidence at the crime scenes suggests that most had had sex before they were killed. Among the victims there has been an actor, a journalist, a banker, a television director, a businessman, a hotelier, a theater critic and a fortune-teller. Ten of the murders remain unsolved. Authorities believe that the killings are not the work of a homophobic serial killer but the result of a series of young male hustlers disgusted with their luck in life and lashing out at their tricks.

The first victim in the series of high-profile deaths was Count Alvise di Robilant. On 15 January 1997, the count was found bludgeoned to death in his Renaissance Florentine home. The former managing director of Sotheby's Italia, the count was an art expert and music scholar whose ancestors descended from the Mocenigo family of Venice and included seven Venetian Doges. His family, whose pedigree is beyond reproach, formerly owned three palaces in Venice, one of which, the Palazzo Mocenigo, was where Lord Byron lived when he wrote *Don Juan*.

The count was described as 'one of the handsomest men in Italy' and, at 72, many women still found him extremely attractive. 'He was divorced from his American wife, Betty, who lives in Rome and with whom he had three sons and was on good terms,' said a family friend. The friend added that the count had been having 'a sentimental life with another woman, also of noble family'. The count's intimate circle, which included members of Italy's leading families, was 'completely above suspicion,' the friend said. 'They belonged to a sphere of people who were not only above board, but lacked the passion needed for such a crime.'

Because there was no evidence of forced entry police suspect the count knew his attacker and may have invited the killer into his home. A local report said that, much to his displeasure, an 'undesirable neighbor' – an East European prostitute – had moved in next door. In frustration the count was said to have tried to have the woman evicted. At first police theorized that the killer could have been a woman because the 'wounds are compatible with a female hand', which led many to believe his neighbor was the culprit. Rumors that the killer was a spurned mistress seeking revenge were also widely circulated through the drawing rooms of Italian society. However, a pathologist's report found that the blows were too deep, and had come from too high an angle to fit the female killer theory.

'The framework of the crime is certainly one of passion,' said Professor Vittorino Andreoli, one of Italy's foremost crime psychologists. 'He is undressed, killed, then covered – if not out of love, then at least out of consideration. It is strange, however, for a woman to kill someone with blows to the head. It is one of the most difficult ways, since one has to hit someone many times, and face the resistance of the victim. It isn't very feminine, whereas the pistol in the handbag is. In short, everything would be a lot clearer if the lover were a man.' Because all evidence indicated a seemingly intimate nature between the count and his killer, police concluded, to the incredulity of his friends and family, that the count had embarked on a secret gay liaison which ultimately led to his death.

The count lived alone on the converted top floor of the fifteenth century palace owned by his cousin. He was well-known throughout Italy for his numerous female conquests, but it was rumored he was bisexual and had begun a homosexual affair before his death. The morning after his death the count's corpse was found by his maid in the drawing-room. It is believed he was attacked first in his bedroom, but died in the adjoining room, next to one of his favorite paintings. The night of his death neighbors said they heard the count playing Bach fugues. Police reported that the piano keys had been wiped clean, suggesting that in fact it was his killer who was the one performing the fugues for the count.

Evidence shows that the apartment had been searched, but no valuables were taken, indicating that the killer could have been searching for letters or photographs that would reveal his identity. The count was found wearing only underwear and his dressing gown, suggesting he might have been intimately involved with the killer before his death. Police determined the killer used a candelabra to hit the nobleman once on the forehead then three more times on the back of his head. Then he covered the body with a bedspread, which is usually done after a crime if the killer is well-acquainted with the victim. Blood was splattered all over the drawing-room walls. The screen of the count's laptop computer was smashed and his favorite painting, St Jerome from the school of Guercino, had been violently scratched. Forensic tests found a slight trace of semen on his lips, though the trace was too faint to determine if it was his or someone else's.

The gay link to the count's murder was further reinforced on 11 August when authorities found 56-year-old Louis Inturrisi similarly bludgeoned in his home in Monteverde Vecchio, overlooking Rome's bohemian Trastevere quarter. Inturrisi, an openly gay American professor, was a lecturer in several Rome universities as well as a restaurant reviewer for the *New York Times*. Like the count he was found half-dressed with pajama bottoms and there was no sign of a forced entry. Investigators reportedly were trying to determine if the count and Inturrisi had any mutual friends or even knew each other.

It wouldn't be surprising if they were acquaintances considering that both flew regularly to New York and traveled in the same cultured circles.

The third victim linked to the case was Enrico Sini Luzi, an elderly Italian aristocrat and gentleman-in-waiting to the Pope. On 8 January 1998, authorities found Sini Luzi, 66, in his apartment near the Vatican with his face pressed against a velvet cushion, a cashmere scarf tightly wound around his neck, and his head bashed in. The amiable and bespectacled former theology professor had been hit on the head more than a dozen times with an antique candlestick. The victim was found in the bedroom wearing only black socks and underwear. He had traces of adhesive on his wrist. The tape marks and scarf suggest he had engaged in 'some kind of erotic sado-masochistic game' before his death. The television was still on and a gay porn video was found inside the tape player. Like the other two victims there was no sign of forced entry and, although the apartment was stuffed with antiques, only credit cards, his mobile phone and a few rings were missing.

The death of Sini Luzi confirmed for many the fear that a homosexual serial murderer was indeed stalking Italian high society. Although he was not openly gay, Sini Luzi's murder had all the trappings of hardcore gay sex-play gone horribly wrong. An aesthete who was described as 'an Oscar Wilde of the provinces', Sini Luzi was always seen around Rome in the company of young men. He frequently took a number of them to his home near the Vatican where he also greeted dignitaries who would come to Rome for an audience with the Pope. His post of gentleman-in-waiting to the Pope is an honor reserved only for chosen Catholic nobility.

Sini Luzi began his services as a gentleman to his Holiness in April 1989. He kept his post until his untimely death, even though he had been arrested years before for having sex in a public bathroom, allegedly with a priest. The Vatican did not comment on his death. However, the Italian newspaper *La Republica* quoted the Reverend Giovanni D'Ercole, an official of the Curia, saying: 'In the face of death, one must only be silent. One cannot express judgments because it is not yet clear how the thing happened.'

Some members of Sini Luzi's family vehemently denied that he was gay. 'He was not a person of "certain habits",' his brother, Lillo, 72, was quoted as saying in *La Republica*. 'Such comportment cannot be reconciled with his morality and the Catholic education he always observed.' Lillo Sini Luzi added that any evidence of homosexual activity found in the apartment was probably planted by the killer to 'trick' investigators.

Because of his position in the Vatican, and like many gay men in Italy, Sini Luzi led a double life that veiled his homosexuality. By day, he obligingly escorted foreign dignitaries on their way to meet the Pope. By night, he cruised the streets of Rome in his black Fiat or sat in a gay bar a stone's throw away from the Vatican drinking ale and looking to meet young men. With the Catholic Church's looming influence and Italy's macho-conservative culture, gay life in Rome is rarely seen or heard.

Two weeks after his murder authorities arrested two men in the town of Avezzano, about fifty miles from Rome. They were found using Sini Luzi's cell phone. One of them, 36-year-old Paul Badea, said he killed Sini Luzi after the aristocrat had picked him off the street and taken him to his house to have sex. Badea's lawyer, Ambrogio Reggio, said his client, who like many other hustlers is a Romanian immigrant, met the victim in October at the Termini railway station. 'Sini Luzi offered Badea a home and a paid job in return for sexual relations,' Reggio told *Deutsche Presse-Agentur*. 'He saw Sini Luzi eight or nine times but did not receive what had been promised. Their last encounter degenerated into a lethal fight when Sini Luzi asked him to do something beneath his dignity.'

A few days after Sini Luzi's death, Reverend Gregory Beheydt, the newly appointed American-born chaplain at the Episcopal Church of All Saints of Milan, was found in his bathroom clobbered to death. The reverend was bound to a chair with his mouth taped shut and had homosexual pornography and videos scattered around him on the floor. Like Sini Luzi and Count di Robilant, the murdered clergyman was not thought to have been homosexual. Martin

Gough, the Anglican priest who found the body, said the reverend had been sheltering two Croats who did housework in exchange for cash and lodging. According to friends, they were the homosexuals. Peter Zivni, a fellow clergyman, said: 'I know that he used to take in Slav immigrants, Bosnians or Croats. They are desperate people and sometimes dangerous. But Padre Gregory trusted them.' Eventually the two Croats were charged with his death.

On 3 April another pillar of Italian society fell victim to the wave of gay-related murders. This time fifty-year-old art-restorer Piero Nottiani was found by his estranged wife bludgeoned to death in his third floor apartment in the Umbrian capital of Perugia. His body was rolled up in a rug and his head had been crushed with a one-foot-tall gray marble statuette of an ancient goddess. Nottiani was chief restorer for Umbria's state heritage department, specializing in Old Master paintings. Again there was no sign of forced entry, suggesting that Nottiani knew his killer. Police found a cooked dinner in the kitchen, a bottle of chilled wine in the fridge and table settings for two, indicating that Nottiani might have invited his killer for dinner. Like the other cases none of the antique furnishings or paintings were stolen. In fact, the circumstances of his murder were eerily reminiscent of Count di Robilant's killing.

But these men were not the only ones to die in similar circumstances: there was Don Pietro Contaldo, 53, strangled in 1995; Emilio Cravatin, battered to death in the same year; Francesco Privitera, 53, bludgeoned in his home in the Prenestina area; Giuseppe Malatesta, 56, a hotelier, found naked and dead; Claudio Pavone, 48, battered with a hammer and strangled with a telephone cord; Vittorio Meloni, a television director, also battered to death; Dante Livorno, 50, a theater critic, strangled with a telephone cord; and Mario Chiarani, a 67-year-old pensioner, found tied to a chair with his mouth taped shut, suffocated. In all, twenty men of similar profiles have been found dead in Rome since 1990. And several others have been found outside the capital. Five of the ten cases solved have led to the arrests of foreign male hustlers.

Gay activists believe there is a clear link between the increase in violence against homosexuals and the influx of East European immigrants, particularly from Romania where homosexuality is illegal. 'Many of them [Romanians] profess they are not homosexuals and are just prostituting themselves. But this is an old excuse used by many rent boys. The truth is that they are gay and are disgusted with themselves because under some communist regimes to be gay was to be a criminal. This self-loathing can quickly turn to violence,' said Andrea di Giambattista, a spokesman for Arcigay, an Italian gay advocacy group.

'The method of killing seems identical,' said gay activist Angelo Pezzana, who doubts there is a gay serial killer at work. 'But the hand which has killed them is not. People who bring home an unknown Albanian or Senegalese are committing a fatal error.'

In the wake of Sini Luzi's killing the gay community took to the streets to express their frustration with investigators who they thought were not giving the murders as high a priority as they would if the victims had not been gay. 'The crime involving Enrico Sini Luzi is only the latest in an incredible series of killings that seem to have no end,' Franco Grillini, the President of Arcigay, said in a prepared statement. Grillini, in a press conference following the murder, asked for a parliamentary inquiry into the mushrooming violence against gays. 'A government intervention is absolutely necessary to break the wave of homicides,' he said.

Massimo Consoli, founder of the Italian Gay Movement, took the blame game a step further, pointing at the Roman Catholic Church itself as the 'primary instigator of discrimination'. Consoli, not mincing words, called on the Pope to publicly condemn the gay killings of Sini Luzi and others that have rocked the nation. 'The real problem of Italian gays is the Catholic Church,' said Grillini, pointing out that the Church has repeatedly rejected any reform that might reduce the 'homophobic atmosphere' its policies have created.

Six days after Sini Luzi's death, Alfredo Ormando, a gay Sicilian writer, attacked the Church's position against homosexuality in dramatic and deadly fashion by dousing himself with gasoline, then torching himself to death in front of St Peter's Basilica. In his suicide note the martyred homosexual wrote, 'I am taking my life because my family and society have rejected me because I am homosexual.'

On a national level the number of anti-gay homicides in Italy has reached epidemic proportions, with as many as two hundred murders going unreported each year. Furthermore two hundred teenagers commit suicide each year because they find it impossible to cope with being gay. 'Italy is still a very macho society where homosexuality is not widely accepted,' Grillini said. 'Intolerance leads to violence, whether self-inflicted or otherwise.' Tolerance towards gays has increased, particularly in the northern cities of Milan and Bologna. But anti-gay feelings are still strong in the south, where hard-line machismo and conservatism prevail. 'We are by now in the face of a real and true national emergency,' said Grillini.

Whether the rash of gay killings in Rome and throughout Italy is the work of a serial killer or the result of a new breed of violent street hustler venting its rage on the older men, no one knows; that is until all the cases are solved. However, though many of the murders fit the Eastern European male hustler killer pattern, others don't. Possibly there could be someone more cultured and educated killing his kin. There could be an affable and attractive killer plucking out Italy's rich and powerful for his own deviant sake. Someone like, for instance, Andrew Cunanan who, in 1997, ended his cross-country murderous gay rampage by killing famed clothing designer Gianni Versace for reasons unknown. So many deaths with so many similarities must involve at least one serial killer. A sadistic killer could be lurking in the shadows of Italian gay society setting up his next kill.

13. CIUDAD JUÁREZ, CITY OF THE DEAD

Since August 1993, Mexican Federales have been baffled by the number of young women found brutally raped and murdered on the outskirts of Ciudad Juárez, an industrial border town next to El Paso with a population of two million. The number of the dead varies according to the sources. Local women's rights groups believe that since 1993 at least 187 women have met violent deaths in Juárez. Of these, many were killed by pimps, drug dealers, husbands and boyfriends. However, at least a third of the deaths remain unexplained and police have no suspects. Authorities believe that about thirty cases have the common thread of torture and rape, suggesting they are the work of one or several serial killers. Independent criminologists from the US believe that between fifty and seventy cases fit a similar rape-torture-murder profile. But FBI agents who visited Juárez found no evidence suggesting there was a serial killer at work. Local authorities all but dismiss the killings as a side effect of the city's mushrooming industrial sector, which brings tides of hungry migrant workers to the area, all desperate for work and money.

Most victims are slender, dark-haired girls between fourteen and eighteen years old who work in one of the numerous American-owned *maquiladora* factories. Many are killed on their way to and from work. Their bodies have been found – sometimes with their blue factory-issued aprons on – dumped in the desert or next to the roads leading to the unlit squatter camps ringing the city. In some cases, the victims are mutilated and horribly disfigured. Objects have been stuffed into their vaginas or anuses, and/or their left breasts have been hacked off. Many are strangled, then stabbed repeatedly. Others were found with their hands tied behind their backs. Some have their panties removed, even if they are still fully dressed. Several men have been arrested in connection with the killings, but the carnage has continued unabated.

The *maquiladora* murders first attracted attention in 1993, when a government psychologist, Oscar Maynes, noticed an unexplainable rise in the murder rate of poor, young, slender women with dark skin and long black hair. 'The authorities were just indifferent,' said Irma Perez Franco, the mother of a twenty-year-old shoe store clerk who was murdered in 1995. During the same week in which her daughter was killed, eight other bodies were discovered in a stretch of the surrounding Chihuahua desert.

'Juárez is the ideal place to kill a woman, because you're certain to get away with it,' said Astrid Gonzalez Davila, a founder of the Citizens Committee Against Violence, a group that works with the relatives of murder victims. 'The failure to solve these killings is turning the city into a Mecca for homicidal maniacs.' Adding to the homicidal maniacs, the local heroin and cocaine distribution networks have made Juárez and its sprawling shantytowns one of the most dangerous places on earth.

While similarities between many of the murders have fueled the theory that one or more serial killers may be at work, local authorities attributed most of the deaths to the growing drug trade and the shifting of traditional values in the region. By and large, Juárez has always been a city ripe with violence, but the growing list of dead girls has become too large to be ignored. 'We don't believe that we do have a serial killer,' said Manuel Esparza, Operations Co-ordinator for the state's Special Prosecution Unit of Female Homicides. 'There are different [methods of operation], different dumpsites and different kinds of victims.'

Some see the heart of the problem stemming from a macho backlash caused by the growing local female labor force in this sprawling industrial Mecca. In the rapidly transforming social hierarchy of Ciudad Juárez women are being victimized for taking the traditional place of men in the work force. Dr Irma Rodriguez Galarza, a forensic specialist, told the *Dallas Morning News* that the cluster killings haunting Juárez and its surroundings may be the result of the psychological crisis affecting Mexican men as they are being phased out of the local labor force.

'There exists a rivalry, professionally and economically, between men and women,' Dr Rodriguez said. 'Women don't stay at home anymore. They have more liberty now, liberty that puts them at risk. I'm sure that the FBI, as experts, will come to the conclusion that this is not the work of a serial killer but of a social criminological phenomena – a product of a loss of values and the influence of drugs and alcohol.'

Women's rights advocate Esther Chavez Cano, who has spearheaded the effort to resolve the killings, agrees that the violence against women in Ciudad Juárez is partially caused by the growing number of *maquiladora* factories that only hire female workers. 'Women are occupying the place of men in a culture of absolute dominance of men over women,' said the 65-year-old retired businesswoman. 'This has to provoke misogyny.'

Plant owners of the 330 *maquiladora* factories say they prefer hiring women because they are 'more nimble and orderly'. However, the standard $3-a-day minimum wage they pay might be the true reason why 70 percent of their labor force is young, female and uneducated. Many of these young women are drawn from the southern Mexican states to Juárez by the promise of work and a better life. Sadly, their hopes for prosperity are quickly dashed by a grim reality of meager salaries, shantytowns, violence and squalid living conditions. 'The women here in Ciudad Juárez are expendable, disposable women,' said Judith Gallarza, a women's rights activist. 'It's a problem of government indifference, of impunity and of machismo.'

Complicating an already complex situation, two federal investigators, Oscar Defassiux Trechuelo and Eduardo Muriel Melero, protested that their investigation was being hampered by state authorities because evidence in some of the killings implicated local police officers. Other reports paint the foreign-owned *maquiladora* factories and the rich who are untouched by the slaughter as the true culprits of this evolving tragedy. 'Even the devil is scared of living here,' a Juárez fruit vendor told a *Harper's* reporter who was in town dredging up stories about the unfolding carnage.

The living conditions for most of these women are less than desirable. Most of the 150,000 factory and assembly plant workers live in wood-and-tarpaper shacks in squalid slums surrounding the city. Many of these shantytowns have no running water or electricity. Factory owners, wishing to maximize their profits, keep their plants in operation 24 hours a day, forcing many women to return to their homes late at night on isolated unpaved roads. Some, unfortunately, never make it.

According to Alma Vucovich, president of the Mexican Congress Committee on Sexual Equality, authorities have not shown much interest in solving the cases, 'because the victims are women and poor, and many times they have no family in Juárez'.

A federal human rights commission criticized state authorities for consistently dismissing the murders, even suggesting many of the victims invited their fate by using too much make-up or wearing miniskirts. 'Girls of eleven and twelve disappear, and the first thing the police say is that they probably ran off with their boyfriends,' said Esther Chavez. 'That's ridiculous.'

Several cases of mishandling of events have worsened the rift between the city's poor and disenfranchised and the police. For instance, when the body of seventeen-year-old Sagrario Gonzalez was found twenty miles from Rio Grande, police informed the media before notifying her next of kin. And when they did finally contact her family they suggested Sagrario had been trying to earn extra money turning tricks, even though she was last seen getting on the bus after her shift in a *maquiladora* factory. Enraged by the apathy of city officials, Sagrario's sister, Geeyamina, started painting black crosses on the municipal lamp-posts to symbolize the senseless loss of her sister's life. Now, most posts in the Juárez sprawl are covered with the crosses. And many makeshift altars have been made on street corners and in police stations.

The first suspect arrested in the case was Sharif Abdul Latif Sharif, an Egyptian-born chemist living in one of the city's wealthy neighborhoods. Sharif was taken into custody in 1995 after a prostitute accused him of raping her at his home. In custody Sharif allegedly confessed to five killings. Since then he has staunchly maintained his innocence. 'I am innocent,' claimed Sharif in a prison interview. 'They are pinning this all on me because I am a foreigner . . . I'm just a drunk, I'm not a murderer.' In 1996 a judge dismissed six murder charges against Sharif, then prosecutors filed new murder charges and threw him back in jail. On 3 March 1999 Sharif was convicted of the 1994 rape and murder of eighteen-year-old Elizabeth Castro Garcia and sentenced to thirty years in prison.

A quick look into Sharif's past reveals a man of great scientific genius as well as a rapist and possible serial killer. By the time Sharif arrived at Ciudad Juárez he was no stranger to sexual violence against women. The Egyptian immigrant had several run-ins with the law in the US before relocating to Mexico. He had two sexual battery convictions in Florida – in Gainesville and Palm Beach – resulting in six years in prison. A third rape charge in Brownsville, Texas pushed him across the border. He also had a history of drunk-driving arrests in New Jersey, Florida and Texas and a 1984 jailbreak charge in Florida that somehow went unpunished.

According to all who worked with Sharif, he was a man of scientific genius as well as a hard-drinking, womanizing charmer who was personable and funny. Several American oil companies considered him a genius of the laboratory and sought his services, regardless of the cost. He was a chemist who, according to a colleague, 'could make a bomb out of Bisquick.' One Midland, Texas, company even hired him from prison, overlooking his obvious psychopathic behavior and helping him fight off deportation. Sharif, in fact, was lucky beyond belief, taking full advantage of his personal magnetism as well as the loyalty of his employers. After two rape convictions he somehow eluded deportation despite a law calling for the banishment of any legal alien who committed two crimes of 'moral turpitude.'

In May 1981, Sharif punched and raped a 23-year-old neighbor in Palm Beach, then claimed they had consensual sex that had got a little rough. With the help of his boss Jim Gambale, the owner of Cercoa Inc., Sharif hired Greg Scott, a highly regarded Palm Beach defense lawyer. Scott was able to plea-bargain the rape charge to five years probation. On 13

August, the night before he pleaded guilty to sexual battery, Sharif attacked another woman at her home in West Palm Beach. 'I was on the floor between the bed and the bathroom,' she wrote in her police statement. 'He began telling me to take my clothes off. I asked him please for a towel, and he said no, kicked me once or twice and said he was going to kill me, and hit me again several times.' Then he calmed down, asked her to fix him a drink, and even asked her for a date the next night.

'The suspect in this case is Sharif Sharif,' an investigator wrote after she reported the attack. 'He . . . has current sexual battery charges pending, using the same motive.' Inexplicably, the second attack was never reported to the prosecutors handling the first rape case. That same day he was released on parole on the first charge he was arrested and charged with false imprisonment and battery. Then he was quickly released on bail so he could return to work. Eventually, on 11 January 1982, he was found guilty of battery for a second time and sentenced to 45 days in jail.

After getting fired from Cercoa, Sharif relocated with two co-workers to Gainesville where they formed their own firm. In Gainesville, Sharif ended a short-lived marriage by beating his wife senseless. A few weeks later he attacked a college student who answered his ad for a live-in housekeeper. 'If you try to escape, I will murder you like the rest of them,' he allegedly told the terrified twenty-year-old. 'I will bury you out back in the woods. I've done it before, and I'll do it again.'

After his arrest for the Gainesville attack several other women called police to report that they had been terrorized by him. 'All were so frightened that they were afraid to come forward,' Gainesville Police Captain Sadie Darnell wrote ten years later to an El Paso federal judge during deportation proceedings against Sharif. 'Some indicated they thought he would kill them if he found out.'

In light of the murder charges against Sharif in Mexico, US authorities have been looking into several unsolved murders in Florida and New Jersey that might have involved the Egyptian chemist. One case in particular, the 1977 abduction and murder of thirty-year-old Sandra Miller in New Jersey, points to Sharif as a viable suspect. Miller was attacked the night of 3 January 1977, when she returned home from her job with Eastern Airlines at the Newark Airport. Her killer was apparently waiting for her when she pulled up at the remote farm where she lived with her five-year-old daughter. Evidence found outside the farmhouse suggests a fierce struggle ensued between Miller and her assailant.

Miller was eventually overpowered and driven away in a car a few miles across the Delaware River into Pennsylvania where she was either dumped on the side of the road, or jumped from the car in an attempt to escape. She died – of a single stab wound – just as a police officer reached her. After learning of Sharif's incarceration for a series of rape–murders in Juárez, New Jersey State Police Detective Chris Andreychak established that Sharif worked at a chemical plant two miles from Miller's home, and they both frequented the same bar. Considering Sharif was an obsessive womanizer and Miller a pretty brunette, undoubtedly they would have met. Comparing her case to other known attacks committed by the brilliant chemist, one cannot avoid suspecting his involvement in her untimely demise.

With Sharif in jail the killings came to a momentary halt, then continued at a faster pace. Authorities theorize that Sharif hired a gang called the 'Rebels' to continue murdering women. In April 1996, police detained nearly two hundred men in a raid on several bars in Juárez. Among those arrested were Sergio Armendariz, a nightclub security guard and leader of the Rebels, and six fellow gang members. Police claim Armendariz – also known as El Diablo – and his gang were hired by Sharif to ritually kill at least seventeen girls. Fortunately El Diablo and the Rebels enjoyed the job of torturing the women on a concrete sacrificial slab before murdering them. Several of the victims had bite marks all over their bodies, three of them matching El Diablo's own teeth. Most of the victims had their skulls caved in. Though investigators believe Sharif, Armendariz and the Rebels are responsible for at least seventeen murders, their arrests still failed to stop the bloodshed.

In March 1999, a team of FBI specialists joined Mexican authorities in the investigation. The involvement of the FBI came after months of meetings between Chihuahua state officials and bureau officials in El Paso. Though FBI profilers have worked regularly with Canadian authorities, the bureau's involvement in the Juárez killings marked the first time federal agents have been asked to assist with an internal investigation in Mexico. The three profilers sent from the National Center for the Analysis of Violent Crime in Quantico, Virginia, visited several of the recent crime scenes and analyzed crime photos and other evidence. After a week of investigation, the team of FBI agents concluded there was no serial killer at work in the area. 'The team determined that the majority of cases were single homicides,' said a statement issued by the FBI in El Paso. 'It is too premature and irresponsible to state that a serial killer is loose in Juárez.'

Contradicting his former employers, famed serial killer profiler Robert Ressler said there could be up to three different killers in action. Ressler was invited to Juárez in 1998 to look into the cases. Chihuahua Attorney General Arturo Chavez said his office sought Ressler's help because, 'we have no one with that kind of experience' in Mexico. During his first of three visits to Juárez, Ressler found that of the then 187 deaths, 76 victims seemed to fit a pattern. Most were women between the ages of 17 and 24, most had been raped and strangled, more than a dozen had disappeared going to or from work at the city's assembly plants.

'I determined that it wasn't one person who was responsible,' said Ressler, who heads the Virginia-based Forensic Behavioral Services, a private company that focuses on profiling, investigations and law-enforcement consultation. 'It's not one serial killer. I think it's probably two or three.' Ressler theorized that an American may be crossing into Juárez and taking advantage of the border's anonymity. He noted that Juárez offers serial killers plenty of dark streets, abandoned buildings and a transient population from which to choose victims: 'It's an ideal situation for an American with money. The environment for trouble is there.'

Another famed criminologist, Candice Skrapec, who is best known for profiling New York's 'Zodiac Killer', spent ten weeks in the summer of 1999 working with Juárez police.

Skrapec, a professor of criminology at California State University at Fresno, said she had identified 67 cases in which she believes serial killers were involved. 'Nothing jumped out at me in terms of Satanic rituals or specific torture, as in cutting off someone's fingers or breasts,' she told the *Toronto Star*. Skrapec's findings suggest that there could be up to four different serial killers at work on the streets of Juárez. The Canadian criminologist said there might be even more murders from before 1993 that could be tied to the suspected serial killer sprees.

Because of his strong family ties to Ciudad Juárez, Skrapec considered Angel Maturino Résendez, the feared 'Railway Killer', a possible Juárez serial killer. 'We are especially concerned because he has lived in two barrios here,' said social activist Chavez Cano. In fact, most of his family lives in Juárez including his uncle, Rafael Résendez-Ramirez, whose name he used as one of many aliases. On 13 July 1999 – urged by his sister and brother – Maturino Résendez crossed the Ysleta Bridge over the Rio Grande into the US, shook hands with Texas Ranger Andrew Carter, and surrendered; thus ended a six-week televised manhunt that made him, at the time, the most wanted man in America. Authorities speculate that the suspect feared that bounty hunters, hoping to cash in on the $125,000 reward offered for his capture, would gun him down. Instead, family members who brokered the surrender claimed the reward for themselves.

In custody Maturino Résendez was charged with allegedly bludgeoning to death nine people. Most of the attacks occurred in the homes of the victims located near the same railway lines he used to travel from state to state. His murderous rampage spanned from Texas to Kentucky, Illinois, and started on 29 August 1997, with the slaying of a 21-year-old college student in Kentucky who was attacked while walking with his girlfriend along railroad tracks. The rest of the killings occurred between September 1998 and 15 June 1999. His last two victims were a 79-year-old man and his 51-year-old daughter who were found dead in their home in Gorham, Illinois, near the train tracks. Fearing the Mexican Government would block the suspect's extradition if he could be handed the death penalty, Texan authorities waited to charge Résendez with any killings until he was in custody in the US. If convicted as a serial killer in Texas, Maturino Résendez is likely to receive death by lethal injection. Because of his familial links to Juárez and the brutality of his murders, the rail-hopping hobo is being looked at as a suspect in at least some of the Juárez killings. All other characteristics of his alleged murders and his victim profiles make him a highly unlikely suspect in a majority of the unsolved Juárez cases.

The next big break in the Juárez case came on 18 March 1999 when a fourteen-year-old girl was raped, strangled and left for dead in a secluded stretch of the desert. The young victim, called Nancy, miraculously regained consciousness and was able to make her way to a nearby ranch to summon help. Now Nancy is talked about with a reverence generally reserved for saints. Young Nancy instantly became a symbol for all those who lost their lives in the surrounding desert, as well as a sign of hope for the surviving women in Juárez. Nancy told police that she had been attacked by the bus driver who had picked her up after leaving her job at a *maquiladora* factory at 1 a.m. Once all the other passengers left the bus she noticed the driver headed in a strange direction. He then told her he was having mechanical problems, stopped, grabbed her by the neck and asked if she had ever had sex. The last thing she remembered before regaining consciousness covered in blood was the driver saying he was going to kill her.

On 1 April 1999, police arrested Jesus Manuel Guardado Marquez, the bus driver who drove Nancy back from work the night she was assaulted. The driver, accused of rape and attempted murder, said he was innocent and blamed the attack on a group of fellow bus drivers. In yet another ghoulish twist to this already ghoulish murderous tale, the drivers, hired by the factories to provide safety for the workers, turned out to be their predators. Marquez, 26, known as Dracula, three more drivers and a US national who was the ringleader, were arrested and charged with seven murders and one rape. 'The belief is that, together, they assassinated several young women,' said Fernando Medina, spokesman for the state of Chihuahua.

Chillingly, the bus drivers also claimed to be on the payroll of Sharif Sharif. Finally, with the April arrests, residents of Ciudad Juárez feel their murderous apocalypse might be coming to an end. With the survival of Nancy, authorities believe they may have an answer to one of Mexico's greatest crime mysteries. 'We can't say we've resolved all the cases,' cautioned Suly Ponce. But, she added, authorities are starting to see the light at the end of the tunnel.

Police confirmed that Dracula admitted having sex with the teenager who accused him of rape, but said it had been consensual. Another victim came forward saying she too had been raped by him. Police also blamed Marquez for the murder of Cargrario Gonzalez Lopez, seventeen, who was found in 1998 in a remote area in northwest Juárez. The driver allegedly also admitted to having sex with Lopez but identified another driver as her killer. Evidence indicates the bus drivers acted together as a gang in their murderous escapades. Prosecutors estimate that between twenty and thirty girls may have been killed by the deadly bus cadre. One driver, Jesus Guardado, re-enacted the crimes for prosecutors and police. 'He demonstrated how two of them would grab the victim by the neck and strangle her between them, often until the vertebrae cracked,' said Juan Carmona, spokesman for the state prosecutor's office. The lethal bus driver added, 'That made such a nice cracking sound.'

According to prosecutors, the drivers said they had been contracted by Sharif from jail so they would kill two women a month and continue the string of killings he was suspected of orchestrating. Sharif allegedly paid them $1,200 a month in exchange for two pairs of panties representing two murders. Since the bus drivers were allegedly addicted to cocaine and desperate for money, they accepted the offer. 'His accomplices say Sharif's idea was to distract attention from himself. With this [plan] he would make authorities and the citizenry think he had nothing to do with the other homicides, since he was in jail,' Ponce said.

Sharif, of course, proclaimed his innocence. 'I've been fighting for my freedom for three and a half years. They accuse me of everything,' he said. Authorities are also trying to trace the origin of the money used by Sharif to pay them. It is believed it came from patents the Egyptian chemist owns in the US on several scientific inventions.

Though charged with seven murders, the five suspects allegedly confessed to committing twenty. Then, in a press conference the suspects claimed their confessions were beaten out of them. 'Torture is more likely when there is political pressure to solve a case,' said Adriana Carmona of the Fray Francisco de Vitoria Center for Human Rights.

Victor Moreno Rivera, the alleged ringleader and only US citizen of the deadly bus ring, said police wrapped him in blankets and nearly drowned him with water. 'I felt death was near,' he said, 'so I told them what they wanted.' At a news conference the five suspects raised their shirts and revealed bruises, abrasions and circular marks they claimed were caused by cattle prods. The prosecutor for the case, Suly Ponce, denied the suspects had been tortured and gave local reporters a videotape of the interrogation to prove the men confessed freely. A spokesman for the government's National Human Rights Commission and the Attorney General's office declined to comment on the alleged police brutality.

Since the five bus drivers were charged with twenty murders, there have been no more killings of young girls that fit the established rape-torture-murder profile of the past. 'Since March, there hasn't been a single case . . . of what we classify as sex murders,' said Juan Carmona, spokesman for the state prosecutor's office. Though women are still being killed in Juárez, the victims are now older, and their bodies are being found in a wider variety of places like houses, hotels or cars. In some cases the killer or killers try to cover up the evidence by burning the bodies rather than simply leaving them in the desert, suggesting they might have connections to the victim. Instead of the strangling and skull crushing involved in the previous deaths the bodies now found have knife and gun wounds.

Washing the blood off their hands, factory owners claimed that the bus drivers were subcontracted to them by a third party, and therefore they could not be held accountable for the killings. However, after six years of carnage, local industry leaders demonstrated their 'heartfelt concern' for the surviving workers by distributing whistles and pepper spray to their employees. But these measures do not provide much comfort for those who find themselves alone on a bus on one of the region's many isolated desert roadways. With 187 women confirmed dead and 95 more missing, life seems to have lost its value in this city of the dead. Unknown, still, is the number of predators roaming the Chihuahua desert waiting in the dead of the night for their next innocent victim.

CIUDAD JUÁREZ UPDATE

On 23 February 2001, Dallas police announced the arrest on unrelated charges of a man whom Mexican authorities suspected of being a serial killer preying on young women in Ciudad Juárez. The suspect, 24-year-old Jose Juárez Rosales, is believed to be a member of a street gang, Los Rebeldes (the Rebels), who are allegedly responsible for the 1996 kidnappings, rapes and murders of at least seven women.

Juárez, an undocumented immigrant, was arrested at his sister's East Dallas apartment by sheriff's deputies on a bond forfeiture charge from a DWI (Driving Under the Influence) case. In custody, authorities matched his fingerprints to a man named in a 1996 arrest warrant for rape, murder and kidnapping of Rosario Garcia Leal.

Alleandro Medina of the Mexican attorney general's office in San Antonio said Mexican authorities expected to charge Juárez with several more slayings once he is deported back to Chihuahua: 'When he arrives in Mexico, he will be a suspect in many crimes.' According to Dallas County Sheriff's Department Investigator Don Peritz, Juárez has not been linked to any crimes in the Dallas-Fort Worth area, but police are searching through unsolved cases similar to those in Mexico. 'We're looking at all of our unsolved murders and sexual assaults that were similar to those,' Investigator Peritz said. 'We're encouraging other agencies to do the same and look at their unsolved murders and sexual assaults.'

Juárez's sister, Sara Rosales, said her brother did not kill anyone and was arrested because Mexican authorities are under intense pressure to find those responsible for the

Ciudad Juárez killings. Mexican police arrested Juárez in 1996 in connection with the slaying of Rosario Garcia Leal. After spending about a year in jail, he was released by a judge who determined there wasn't enough evidence against him. Authorities appealed the ruling and a different judge issued a new arrest warrant for him, but by then Juárez had fled across the border to live at his sister's house.

Esther Chavez Cano, director of the Casa Amiga rape crisis center in Juárez, acknowledged that although Mexican authorities have arrested three sets of suspects in relation to the killings, the pandemic violence against women in Ciudad Juárez continues unabated. 'The deaths continue and the authorities keep telling us the same thing – that it's Sharif. They have no credibility,' she told the *El Paso Times*.

14. THE PSYCHOPATH OF COSTA RICA

Since 1986 the unidentified predator known as the 'Psychopath' has been roaming the southern edge of the Costa Rican capital of San José, attacking young couples parked in secluded areas in a densely forested area known as the 'Triangle of Death'. To date the mysterious killer is believed to be responsible for nineteen deaths. The killer often waits until the unsuspecting couples start making love before shooting them in the head with a high-caliber weapon. Authorities – with the help of FBI profilers in Quantico – have drawn up several psychological profiles of the killer, including one 'Rambo' theory that portrays him as a deranged former soldier or police official. Another profile paints the killer as the unhappy son of a wealthy landowner savagely lashing out at his domineering mother.

In 1997 authorities announced the Psychopath may also be responsible for the disappearances of thirteen other people who vanished in the Triangle of Death. 'We don't know for sure whether the others were his victims, but we can't discount that at all,' said Francisco Ruiz, a spokesman for the Judicial Investigative Organization (OIJ in Spanish), Costa Rica's version of the FBI.

'Let's not rule out that there are other bodies buried in the area,' added Linette Saborío, the present director of the OIJ. Since the thirteen disappearances were announced, two presumed victims have been located alive.

For a nation known for its peaceful disposition, the Psychopath case has been a thorn in the side of Costa Rican law enforcement since it was first uncovered. During the last two OIJ administrations, each incoming director vowed to make the apprehension of the killer its highest priority. According to Director Saborío every officer in Costa Rica dreams of arresting the perpetrator: 'There is not a single police department that is not doing something in this investigation.' In a 2 November 1996 interview Saborío said,

'I think the mystery is about to be solved.' Since then, the Psychopath has claimed two more victims while authorities are no closer to uncovering his identity and stopping his lust for blood.

With a population of 3.7 million people, Costa Rica has been known as a safe refuge in the historically violent Central American region. During the '80s, while neighboring nations endured lengthy civil wars, Costa Rica prospered from fruit exports and tourism. Called by local politicians a 'perfect country', Costa Rica has not had a standing army since 1948. It is not the place one would expect to find a serial killer. But there is one – effective, elusive, cruel, and deadly. Emerging from the coffee bushes like a real-life bogeyman and disappearing back into the night leaving a trail of death in his wake.

The killer's murderous spree began on 6 June 1986, with the butchery of seven women and girls who were returning from a religious function in the Cruz de Alajuelita. In the Alajuelita Massacre, considered Costa Rica's most heinous crime, the killer or killers unleashed a sordid assault against two adult women and five young girls. When the smoke settled, all of them were murdered with .45-caliber gunshots to the head. Three of the girls were also raped. Authorities believe four men, including the Psychopath, were involved in the carnage.

Following the Alajuelita Massacre all other Psychopath attacks – except two – have been on loving couples parked in the Triangle of Death. The first couple attacked was 27-year-old Roberto Castro Mora and his girlfriend, nineteen-year-old Francis Salazar Suárez, who disappeared on 14 December 1986. Next came 23-year-old Juan Guillermo Nájera Monge and his girlfriend 21-year-old Damaris Rodríguez Martínez, who vanished on 7 February 1987, from the same general vicinity in the La Amistad Park. Five days after their disappearance, the body of Nájera was found in a shallow grave by a Boy Scout troop searching the area. Under him police found Roberto Castro, who had been killed nearly two months before. On 22 February the body of Damaris Rodríguez was found hidden five hundred yards away; ten

THE PSYCHOPATH OF COSTA RICA

days later Francis Salazar was discovered one hundred yards from Rodríguez's grave. Both women had small knife-like mutilations on their breasts and genitalia.

The elaborate positioning of the bodies indicated the killer spent time at the crime scene after their deaths. First, investigators theorize, the killer hid Castro's body, then dragged the body of Salazar more than five hundred yards through the brush. Two months later, he returned to the same area in the park and re-created his murder fantasy by killing a new couple and following the same elaborate post-offense ritual. Coincidentally, the two slain women were close friends, worked together and lived next to each other. And the first murdered couple knew one of the suspects eventually charged with partaking in the Alajuelita Massacre.

The next Psychopath attack – and perhaps the first one in which he acted alone – was on 14 June 1987. This time the killer shot 24-year-old Ligia Camacho Bermœdez through the window of her bedroom while she calmly read on her bed. This case is the most puzzling, and perhaps the most revealing, of the Psychopath rampage. Because this attack is so different to the others, investigators believe it holds the key that will eventually unravel the mystery.

The night of her murder, Ligia's boyfriend left her house in Desamparados no later than 10 p.m. and headed to his home in Patarrá on the bus. Somewhere around two in the morning Ligia's mother heard what she thought was a knock on the door followed by someone shouting: 'The police are in trouble.' The mother of six answered the door, saw no one outside and returned to bed. According to investigators the killer shot Ligia from no more than six inches outside the window. Ligia's bed, according to the crime report, was about two feet from the glass, which places the victim and the killer at less than three feet from each other at the moment of the killing, which might suggest they were talking to each other. No one in the house heard the gunshot, leading detectives to believe the killer used a silencer.

The OIJ theorize that Ligia, who worked at the National Blood Bank, might have had information identifying the killer or killers of the women in Alajuelita and the two couples in the La Amistad Park. Throughout the Psychopath investigation, several of the suspects considered in the case were somehow connected with Ligia. Following the murder her boyfriend was arrested and detained for several hours until it became obvious he had nothing to do with it. Two other men, a driver and a co-worker at the National Blood Bank, were also arrested and quickly dismissed as legitimate suspects.

Between 1988 and 1989 four more murders were attributed to the Psychopath. On 25 August, 1988 Aracelly María Astœa Calderón, 15, and her boyfriend, Víctor Julio Hernández Sánchez, 18, died of multiple gunshot wounds in San Vicente de La Unión. Then, on 21 April 1989, Marta Miriam Navarro Carpio, 28, and her boyfriend, Edwin Mata Madrigal, were found in the Lomas de Ayarco ranch in Curridabat. He died of a gunshot wound to the head; she was shot in the head and the face. Then her body was covered with several heavy rocks. Some investigators believe that the rocks could not have been moved by only one person, suggesting that the Psychopath is indeed at least two men acting together.

Then, for five years, the Psychopath disappeared from the face of the earth. During the five-year lull the Psychopath was believed to either have been satisfying his murderous fantasies with someone, in jail for an unrelated offense, or abroad where he continued killing. On 17 March 1995 the Psychopath shocked his way back to national headlines with the murder of Marjorie Padilla Sequeira. On her way back from celebrating her twentieth birthday Marjorie was accosted by a stranger on a bridge five hundred yards from her home. Following a short struggle the young woman turned to run but her attacker mortally wounded her with a gunshot to her back. Just as quickly as he appeared, the perpetrator vanished into the coffee bushes flanking the road leaving the dying young woman on the ground. Forensics determined Marjorie was killed by the same .45-caliber munitions used in all other Psychopath killings.

Though her death has been linked to the Psychopath by OIJ agents, her mother, Carmen, doubts his involvement in the case. Other than using the same type of bullet, nothing else links Marjorie's death to the others. All other Psychopath killings have been perfectly organized, perfectly orchestrated, perfectly executed. But Marjorie was a victim of opportunity; nothing indicated that her killer was following a plan.

A year later, in late October 1996, the Psychopath struck again in the Triangle of Death. A pair of young lovers, Ileana Alvarez, 23, and Mauricio Cordero, 24, were ambushed in their car as they were parked next to the road in Desamparados. Two days after they were reported missing, their bodies were found in a shallow grave under banana leaves about half a mile away from their vehicle. Alvarez was found naked dumped on top of the fully dressed Cordero. Her handbag and clothing were sandwiched in between them.

The lovers were described by all who knew them as hard-working youngsters with promising futures. Ileana worked at a supermarket and was studying microbiology at the University of Costa Rica. Mauricio worked with the Costa Rican Airlines (LASCA) and had recently started a second job with the Tico Pager services. 'In the brief time he was here, we knew him as a good person and a team player,' said Xinia Zœóiga, his manager at the pager company. Mauricio and Ileana began dating six months before they were killed.

According to several crime scene analysts, the perpetrator seemingly scouted the area thoroughly before attacking. Rafael Monge, a caretaker at a nearby ranch, said three weeks before the murders of Ileana and Mauricio he saw a gray pick-up truck leaving the area at around 5 a.m. A similar truck was seen leaving the vicinity the night of the murders at about 2 a.m. Several weeks later investigators located the reported truck and determined it was unrelated to the case.

At the October 1996 crime scene, the perpetrator was careful not to touch anything and to cover any forensic evidence he might have left behind. Pieces of black tape found on the ground suggest the Psychopath used the tape to mask the soles of his shoes. 'We're facing an experienced and cold-blooded criminal,' said the former director of OIJ Gerardo Lázcares. 'It's a huge challenge.' Like other victims of the Psychopath, Ileana Alvarez and her boyfriend Mauricio Cordero were killed under a night of the full moon. The killer first confronted them in their car, then took them to another location where he raped Ileana and shot them both dead. Police theorize he approached the car undetected and surprised the young couple in the throes of passion with his gun drawn. He then led the two lovers uphill several hundred yards into the brush where he killed Mauricio, then raped and killed Ileana.

Bloodstains found several feet from their final gravesite suggest that there was a brief struggle between the killer and one or both of the victims. Investigators believe the Psychopath shot Mauricio three times in the head when the youngster tried to attack him. Then he undressed Ileana, raped and tortured her, and ended her life with a single bullet to her forehead. Ileana had scalpel-like cuts in her breasts, buttocks and genitalia that were similar to knife marks found on the bodies of two victims found in 1987: Francis Salazar Suárez, who died on 4 March, and Damaris Rodríguez, killed on 22 February.

In January 1997 an OIJ officer and a translator flew to Quantico, Virginia to discuss their case files and crime scene photographs with FBI profilers. 'We want to solve this case this year,' Investigator Ruiz told Costa Rica's La Nación newspaper. Over the years Costa Rican authorities have created several psychological profiles of their killer, but with the help of FBI agents in Quantico they hope their new, more detailed profile will lead to the final capture of the maniac. The FBI profile of the Psychopath indicates the suspect is a highly intelligent individual with no college education and a history of psychiatric problems. He is probably white, middle-class, in his mid-thirties to early-forties, and is in good physical shape. Financially, he is believed to be making enough money to get by. He might have some sort of military training and a passion for hiking and hunting, explaining his familiarity with the forested areas surrounding the crime scenes. According to Gerardo Lázcares, 'We are convinced that he is a man who has been traumatized by his involvement in war.'

Evidence suggests the Psychopath approaches his victims in a police uniform, which enables him to gain immediate control of the situation. OIJ agents said that they had a composite sketch of the killer from two surviving couples who were approached by someone pretending to be a police officer and managed to escape. After looking at the suspect's handling of his weapon, the munitions he used, and his control of the crime scene, FBI agents confirmed the killer used to be, or still is, in the Costa Rican police force. 'This man thinks like a cop,' said Lázcares, adding that he doubts the suspect may have any links to the OIJ. 'I would say he is a former cop with a desk job.'

The Psychopath is thought to lead a double life in which by day he is an unremarkable, normal individual, and by night turns into a bloodthirsty vampire, sweeping on his victims as part avenging angel, part bird of prey. On the one hand he is believed to be the son of a politically powerful man who is protected by his influential family. On the other he is believed to be a former guerrilla and/or veteran from the wars in El Salvador and Nicaragua. Because of his total control over the crime scenes, investigators theorize he is not acting under the influence of alcohol or drugs.

Police believe the killer plans in advance every step of his attacks down to the smallest details, carefully staging any evidence he chooses to leave behind. The hard-to-reach locations of the dumpsites also suggest that the killer scouts them out and carefully plans every move. In some cases the killer has left markings directing police to the bodies. It is unclear if he left any markings at the most recent crime scene. A classic organized killer, the Psychopath relishes being in complete control of his sexual fantasy which has, over years, become more elaborate and detailed. Like other organized serial killers the Psychopath comes prepared to the kill-site with the murder weapon, prepares the kill-site, and follows a clearly rehearsed post-offense behavior. The fact that he spends time at the site after the murders reflects that the killer feels comfortable in the crime scenes and thinks in a clear and organized manner.

The suspect is most definitely the dominant partner in any relationships he has with women, which might explain why he is single, separated or divorced. He is probably sporadically employed or under-employed and keeps a flexible schedule. If he works he has a blue-collar, labor-intensive job, or might work the graveyard shift, though, when he's not working, he still keeps late hours. The most dominant person in his life is his overpowering mother who might have abused him physically or psychologically when he was young. Rafael Guillen, a former director of the OIJ, said he believes the killer has been carrying out his crimes in revenge for something that happened to him years ago.

Certainly, the crimes of the Psychopath are sexual in nature. 'He is a man that could be described as a lust murderer who is trying through his victims to satisfy his sexual fantasies,' stated a 1996 OIJ press release. The OIJ release also theorizes that the killer could have repressed homosexual tendencies that fuel his hatred towards women. Fernando Garzonsa Meseguer, a forensic doctor who examined the victims attributed to the Psychopath from the mid to the late '80s, doubts that the killer's motivation is sexual in nature. Instead he believes the killer wanted to exert his power over his prey. 'The Psychopath wants to hurt, kill, humiliate his victim,' said Dr Garzonsa. 'His actions do not include sexual desire, though he does conclude his assaults sexually.'

In an interview with *La Nación*, Dr Minor Aguilar of the OIJ noted that the behavior of the Psychopath illustrates the cyclical nature of his crimes. For long periods of time he maintains his murderous instincts in check before succumbing to the need to kill. These periods could be associated with extended trips to different areas of Costa Rica or to another country. 'He is a person who is socially inept, who is almost always hostile and aggressive, though it is unlikely his criminal nature affects his performance at work,' said Dr Aguilar. 'His psychosis does not necessarily affect other parts of his personality.'

Because of the mutilation of the genitalia of several female victims, Dr Aguilar believes the killer is motivated by some unnamed childhood sexual trauma: 'It seems that the sexual history of this individual is dictated by the feminine figure, which he finds traumatic and rejects.' Many studies indicate that people who endured sexual and psychological abuse as children suffer from Post-Traumatic Stress Disorder as adults. This could be the case with the Psychopath.

Part of the task force investigating the killings has followed the movements of at least five individuals. Two other suspects, Luis Monge Sandí and Arnoldo Mora Portilla, have been tried repeatedly for participating in the Alajuelita Massacre, but neither one is believed to be the Psychopath. Four months after the massacre Sandí, known locally as 'Tres Pelos', and Mora became suspects in the Alajuelita case when a M-3 submachine gun they stole was linked to the killings. The machine gun was stolen on 8 March 1986 from the home of former Public Safety Minister Rodolfo Quirós. In two trials in 1990 and 1991 prosecutors accused Tres Pelos and Mora of using the weapon in the massacre. Both times the cases against the two men ended in mistrials because of procedural errors.

During their first trial in 1990 Sandí was found guilty of seven murders and two rapes though no evidence placed him at the crime scene. Mora, who was charged with one rape and aggravated assault, was linked to the crimes by bite marks matching his teeth on the body of one of the victims. Mora was found guilty on both counts, handed a twelve-year sentence, then released on parole because he was a minor at the time of the killings. Days before the start of the third trial Tres Pelos was murdered while getting into a car outside his home by two men who escaped on a motorcycle. Before escaping the crime scene, the killers took a satchel belonging to Tres Pelos. Strangely they did not take his wallet, jewelry or any of the other valuables in his car. According to his mother, Tres Pelos carried the proof of his innocence in the Alajuelita Massacre inside the satchel.

As the date of his third trial was announced he allegedly told his mother, 'Don't worry, in this satchel I have all the proof I need to get out of this mess. I'm not going to take the blame for something I didn't do.' His mother, Doóa Zoraida, believes her son was killed because of the content of his satchel. As of the date of this writing, his murder remains unsolved and police have no suspects. Two weeks after the murder of Tres Pelos – and a five-year halt in the killings – Marjorie Padilla fell victim to a bullet of the Psychopath. Authorities speculate that her death was merely a reminder to the nation that the Psychopath was still alive and raising hell.

The main piece of evidence linking all murders has been the type of munitions used by the killer. According to Guillermo Sáenz, former Director of the Civil Guard, the killer uses a particular type of .45-caliber bullet that was made in the US before 1953. This type of munition was donated to Costa Rican law enforcement by the US decades ago. Presently, it is only available locally on the black market or from the National Armory. Police think the killer probably obtained the bullets from the black market or from an unsuspecting individual in the police force. That is, if the perpetrator is not presently or formerly a member of the force himself.

In February 1999, OIJ agents collected nine bullet casings found at the Alajuelita crime scene and four casings from the missing gun and sent them to the FBI in Quantico for analysis. The FBI lab was unable to find an exact match in both sets of casings, bringing into doubt the involvement of Mora and Tres Pelos in the Alajuelita killings.

Forensics of the bullets used in the last two murders attributed to the Psychopath have led authorities to re-think their initial theory that the killer used an M-3 submachine gun. New evidence suggests that the Psychopath uses a .45-caliber handgun – perhaps with silencer – manufactured in the US, by Federal Ordenans, or in Spain, by Apache. Both these .45-caliber weapons leave five microscopic grooves carved into the bullet as it leaves the barrel. Other .45-caliber weapons tend to leave six grooves. The marks on the bullets could also be explained by dirt inside the barrel scratching the projectile suggesting that the perpetrator was not taking care of the weapon or that he keeps it buried underground. This theory has all but been dismissed because such behavior would wildly contradict the general profile of the killer.

For over a dozen years investigators have been trying to locate the Psychopath's weapon. This search has taken agents to Panama and Nicaragua. In 1992 OIJ agents learned that a similar weapon had been allegedly sold to a drug lord by a former Costa Rican diplomat who at the time was considered a suspect. The suspect lived in the town of Tres Ríos and was believed to possess a small arsenal of high-caliber weapons. At the time the OIJ believed the individual participated in at least five of the killings. The ex-diplomat was taken off the suspect list after he proved that he was outside Costa Rica at the time of some of the killings.

Another suspect, whose name has not been released to the press, was identified as the son of wealthy parents who joined the Nicaraguan revolutionary FSLN army in the '70s and later was rumored to have died in battle. The suspect was first looked at following the Alajuelita Massacre and was believed to be somehow associated with Ligia Camacho Bermœdez. But news about his alleged death on the battlefield led to him getting dropped from the suspect list. In January 1995, the suspect reappeared in Costa Rica leading to a wave of speculation by investigators that he was, indeed, the mysterious killer.

Considering his furtive nature, his relation to Ligia Camacho Bermœdez, his military training, his access to .45-caliber munitions and his ability to survive in the wild, the unnamed man was, for all purposes, a legitimate suspect in the case. Fueling speculation that he was the killer was the fact that Tres Pelos was murdered two months after his name appeared in the Social Registry. Then the suspect found out he was being investigated on 17 November 1998, when he read an article by Ronald Moya about the Psychopath in the Sunday Edition of San José's *La Nación*. Though the writer did not name him, he recognized himself in the description of the individual suspected of being the killer. A week after reading the article the suspect contacted authorities to clear his name. The 43-year-old ex-revolutionary could not have been the killer, he revealed, because he was in jail in Nicaragua when the October 1996 double murder of Ileana Alvarez and Mauricio Cordero occurred. Authorities have also noted that he was in jail in the United States during two other attacks.

On 26 June 1998, the OIJ announced the arrest of a new serial killer operating in the Triangle of Death. The new killer, identified as a 52-year-old local construction worker, is said to have raped and murdered at least four women. An avid hunter and the father of eleven, the new suspect is said to have killed his victims with a hunting rifle. OIJ director Saborío disclosed that the investigation into this unnamed individual was triggered by information uncovered through tips in the case of the Psychopath. Though the suspect has a history of aggressive sexual behavior and frequently hunts in the forested areas of the Triangle of Death, he is not considered to be the feared Psychopath.

The last case linked to the new suspect was the 17 May disappearance of Liliana Chavarría, a resident of Tres Ríos, with whom the man had a close relationship. The other cases involved are as follows: Ana Patricia Navarro, who disappeared on 19 June 1991, after she left work for her home in Patarrá; Annia Arce, who was never seen again after she left work on 20 February 1989; and a Salvadoran woman, who lived in Hacienda Vieja of Curridabat, but whose name and date of disappearance have been withheld by authorities.

On 13 April 1999, Guillermo Benavides, head of the Serial Homicide Investigation Unit, mysteriously announced that a key piece of evidence was uncovered in their ongoing investigation of the Psychopath. 'It's a strong and interesting piece of evidence which I can't talk about. We can only confirm that our team found something very, very important about the crimes of the Psychopath.' No further details have been made available. In any case, as the years roll by, the Psychopath remains at large, planning his next kill. Hopefully, one day, he will commit a mistake and will be stopped before he kills again. But all evidence points to someone for whom only death will stop the lust for blood.

15. THE HIGHWAY MANIAC

Since 1997 Argentina's 'Highway Maniac' has claimed possibly up to twelve women from the streets of the coastal city of Mar de Plata. In a little more than a year the naked bodies of five women appeared along highways outside Mar de Plata and eight other women have gone missing and are presumed dead. All victims, except one, were known prostitutes or had histories of prostitution arrests. Most of the victims found were strangled as well as mutilated and dismembered. One victim had the word 'Puta' (whore) carved on her back. Police, after more than three years investigating the crimes, have no clue to the identity of the killer. In fact, they are not even sure if they are dealing with one or several different killers.

Many of the theories surrounding the case paint the Highway Maniac simultaneously as a lone-wolf killer, a gang of killers, a sexually dysfunctional psychopath, a corrupt cop, an HIV-infected predator and/or a vengeful drug trafficker. Forensic pathologist Jorge Tonelli, noting the precise mutilation and clean dismemberment performed on the victims, confirmed that the Maniac could be a butcher, fish cutter, or even a surgeon. 'We are facing a maniac,' Tonelli told Argentina's *Clarin* newspaper. 'He has a severe conflict with everything feminine. His psychological profile suggests someone who is impotent, fearful of the opposite sex and has a raging Oedipal crisis. He sees women as an object from which he can extract revenge for his own inadequacies. That's when he decides to kill.'

Police believe the killer could have contracted AIDS from having previous sexual relations with prostitutes and now, in an act of revenge, is killing those whom he blames for his infection. That would explain both why most of the victims were prostitutes and why, even if the victims were found naked, he did not rape them. Profilers believe the killer probably grew up with an overbearing mother who might have also been a prostitute. Another theory posits that the killer lost his wife to prostitution and now is extracting his revenge on the other prostitutes.

The killer is believed to be between 25 and 40 years old, of a middle-class background, and probably suffered abuse as a child. Authorities think he takes the victims somewhere, perhaps his home, where he tortures them before strangling them to death. Then he 'poses' their remains near roadways outside the city. The killer could be sexually impotent or suffer from some other sexual dysfunction that leads his pronounced hatred of women. Investigators believe the killer tortures his victims and mutilates their genitalia because of this hate. Police reported the fiend used a blowtorch on two of the bodies recovered. It is unclear if the women were blowtorched while still alive or post-mortem.

The first victim in the serial pattern was found by a trucker on 1 July 1996. The victim, identified as 27-year-old Adriana Jaqueline Fernandez, was an Uruguayan artisan living in Mar de Plata. She had been strangled with a cable then dumped naked in a stream under a bridge over Highway 226. Unlike the others who followed, Adriana was not a prostitute, did not have children, and showed no signs of torture. The next victim, 35-year-old Maria Esther Amaro, was found on 29 November. She too was strangled and dumped naked on the side of the road, though this time it was Highway 55. Ligature marks on her wrist suggested that she was bound. Cuts on her knees indicated the killer forced her onto her knees. The killer cut her, post-mortem, from her stomach to her chest. On her back the killer inscribed the word 'Puta' (whore) with his knife. Like other victims who followed, Maria Amaro worked as a prostitute in the La Perla district. Like the others she had children and was mutilated by the killer's knife.

On 15 January 1998, Vivian Guadalupe Spindola, 26, vanished from La Perla. Five days later her two legs and an arm – missing the hand – were found near an area called Los Acantilados. Two days and ten miles away her torso was discovered by a truck driver near Highway 88. Her head was never found. Vivian was identified by a tattoo near her pubic area. The next victim, 26-year-old Mariela Elisabeth Gimenez, was last seen on 4 May as she boarded a bus on her way home. Her mutilated corpse was discovered on 13 May near Highway 88, about thirty miles from Mar de Plata. She had her buttocks sectioned. Also her arm and part of her shoulder were missing. She had cut and ligature marks around her neck. Forensic evidence determined she was mutilated post-mortem.

Chief Investigator Jorge Luis Acosta told *Clarin* that forensic evidence at the crime scenes suggests that the killer was working alone. The Maniac, he believes, careful to plan his attacks, brings weapons and tools with him, and has locations pre-scouted and prepared for his attack and his post-attack routines. Acosta believes investigators got close to the Maniac after the fourth victim was found. Since then the killer changed his MO drastically, hiding most of the subsequent victims' bodies instead of displaying them at the crime scene.

Suspected victim number five, Ana Maria Nores, 26, was last seen alive 19 July. She was two months pregnant when she disappeared. A mother of four, she too worked as a prostitute in the La Perla red-light area. Like the other victims, Ana Maria was skinny, had long, curly black hair, dark eyes and pale skin. Chillingly, four friends who worked with her in La Perla said that days before she had commented that she would be next. Following her disappearance, someone, perhaps the killer, called authorities and told them to look for the victim's remains in a field next to Highway 88. No remains were found there. Then the alleged killer called a local reporter in Mar de Plata and said: 'She will not be the last one.' The caller never called again. Authorities assume it was a prank call. However, they are not discarding the possibility that the Maniac was the man on the phone. 'You can expect anything from someone as mentally unstable as this guy . . . even a phone call to show his disdain for the investigation,' an unnamed police source told a reporter for the *Clarin*.

With the help of two helicopters and more than two hundred officers on foot and horseback, authorities launched a massive search of the outskirts of the city. With the disappearance of Ana Maria the women of Mar de Plata said they had had enough. Graffiti on the streets clamored for the arrest of the Maniac and a resolution to the growing murder mystery. Authorities, some women thought, were not doing enough because the victims were prostitutes and poor. On 22 July a group of women took to the streets of the La Perla red-light district and marched to the Regional Police Station. There they confronted District Attorney Susana Kluka and demanded a stop to the murders. 'Like anyone who disappears, the dead women deserved to be heard,' said a petition they handed to the District Attorney. 'We only hope justice is served. All the murdered women had families and children.'

While investigating the Nores disappearance, authorities discovered that another prostitute, 36-year-old Patricia Prieto, had not been seen since 23 February. Prieto, who was known on the street as *La Dominguera*, left her five-year-old daughter at home the night of the 23rd and never returned. She was reported missing in July when the father of the child went to court to gain custody of the little girl who had been abandoned at home. The next to disappear was 26-year-old Silvana Paola Caraballo. She was reported missing by her building manager on 20 October. He discovered she was missing when Silvana's six-year-old daughter came to him crying and saying her mom never returned from work. As the Maniac victim profile would indicate, Caraballo, who was also studying architecture, had a history of prostitution arrest. She was last seen near the La Perla neighborhood.

Three months later, on 14 January 1998, 25-year-old Veronica Andrea Chavez was reported missing by her mother after she failed to return from work. According to Palmira de Jesus Diaz, her mother, Veronica worked as a hat-check girl at a local club and as a cleaning lady at a law firm. Police determined that in fact Veronica did not work in either place. Though no evidence suggested she worked as a prostitute, authorities discovered she did have friends in 'the life'. One of her prostitute friends assured authorities that the young woman was not selling herself. 'If she was ever seen in the stops around La Perla it was because she was visiting me,' the friend told *Clarín*. Chavez had no arrest history.

On 14 July district attorney Marcelo Garcia Berro was identified as a person of interest in the Maniac investigation. Berro's name was found in Veronica's phone book. Veronica was also seen by a former policeman, the night before disappearing, getting into Berro's car. Berro said he had known Chavez for more than a year, adding that he had last seen her in December. Investigators believe Berro was not completely truthful about his relationship with the victim. Investigators also determined that Chavez had recently placed more than twenty calls to Berro's office and to his cell phone. As of this writing there have been no further news reports about Berro's status in the Veronica Chavez investigation.

Veronica was also associated with three policemen, two of whom are also mentioned in the investigation files of two other victims, Ana Maria Nores and Silvana Caraballo. Nores' mother said that the policemen wanted to use her daughter as bait to catch the feared killer. Other women who knew the missing prostitutes believe the cops were using Nores and Caraballo to sell drugs. One theory bandied around is that the Maniac is a corrupt cop who is taking money from the women so they can continue working the streets. Like other predators hunting prostitutes, the Maniac might also be involved in using and sharing drugs with the women. Other profiles also point at police-type figures as possible suspects. Attorneys for the families of Nores and Caraballo said in court that they doubted the disappearances of their daughters were related to the Maniac case. Instead they painted a picture of corrupt cops manipulating street women into selling drugs, then murdering the women if they threatened to quit.

Victim number nine (and the fifth set of remains recovered) was discovered on 20 October 1998. Two kids playing in an empty lot in the outlying neighborhood of Las Heras found a pair of female thighs in a bag. The thighs were cleanly cut from the knee to the groin. The bag they were in was covered with a black coat. Next to it they noticed two cords, one made of thread and the other nylon, and a little charm necklace. The next day a schoolteacher walking to school found three bags of bloodied clothes less than fifty yards from the first crime scene. With the help of the clothing, the victim was quickly identified as 25-year-old Maria del Carmen, a native of Rosario. Maria del Carmen lived in Mar de Plata with her godparents, who thought she worked as a waitress. However, authorities determined that she actually worked as a prostitute. Unlike the others, she worked primarily in the port area.

In January 1999, after more than two frustrating years of failed leads, the Maniac investigation was taken over by Deputy Chief Maria Cristina Ortiz. In her new role as lead investigator, Ortiz decided to restart from scratch. With the help of four other senior officers Ortiz hopes to crack the mystery by re-examining the evidence with a fresh mind. 'He could be a serial killer or maybe several killers,' she said at the press conference announcing her new assignment. 'He could be anyone. At this time we have no real leads. Perhaps the killer is sitting in the corner bar having coffee.' Since then, three more women have gone missing.

The first woman to disappear in 1999 was thirty-year-old Claudia Romero. 'She would have never left on her own volition because she loved her family too much,' her husband, Carlos Bardazza, told the *Clarín*. Romero, who had a history of arrests for prostitution, was last seen at her 'stop' in the city center on 1 March. Her husband said she used to work around La Plata, but she had problems there with some of the other women. Romero had a three-year-old daughter and she was three months pregnant. On 11 September, Sandra Carina Villanueva, 26, vanished. Like Romero she had a history of prostitution arrests and was last seen in the center area of Mar de Plata. As of this writing the twelfth and last missing woman in Mar de Plata disappeared on 30 October. A mother of four, 33-year-old Mercedes Almaraz was last seen strutting in the La Perla district. According to authorities, Almaraz, a known prostitute, would leave her children at home with a sitter for two to three-day periods while she would do a drug run for a local drug dealer. Although she could have easily disappeared on one of her runs, authorities believe she closely matches the Maniac victim profile and should be considered part of his victim list.

Since the killings started prostitutes in La Perla have been wearing hidden microphones and carrying knives to protect themselves. One woman wearing a mike told the *Clarin* she hires someone every night to sit in a nearby car and listen for any suspicious interaction with her clients. A prostitute named Sandra, talking to the newspaper about the suspected killer, said: 'He's someone who has several cars, who plans everything, who is always searching, and chooses you. It's possible that I've already been with him.'

Yanina, another prostitute, who has armed herself with a knife, added, 'We know that we could be the next ones, but he doesn't know that we're ready for him. Because if we don't get him, who will?' Both Sandra and Yanina said they hope to come face to face with the killer.

'Before every night I cross myself and I ask the Virgin to bring me the killer,' Yanina said. 'Then he'll get what he deserves.'

In March 1999 the Governor of Mar de Plata announced a reward of $500,000 for any information that would lead to the capture of the dreaded killer. Soon after the announcement a witness, whose identity has been kept secret, fingered a man living in the neighborhood of Quelmes in Buenos Aires as a possible suspect in the killings. The suspect is believed to be the son of a wealthy family who, thirty years ago, was interned in a hospital for the criminally insane after he dressed up as a woman and murdered three prostitutes in Buenos Aires. In 1995, six months before the first known Maniac murder, the alleged suspect was declared cured and released from the Neuropsychiatry Institute of the State Penitentiary Service. Dr Jaime Montero Vasquez, the doctor who signed his release, has since been relieved of his duties after he also released several other dangerous criminals.

The suspect, who has not been named, is believed to be around fifty years old and suffering from acute schizophrenia. His family owns several properties in Mar de Plata which he, at times, manages. 'He is not a person with homosexual tendencies, but someone who enjoys killing women. In the past incidents he wore his victim's clothing.' Investigators theorize that the suspect might be working in conjunction with a relative who lives in Mar de Plata who has also manifested similar psychopathic tendencies. As of this writing the suspect and his cousin have not been publicly identified and there is no record of whether they have been found, questioned or perhaps even taken off the suspect list.

On 13 April 1999, Eduardo De la Cruz, the Prosecutor General of the Supreme Court in Buenos Aires, called the FBI and French authorities for help in solving the Maniac case. De la Cruz particularly hoped that French and American authorities would help in profiling the suspected killer. 'We've established contact with officers in other countries, specifically France and the United States, to tap into their knowledge of serial killer investigations,' said De la Cruz. On 28 May Alain Pérez, a former investigator in France, came to Argentina to advise investigators. After his arrival he said he was 'confident' the case would be 'resolved favorably' and that the perpetrator will be brought to justice. 'Perfect crimes do not exist,' he told the Argentine press. 'Sooner or later we'll catch the person or persons responsible for so much death and suffering.' In a press conference Pérez told the suspected killer, 'If you're watching or listening, it's time to surrender and ask for the forgiveness of God because you've caused great harm.'

According to Pérez's profile, the Maniac 'commits crimes that seem to him perfectly normal. He also wants to play games with police and, perhaps, interject himself into the investigation.' He is considered to be someone who is 'seductive, very intelligent, with a pleasing demeanor and a strong physique.' It is believed the killer purposely leaves certain personal items of the victims next to their bodies to facilitate their identification. 'It's a way to feed his ego and to make sure he is attributed the murder,' said the profiler.

But with twelve murders under his belt, the Maniac has obviously a well-fed ego. Not unlike other predators in this book, the Maniac's *lustmord* will still need to be satisfied. And more women of the night in Mar de Plata will fall prey to the predator's claws, never to be seen alive again. Having proved himself a capable killer, police can only hope for a mistake on his part or a lucky break that will lead to his arrest and the end of the slaughter. Only then will the women of Mar de Plata stop living in fear of 'being next'.

16. SERIAL KILLING IN BELIZE

Something evil is brewing in the tropical paradise of Belize. A vicious serial killer, dubbed 'Jack the Butcher' by the local media, is roaming the streets of Belize City; he has raped, murdered and mutilated at least four young girls. Until now Belize has been known worldwide for its coral reefs, jungles and its limitless scuba diving. But not any more. With its peace and tranquility shattered, 'Belizeans are horrified and in a state of shock that something this outrageous can happen in our country,' said Police Spokeswoman Christy Castillo. 'Things like this just do not happen here.' The last of Britain's colonial territories, Belize once prided itself on being the type of place where everyone knew each other and people looked after their neighbor's children.

A peaceful place, that is, until a year ago, when the body of the first mutilated victim turned up on a deserted road outside the capital. In less than a year four girls have been killed in the same brutally sadistic manner. Adding to the nationwide horror three more girls have been raped and murdered by family friends or relatives who are now in jail. With more and more young children from poor families and broken homes being lured into trading sex for money, child abuse has become a national tragedy and a rising tide of sex crimes could rot the nation to its core.

In the '80s and '90s Belize, a tiny Central American nation of 230,000 people, prospered from tourism and the export of sugar, citrus and bananas. But the recent crash in the banana and citrus markets led to the relocation of at least 100,000 Belizean workers to Miami and other parts of the US in search of better paid jobs. Thus Belizean society was left a dysfunctional shell of its former self with grandparents and grandchildren running the show and unable to cope with the pressures of the modern world. Also a wave of Honduran and Guatemalan refugees pouring through its borders has changed the face of Belize's once homogenous population and brought uncertainty to its national character.

Many think Belize is being victimized by the changing times: the mind-numbing effects of satellite television, the massive relocation of its workforce, and the new wave of Spanish-speaking refugees. No longer do elders sit on their porches checking on the kids playing outside. Instead they are watching the sex and violence churned out daily by the sixty channels available on their satellite televisions. Zaida Young, a research information officer for the National Organization for Protection From Child Abuse, believes the growing problem in Belize is rooted in the need for money by families with no one working abroad. Some children, she believes, are exchanging sexual favors for money and treats, which in effect could be contributing to their untimely deaths. 'Many children are getting sexually active for money,' she told the *LA Times*. 'No one has talked about it until now. Children from poor, single-parent families are being lured to their death.'

But the flow of crack cocaine and the rise of innercity gang warfare in Belize City has irreparably damaged the daily life for all. Authorities say the cocaine problem reached a peak in 1993 and has been steadily brought under control. Still, urban crime is on the rise due mostly to a wave of Belizeans moving back home from the US. With this repatriation, typically American problems like gangs and drugs have returned to Belize. According to Karla Heusner, the first journalist to bring international attention to the series of murders, Belizeans were caught by surprise by the skyrocketing urban crime rate. Heusner noted that the sharp rise in crime stems from many local youngsters who grew up in the US where they learned to gang bang and deal drugs; 'they were educated abroad' and then were deported back to Belize. 'The crack problem messed everything up,' Heusner said in a telephone interview. 'Now there's lots of hold-ups, people shot after being robbed, daytime killings, defiant stuff.'

Most troubling though is the sudden appearance in 1998 of a sadistic lust murderer preying on the innocent and young. Being the first case of serial killing in the nation, local police have proven to be inadequately prepared to deal with the situation. 'The main problem we have had with these cases is that we have never had to deal with anything remotely this evil in our history,' said Police Spokeswoman Castillo. 'Though this might seem primitive, most of our murder cases in the past were straightforward and were solved with the help of eye-witnesses.' In these cases, however, only the mutilated remains of the four young girls speak of the monstrous nature of the roaming killer.

'If someone had told me five years ago that this could happen in our community, I would not have believed them,' said Jennifer August, vice-chairwoman of the Belize Organization for Women and Development. But it is, and the blood of the four innocent girls whose lives have been cut short is a testament to changes tearing apart the nation.

Heusner believes the killer is probably from the US. Because serial killers tend to kill members of their own race, Heusner theorizes that the predator is African-American. Furthermore, she believes, the killings probably involve a couple of men coming from Los Angeles or Miami who have friends in Belize providing them with the girls. Perhaps, she speculates, 'they are part of a sicko video ring that is taping the murders.' The affable journalist said the Belizean Tourist Board 'freaked out' when they saw she filed a story on the killings with Associated Press. Belize as a nation seems to be in denial about the growing crime on its streets. Though the government sees the country as a place where there's hardly any crime, newspaper and radio reports paint a different picture.

Not being prepared or equipped to handle the investigation of the serial killings, Belizean authorities turned to the FBI and Scotland Yard for help. 'Until the end of last year, our forensic capability was severely lacking,' said Police Spokeswoman Castillo. 'It wasn't until November 1999 that officers were trained in DNA-testing and such. Now fingerprinting is becoming big, but maybe it's too late. This is why the FBI was asked to help.' The FBI offered aid and sent agents to train Belizean officers in profiling and evidence-gathering techniques. However, FBI agents have not been directly involved in the investigation. Authorities have sent fibers and swabs taken from the four victims for DNA-testing in Quantico. Incoming Police

Commissioner Hughington Williams suggested that either the FBI or Scotland Yard would soon send agents to help local police track the sadistic killer. Local journalists believe the FBI agents have already got involved in the case, which explains the sudden news blackout that has fallen over the investigation.

Britain's Scotland Yard offered to help after British troops stationed in Belize came under suspicion. Belize, a former colony, has a garrison of one hundred British troops helping the Belizean army train for guerrilla warfare in the event of an invasion launched by neighboring Guatemala and/or Honduras. Because locals are convinced none of their own would rape, murder and mutilate their children, the British 'squaddies' – as they are known – have become the prime suspects. In the words of one soldier: 'It's like the Wild West, and we're the strangers in town, the number one suspects.'

On 17 November 1999, the Yard said it would assist in the investigation. Former Police Commissioner Ornell Brooks told London's *Mirror*: 'We just hope Scotland Yard can succeed where we have failed. This man must be stopped before he kills again.'

Suspicion that the killer is a foreigner grew after an alleged attempted abduction of a fourteen-year-old girl by a man wearing gloves and a stocking mask who jumped out of a car. Locals believe the foiled abductor was attempting to hide the fact that, unlike most Belizeans, he was white. After the attack was investigated by authorities, the veracity of the fourteen-year-old's account remains, at best, tenuous. Nevertheless the off-duty squaddies are still glared at as they stroll through the streets of the city. 'It wasn't always like this,' an unnamed soldier told the London *Mirror*. 'But the girls' deaths have changed attitudes. Now there is an atmosphere of fear and paranoia.'

A Belizean national added: 'We suspect everybody. This is a small country and it is being torn apart by suspicion.'

All four serial killer victims have been abducted in Belize City and were found dumped on the outskirts. The first three were found in roads and easily accessible swamp areas, suggesting the killer wanted their bodies found. The fourth victim was left in a quarry. Since the killings started, three other young girls – in unrelated cases – have been raped and murdered: one in a Belize City suburb, and two in rural areas in northern Belize. Another youngster was reportedly raped, beaten with a rock and left to die in the southern town of Dangriga. Fortunately, she survived. And yet another girl has been reported missing. Though family members think she might have run away from home, she too could have fallen prey to the sadistic killer.

Five men in Belize City have been arrested for the one killing in the suburb of Ladyville. The killing was at first believed to be drug-related, then a more callous sexual revenge scenario emerged. The suspects were released for lack of evidence but still remain under investigation. Subsequently one of them was killed execution-style while he was sitting in his car with his brother. Another man was arrested in the capital in connection with one of the serial killings after it was determined he had contact with one of the girls the morning of her abduction. He too was released after the fourth victim disappeared while he was in custody. Two men in Northern Belize have each been charged with one of the murders outside the city and are presently awaiting their respective trials.

All victims of the serial killer have been poor, young, and from single-parent homes. The first little girl to disappear was thirteen-year-old Sherilee Nicholas. She was last seen heading to school on 8 September 1998. Her decomposing body was found on 9 October partially submerged in water in a mangrove along the Western Highway eight miles from Belize City. She had been raped, then stabbed more than forty times in her chest, hand and head. Investigators believe the youngster tried to fight her attacker off. 'The girl died as a result of internal and external hemorrhage due to the stab wounds that she received,' Lead Investigator Sergeant Francisco Patt told the Belizean Channel Five News. 'She was stabbed on the left side of the chest and in the right palm of her hand. To me it looks like she was defending herself.'

Forensics determined that Sherilee had been dead for only two days. Ominously, her corpse was covered with the clothing and sneakers belonging to the second girl to vanish,

KILLERS ON THE LOOSE

nine-year-old Jay Blades. 'I know that dress,' said Sharine Garbutt, Jay's mother. 'It's my daughter's.' It is unknown how Jay's clothing and shoes ended up on Sherilee. Authorities theorize that either both girls knew each other and might have traded clothing or the killer, in a macabre gesture, returned to the crime scene to place Jay's dress over Sherilee's body. Jay left for school the morning of 7 October and never made it to her classroom. According to Garbutt, Jay frequently ran away from home, but would return several days later. This time she never returned. Her skeletal remains were discovered on 7 June 1999, eight months after she went missing. Authorities found evidence that the child was raped and mutilated by her attacker. Next to her body police found a knapsack with books and other school materials belonging to Sherilee Nicholas. Fearing a mistake in identification, authorities exhumed Sherilee's body against her mother's will and sent DNA-samples to the FBI lab in Quantico for examination.

While Jay was missing three more girls were murdered, though only one of them was a victim of the serial killer. The first murder was of Samantha Gordon, fifteen, who disappeared 6 November and was found two days later naked a few yards off the coast with numerous cuts and bruises on her back and knees. According to Assistant Inspector Simeon Alvarez, the former head of Belize's Crime Investigation Branch (CIB), Samantha was last seen around eight o'clock in the evening boarding a vehicle heading towards Ladyville, a suburb on the outskirts of the city. Authorities believe she was first sexually assaulted, then either given an overdose of drugs or strangled before her naked body was dumped into the sea.

According to Elise Gordon, her mother, Samantha would never have got into a car with a stranger. Her mother, distraught, said: 'She was happy, laughing, talking. I mean, we are not a household of violence.' What she finds most disturbing is that her daughter may have died at the hands of someone she knew. 'Samantha was dressed, she wasn't naked, she had on clothes. Where are they? Did anybody look for them? She had on jewelry, they are all gone. Did anybody look for them? She had on a silver Timex; she had gold earrings; she had on brand new Nike tennis shoes. The clothes she was wearing, she had just took out from the post office. It was sent to her from California.'

Gordon, authorities believe, was not a victim of the serial killer. Her death was first attributed to a drug deal gone wrong involving her brother and the five men who were arrested for her murder on 4 July. Further investigation has characterized her death as a revenge killing involving sex rather than drugs. According to Belize's former Attorney General Adolf Lucas, authorities, being pressured to find viable suspects, rushed the arrest of the suspects and his office eventually had to release them for lack of evidence. Perhaps coincidentally, six months later, Lucas lost his job. It was rumored, though not proven, that Gordon gave the AIDS virus to one of the men arrested for her death. Allegedly the infected man ordered her killing in revenge for her passing the virus on to him. The man hired four killers who allegedly took Gordon to a basketball game, and then left in a car with her to Ladyville where the man who ordered her hit was throwing a party. Shortly after, she left the party with two of the suspects and was never seen alive again.

One of the men arrested for the Gordon murder, 25-year-old taxi driver Frederick Neal, was, along with his brother, shot to death execution-style on 26 January 1999. Tellingly, his brother, Vincent Jones, 26, was scheduled to appear in court to answer charges of assaulting Samantha's brother, Mark Gordon. Though investigators have not revealed if their deaths were in any way connected to the Samantha Gordon case, circumstantial evidence points straight to it. As of this writing one suspect, Shelwyn Grey, was arrested for the double murder, but later acquitted for lack of evidence.

Adding to the national sense of horror, the next victim unrelated to the serial killer, thirteen-year-old Becky Gilharry, was raped and strangled by a family friend in the San Antonio village outside Belize City. Her mangled body was found on 15 February in the grounds of the Santa Rita Maya Ruin on Corozal. Robert Hill was arrested for her killing. Hill allegedly got up after having dinner with Becky's family, said he had to make a phone call and left with the girl. Becky never returned, and the man had no explanation for her disappearance. The next day, when her body was found, the man was promptly arrested. As of this writing Hill has been charged with murder and is awaiting trial. Police believe, without a shadow of doubt, that Hill will be convicted for the rape and murder of young Becky Gilharry.

The next serial killer victim to disappear was twelve-year-old Jackie Fern Malic. Like Sherilee Nicholas and Jay Blades, Jackie vanished on her way to school in Belize City. Her body was found on 24 March – two days after her abduction – in a feeder road off the Western Highway near where Sherilee's body was recovered and, eventually, Jay Blades' remains would be discovered. The minor – who was found still wearing her school uniform – was stabbed thirty to fifty times in her face, vagina, buttocks and right knee, and her left arm was violently amputated from the elbow down. Investigator Alvarez said the schoolgirl was not wearing any underwear when her body was found, suggesting she was sexually assaulted before she was murdered. Forensic analysis determined she had a large amount of semen in her body indicating she could have been raped by more than one individual.

Police Pathologist Dr Mario Estradabran said Jackie had been slowly tortured and mutilated by someone who knew what he was doing and took great pleasure in it. 'The attacker had a lot of time to inflict injuries on Jackie Fern Malic's body. He was enjoying the procedure that he was performing.' Estradabran believes the attacker could be trained as a butcher, doctor, or someone familiar with surgical tools. Based on his experience and autopsy findings, Estradabran concluded that Malic and Sherilee Nicholas were killed by the same weapon and person.

Adelma Malic, Jackie's sister, told police that Michael Williams, a forty-year-old auto mechanic and family friend, offered the two girls a ride to school the morning of the disappearance. Adelma said that although they were friendly with Williams they refused his offer and kept walking. Both girls arrived at the school compound where the younger sister went to her class. Jackie, however, never made it to hers. Police questioned Williams as a possible suspect and released him after 72 hours for lack of evidence. According to his lawyer, Kirk Anderson, Williams was seen in his garage by numerous people, including a policeman, on the day of the disappearance.

Two weeks prior to the disappearance of Jackie Malic, Williams allegedly contacted a pharmacist to purchase a 'knockout' drug that would put down a child between the age of twelve and thirteen. His alibi for purchasing the substance was that there were young people going into his garage to steal his food and drinks and he wanted to catch them. Hours before a police press conference following his arrest rumors were flying that his attorney himself might be arrested. According to Assistant Inspector Eli Salazar, Williams's common-law wife, Julie Staine, claimed the attorney told her to get rid of the clothing Williams was wearing the day of the abduction. 'During our investigations yesterday, with the death of Jackie Malic we received information from the common-law wife of Michael Williams, Ms Julie Staine, that she received a call from Kirk Anderson, attorney for Michael Williams, informing her to dispose of some clothes that we were going to search for at her residence which were supposed to be evidence against Michael Williams in the case of Jackie Malic.'

When a 23-year-old acquaintance said she had been molested by Williams when she was a child and another family friend said Williams had touched her inappropriately when he was giving her and her family a ride, the forty-year-old mechanic was re-arrested. On 6 April he was formally charged with the mutilation and murder of Jackie Malic. At a press conference on 9 April at the Raccoon Street Police Station, former Police Commissioner Ornel Brooks outlined the evidence, both circumstantial and forensic, that police gathered against the suspect. While detectives established a close relationship between Williams and Malic's family – which would explain why Williams offered the two girls a ride to school – they also 'established the presence of the deceased Jackie Malic in Williams's car around midday on the day of the 22nd – the day of the disappearance.' This evidence, based on a witness account, was never corroborated. The Director of Public Prosecution eventually dismissed the case against Williams because of lack of evidence and – more indicative of his innocence – the murder of a fourth serial killer victim while he was in prison.

The victim, nine-year-old Erica Willis, was reported missing the morning of 26 June. Her decomposing remains were found in the back of a quarry by a passerby on 17 July. Her mother recognized her remains by her hair band and a Tweety Bird ring next to her calcified hand. Though evidence suggested she too was raped, the advance state of decomposition of her remains made it impossible to determine whether she was mutilated like the others.

On 13 April in Orange Walk, just north of Belize City, ten-year-old Karen Cruz disappeared while her mother was waiting on the front veranda of her home for her to return from her aunt's house. Belize, as a nation, panicked with the news of the new disappearance. When her body was found the next day in a stadium three blocks away, police arrested her uncle by marriage who lived next door. Authorities believe the uncle, Antonio Baeza, who had been stalking the girl, got drunk, then raped and killed the ten-year-old. Baeza has been charged with murder and is awaiting trial in Belize's supreme court. Authorities are confident Baeza is the killer and will be found guilty when he is put on trial. Since young Karen was found dead, no other youngsters have been reported murdered in Belize. Another girl, Gertrude Palacio of Punta Gorda Town, has been reported missing since December 1998 and is presumed to have met the same fate as the others. Members of her family, however, believe the girl might have just run away and sooner or later will reappear alive.

Two of the presumed serial killer victims, Sherilee Nicholas and Jackie Malic, reportedly were mysteriously obtaining treats, clothing and money from someone off the streets. Though Sherilee's mother was very poor and could not afford to buy her a school uniform, her fourth-grade teacher Erminda Reid said the youngster would frequently return late from her lunch recess with expensive fruits and other treats that are customarily sold from carts in the streets.

Jackie Malic also brought clothes and money to her grandmother's house and no one knew where she obtained them.
Jackie's grandmother, Deonicia Cadle, said the twelve-year-
old never got into trouble, but police claim her friends at
school told a different story. According to Investigator Alvarez
students at the St Ignatius School said Jackie was occasionally
absent from school and sometimes had an unsuitable amount
of cash on her. Investigators speculate that both Sherilee and
Jackie could have been trading sexual favors for money and
treats. Another theory is that the killer, or agents acting on
behalf of the killer, gained the trust of the young girls with
gifts before kidnapping them.

The grisly murders of Jackie and Sherilee brought fear to
all parents in Belize. Addressing the murder of Jackie Malic,
Prime Minister Said Musa said: 'Clearly it is very shocking
when anyone dies or is killed but it is even more shocking
when a young innocent person is killed in this fashion. It's a
horror. It's horrifying and it's even more frightening to think
that there might be a very sick criminal out there who is
perpetrating these murders and abusive acts and the violation
of young people. It's horrible as a society. We have to think
hard about how we are going to fight this thing. It's like a
situation in England with "Jack the Ripper". This type of
crime, the police can do anything possible but you may not
be able to break it easily. You are dealing with a loner –
possibly, a lone sick mind out there who has launched an
operation on how to deal with these things. So it really is
going to tax us really hard to deal with this problem but we
have to deal with it.'

During Jackie's funeral on 27 March her classmates lined
the streets with signs demanding justice. Following the
services an emergency Children's Summit was convened by
the National Organization for the Prevention of Child Abuse
(NOPCA) and UNICEF. Dolores Balderamos Garcia, the
Minister of Human Development, Women and Youth, and
one of the more vocal politicians addressing the senseless
slaughter, said it was imperative to discuss family violence
and the particularly alarming situation of rampant sexual
child abuse. In a public statement following the meeting the

Minister stated that these acts of terror, which began with Sherilee Nicholas, 'must be abhorred by each and every law-abiding citizen in Belize and should be recognized as a blatant disregard for law and order and the sanctity for human life.'

Lorna McDougal, the director of NOPCA, said she has been overwhelmed by the recent heightened awareness on child abuse. Though she is saddened by the fact that it took the deaths of Sherilee Nicholas, Samantha Gordon, Rebecca Gilharry and Jackie Fern Malic to see any firm action take place. 'It is sad that it had to take that for this kind of action to emerge,' McDougal told the Belizean Channel 5 News. 'As you say we have been talking about child abuse since 1992. We have been like the lone voice calling out in the wilderness and there was a lot of denial, skepticism, cynicism about the whole issue of child abuse but now it is out in the open and the silence has been broken, so to speak.'

In an e-mail interview Police Spokeswoman Castillo said: 'Child abuse exists in all forms in Belize and while many are trying to do all they can to help the children, empowering them with rights and education, they are also teaching adults what abuse is and why it's wrong.'

The murder of Jackie marked a change in the attitude of the residents of Belize City. At the Children's Summit Prime Minister Said Musa announced he had come to listen to the children because they could shed some light on why these crimes were continuing. When a little boy asked the Prime Minister, 'Why are there special police to protect the tourists, but not the children?' Musa answered that it was time to create a special task force to deal with these crimes against children. After the summit a nationwide 8 p.m. to 6 a.m. curfew was imposed for anyone younger than sixteen. Wardens were also placed at all schools and parks to monitor children and watch for suspicious individuals. Parents began walking their children to school. The citizens of Belize decided there would be no more abductions. The nation itself banded together to protect their young.

When Erika Willis was found, the horror of yet another murder was marked by a candlelit procession of 1,000 tear-soaked people marching through the streets of the city. 'Belizeans cried out for justice; they cried out for their loved ones; and they cried out for the peaceful country that was changing before their eyes,' said Police Spokeswoman Christy Castillo. Inspector Alvarez told Channel 5 News, 'Indeed we have four cases that are unsolved at this time but again we have to understand that without the assistance of the general public the police will not be able to solve these heinous types of crimes. And definite I am of the belief that someone is out there who saw when these crimes were committed and if these people would come forward to the police the crimes will be solved.'

Many of those present at the vigil, including City Councilor Lilette Barclay Waite, Monsignor Dorick Wright from the Catholic Church, Pastor Ashley Rocke, and June Gabourel, the mother of Sherilee Nicholas, voiced their horror over the death of the young girls and demanded a more aggressive approach by police to solve the killings. Mrs Gabourel said the news of each murdered child since her daughter's death has been like opening the wound all over again. Councilor Waite added she hoped the vigil and procession served as a cleansing for both the society and the streets. Since the discovery of Sherilee's remains, her mother has adorned the family home with her daughter's artwork, yellow ribbons and a brand new outfit her daughter never got to wear. Gabourel believes by keeping Sherilee's memory alive, both society and the authorities will not forget what happened and will one day bring the killer to justice.

Until then, Belizeans better keep a watchful eye on their young.

17. THE PERTH SERIAL KILLER

There is a suspected serial killer in the Australian city of Perth who is believed to have kidnapped and murdered three women. The three victims were last seen in or around the posh Continental Hotel, a popular nightspot in the ritzy suburb of Claremont. All three women were pretty, young and blonde, and were strikingly similar in appearance. Also, all went to the same prestigious school in Perth, the Iona Presentation College. Police have offered a $195,000 reward for information leading to the capture of the presumed killer.

'We are looking at the same offender, a serial offender for the three offences. However, he may have an accomplice,' Police Superintendent and lead officer in the investigation Paul Ferguson said. The killer, according to police, is more dangerous because he is comfortable in the area and blends in with ease. He's probably well-dressed, intelligent, sociable, and has a friendly demeanor veiling his predatory instincts.

'He's not Quasimodo. He's not a hunchback in the belfry. He's a person who is non-threatening and fits into society particularly well in Claremont,' said Sergeant Tony Potts, a police officer on the Macro Task Force that was set up to hunt the killer.

The last known victim, Ciara Glennon, a 28-year-old lawyer, disappeared on 17 March 1997, after leaving the Continental Hotel following a St Patrick's Day celebration. She was the third woman to disappear from the area in little more than a year. The second to vanish was Jane Rimmer, a 23-year-old childcare worker. She was never seen alive again after leaving another nightclub in the area around midnight on 9 June 1996. The first and youngest to go missing was Sarah Spiers, an affable eighteen-year-old legal secretary. She disappeared in the early hours of 27 January after visiting the Continental with friends. Her body has yet to be recovered. 'The inference is irresistible that she is a victim of the person who has claimed the lives of Jane and Ciara,' Sergeant Potts told the AAP News Service.

Rimmer's corpse was the first one found. It was discovered in a swampy shrubland 25 miles south of the city two months after her disappearance. It was naked and in an advanced state of decomposition. 'As terrible as this discovery is, it is a major breakthrough for the investigators of the task force,' said Police Superintendent Ferguson. 'The discovery of the body will have a significant impact on the person responsible and will result in him being preoccupied and distracted.' Ciara Glennon's corpse was found in a shallow grave some forty miles outside the city, three weeks after her disappearance. Police have not officially given details on how both Glennon and Rimmer were killed but they have implied that the women were strangled.

Because of the long distances the killer covered to dispose of the victims, police believe he enjoys driving and might work professionally as a driver. Based on evidence found near the bodies, police reported that the killer washes his car after dumping the bodies at the crime scenes. 'Serial offenders of this nature have been found to be compulsive drivers who spend a lot of time in their vehicle and are concerned with the appearance of their car,' said Ferguson. 'It is likely the individual responsible for these disappearances spent time cleaning or polishing the vehicle he used following the disappearances.'

Police suspect the killer could be a person in authority, such as a police officer or security guard, or perhaps just poses as one. 'These are not random attacks,' said Ferguson. 'The person or persons responsible are very organized. The age and type of women targeted show these attacks don't just happen anywhere, to anyone.' Criminologists have profiled the killer as a 'verbal, intelligent man who has been able to get the trust of his victims'. Police are especially disturbed by the ease with which the killer snatched his victims from the midst of friends in familiar territory, and how he disappears without trace.

Another theory paints the killer as a cab driver, which would have the victim walking straight into the predator's hands. Detectives have been taking fingerprints and saliva samples from Perth's 3,000 licensed taxi drivers and warnings have been posted around the city advising young women not to travel alone at night. Since authorities voiced their taxi driver theory, night-time taxi trade has dropped by at least forty percent. Investigators have also used polygraph tests – a first for Australian murder investigations – to weed out 54 suspicious individuals. 'They were people without an alibi, but there was some other component of complicity; crimes of violence against women, being there on the night, a number of things,' Sergeant Potts said. 'What's happening now is as we work through this vast amount of information we are establishing a pool once again of people who will need to be processed in a similar manner.'

The Macro Task Force, which includes 'dozens of officers', has become a high-tech 'processing center' for information and evidence management. 'We've had, since Sarah Spiers went missing, probably eighty thousand pieces of information we've had to look at, prioritize and give out for inquiry,' explained Potts. To help Australian police catch their killer Scotland Yard has established a computer link-up with the task force to guide them through the Holmes computer program developed by the British police to solve serial killings. Also, agents from the FBI have gone to Perth to assist investigators with the complexities of the investigation. 'Serial killers are historically difficult to catch,' said Sergeant Potts. 'It would be foolish of us to say we're going to catch him tomorrow, but we're confident we will catch him.'

Only one suspect has been isolated in the case, but police have been unable to gather enough evidence to charge him. The suspect, a 41-year-old public servant whose name cannot be printed for legal reasons, spoke out to the media in frustration after enduring nearly two years of surveillance. Not mincing words, the suspect, hoping to put an end to his nightmare existence, begged authorities to either charge him with the killings or leave him alone. 'It's going on and on and on,' he said at a press conference on 16 January 2000. 'Quite often I hope it's all going to end. I pray about that sort of thing. I tend to do that daily. Like many people who have suffered major traumas, I hope in a higher being.'

Though he admits that his behavior around the time of the three killings was strange, he feels that twenty months of constant surveillance is more than any man – guilty or innocent – could bear. At the time of the killings the suspect was allegedly spotted cruising repeatedly around the streets of Claremont. 'I obviously brought it on myself. I had been nosing around, sticking my nose in where it shouldn't have been,' he said. 'I got caught up in it. I was obviously causing concern. I guess if the police have got someone who was acting a bit differently, they have got to be cautious.'

Since the surveillance started the 41-year-old loner who allegedly suffers from depression, was forced to sell his home and move in with his parents. 'It was difficult but I got used to it,' he said of the surveillance. 'That's why I came back home. I didn't feel comfortable on my own.' Still, the man is frustrated by the police's efforts to keep him in check. 'I've tried to help the police as much as I can, and so have my family, but I can't prove anything. I can only give the police facts but it's hard for an accused or a suspect to prove one hundred percent they are innocent.' Pointing to the fact that there have been no serial killings since the suspect was put under surveillance, police say the surveillance is being carried out for the good of the community. 'It was a long time after the last woman went missing that they started watching me,' he said. 'And nothing had happened in that time.'

Police, who have no intention of lifting their surveillance on the man, said they would welcome the chance to put their evidence against the suspect before a court of law. 'I think it is a case of them wanting to make the public feel safe and maybe hoping, on the off-chance, that they may have someone. Obviously they don't know the truth of the whole matter, the exact events. They have told me that. Maybe they don't have much evidence at all about anything.'

Crime Consultant Mark Devenish-Meares believes authorities are after the wrong individual. In fact, he thinks, if the suspect were the killer, he would be happy about the surveillance. 'They could actually be stopping him acting in a way he doesn't like,' he said. 'Many people seem to think that serial killers enjoy what they are doing or what they have done. It may be true that they enjoy the act but afterwards might think, "Jesus Christ, what have I done?" Serial killers may be troubled by their own behavior. They may struggle with themselves for some time.'

Kevin Durkin, Professor of Psychology at the University of WA, believes the longer the stalemate goes on, the less likely the suspect is to crack. 'He knows that, guilty or otherwise, a stalemate has been reached,' the professor told the Australian News Network. 'There may be a sense of alienation, something unreal. He might feel the surveillance has become part of his normal life but, unless he is an especially robust person, he will be liable to pressure. He may not be aware of the stress he is under from the surveillance.'

Australia, surprisingly, has had more than its share of serial killers, with most having been active in the southern section of the nation. Ivan Milat, Australia's best-known serial killer, carved himself a name in the annals of Australian crime history by murdering seven hitchhikers in the Belanglo State Forest in New South Wales. Like convicted Alaskan serial killer Robert Hansen, Ivan enjoyed hunting down his victims like animals, giving them a head-start before hunting them through the bush. His murder spree spanned the period from September 1992 to November 1993. Milat was arrested in 1994 at his home on the outskirts of Sydney where police found gun parts, ammunition and knives used in the killings, as well as camping equipment said to have belonged to some of the murdered hitchhikers.

Milat, who was 51 at the time of his arrest, was known as the 'Backpack Murderer'. The brutality of his attacks both captivated and horrified the Australian public. Some of the victims were shot, others stabbed, and one was decapitated with a sword found in Milat's mother's apartment. Of the seven killed, five were European tourists in their twenties lured to Australia by its reputation as a safe haven for budget travelers. The other two victims were teenagers from the Australian State of Victoria. Two of the dead were young British women whose disappearances led to the grim discovery of Milat's handiwork.

After the discovery of seven bodies the police launched the biggest manhunt in Australian history, which eventually led to Milat's arrest. The star witness for the prosecution was another British tourist who escaped from the madman's car to avoid certain death after Milat pulled a gun on him. On 27 July 1996, after a four-month trial and three and a half days of deliberation, a jury of seven men and four women convicted the former road worker of murdering the seven backpackers. Milat's lawyer tried to pin the murders on, first, Ivan's brother Richard, then, on his other brother, Walter. Many believe the former road worker with an unhealthy obsession for guns and hunting may not have acted alone and perhaps was assisted by his brothers.

More recently, in 1999, Australian police uncovered eight bodies hidden in acid vats inside an abandoned bank vault and three more buried in a back yard in the southern city of Snowtown. The suspects, Robert Joe Wagner, 27, John Justin Bunting, 32, and Mark Ray Haydon, 40, allegedly were involved in a social security fraud scheme in which they were cashing the pension checks of their victims. However, neighbors said the three had a deep hatred for homosexuals, pedophiles and Asians. Wagner, a member of the neo-Nazi National Action group, had been allegedly seduced as a teenager by one of the victims, a convicted pedophile named Barry Lane. Before the discovery of the bodies in Snowtown, Australian authorities thought they had a vigilante-type serial killer on the loose targeting pedophiles. Now police see the case more as a group of grifters who knew each other and were preying on themselves.

Other Australian serial killers of note have been Catherine and her husband David Birnie who were sentenced to life in prison for the rape and murder of four young women in 1986. In an attempt to spice up their sex life, the Birnies cruised the streets of Perth searching for their prey. In all they abducted five women who they later bound, gagged and chained to a bed in their suburban home; David would then rape them repeatedly. Once the couple grew tired of them they would either strangle and/or stab them to death. Then they would bury the victims in a national park outside the city. The would-be fifth victim managed to escape the house through an unlocked window while the Birnies tried to negotiate a cocaine deal in the adjoining room.

Eric Cook, another Perth killer, confessed to committing eight murders between 1959 and 1983. Six of the killings got him sentenced to death by hanging. Moments before being hanged he swore over a Bible that he had committed two other murders for which two men had already been convicted. Cook's five-year murder rampage changed the laid-back and trusting attitudes of the citizens of Perth for ever. In fact, his robbery and murder spree led the West Australian Government to order the city of Perth to keep its streetlights on at night.

Further south, in Adelaide, seven young women were plucked from the streets to be raped and strangled by Chris Worrell. Five of their bodies were found buried in bushland near Truro. Two others were unearthed nearer to Adelaide. Between 1975 and 1976 Worrell, who was bisexual, and his homosexual friend, James William Miller, became known as the Truro Murderers. Worrell himself died in a car crash. Police did not suspect that they were the killers until an acquaintance told police that Miller, during Worrell's funeral, said the two of them 'had done in' some girls. Once in custody Miller promptly confessed. He is now serving six life sentences even though he contends that he never killed anyone.

John Wayne Glover, known as the 'Granny Killer', was responsible for a series of brutal hammer attacks on old ladies on Sydney's north shore. An affable pie salesman who led a seemingly respectable life with his wife and two daughters, Glover also had a history of indecent assault on older women in nursing homes. He was caught in the late '80s after police were alerted to one of the assaults. When an officer called his home and left a message to contact him, Glover attempted to commit suicide. Convicted of six murders, Glover blamed his mother-in-law and his mom for his hatred of older women. Both of them died a year before his killing spree began.

Former postal worker William McDonald murdered four ageing drunks in Sydney in the early 1960s. As a signature he severed their genitals and took them home in plastic bags, earning him the moniker 'The Mutilator'. McDonald was caught three months after he was ruled dead when a former co-worker who went to his funeral saw him walking down

Sydney's George Street. When police scoffed at the man's story he went to the *Daily Mirror* which sparked the investigation into McDonald's faked death with the legendary headline: 'Case of the Walking Corpse'. When the coroner's office exhumed the corpse that had been buried they discovered it was not McDonald's and that it too had mutilated genitals. The Mutilator was arrested in Melbourne where he confessed to the five Mutilator murders as well as a strangulation death in Brisbane.

On 24 January 1999, authorities announced that an Ivan Milat-copycat serial killer is stalking the Queensland–New South Wales border region and has murdered at least three female hitchhikers over the past two years. The latest reported victim was Lois Roberts, twin sister of Australian actor Rhoda Roberts. Her body was found on 8 January in a shallow grave in the Whian State Forest, about fifteen miles from Lismore. She was bound with rope and electrical cord. In October 1997, the body of shop assistant Lee Stace, sixteen, was found in a shallow grave in scrub near the coastal resort town of Yamba. In November 1996 the badly decomposed remains of twenty-year-old Ineka Hinkley were found in the Bongil State Forest, about eight miles south of Coffs Harbor.

A task force, codenamed Metz, was set up to investigate the slayings. The leader, Acting Detective Inspector Peter Gallagher, confirmed the operation was also looking at a number of other murders and disappearances. In a surprising turn, Milat sent a letter through his support group to the Queensland regional crime co-ordinator, Detective Inspector Jeff Oliphant, claiming that he knew the identity of the new killer. As of this writing there is no indication that Inspector Oliphant has contacted the killer.

Investigators agree that the first 48 to 72 hours are critical in solving a murder case. Research has demonstrated that in 66 percent of solved homicides the suspect is taken into custody within 24 hours. If the case is not solved within 48 hours, the chances of it ever being solved fall markedly. In Perth, it's been three years since the last killing. Taking the above-mentioned research into account, unless the killer commits a grave mistake, confesses voluntarily or claims another victim, it is highly unlikely the murders of Ciara Glennon, Jane Rimmer and Sarah Spiers will ever be solved. The same can be said about the three Queensland–New South Wales hitchhiker victims.

18. SOUTH AFRICA'S SERIAL KILLER EPIDEMIC

South Africa is fast becoming the serial sex-crime epicenter of the world, with at least five separate serial killers active and at large today. The serial killer explosion began in 1992 with the abolition of apartheid. No one really knows whether there was serial killing before because there are no records or data confirming or denying it. But since 1992 the number of maniacs on the loose has mushroomed out of control. Between 1994 and 1996 seven high-profile serial killers have been arrested in South Africa: four around Johannesburg, two in Cape Town and one in the KwaZulu Natal region. The killings have terrified the nation, particularly in and around the industrial heartland of Johannesburg where, during the mid '90s, 52 of an estimated 75 serial murders were committed. Sources claim that since 1994 no less than thirty serial killers have been arrested throughout the republic.

Addressing the unprecedented level of violence in South Africa, Dr Micki Pistorius, head of South Africa's Police Service Investigative Psychology Unit (IPU), said: 'I am not prepared to guess how many killers are at large, but we could be facing an epidemic in the future.' Dr Pistorius, the most prominent profiler of the IPU, believes there has been a definite escalation in serial killings: 'The escalation in the population, in crime and violence, and the role of the media are all contributing factors.' Furthermore, she thinks that the problem will only get worse. 'We must remember that we are not the only country with this problem, but our socio-economic conditions indicate that we could become a focal point in the world.'

Others disagree, citing that South African authorities only started acknowledging serial killings after 1992. With no past records of serial slayings in existence, Dr Rika Snyman, a criminologist of the University of South Africa, believes the lack of data has created the impression that South Africa was previously free of serial murder. 'I personally do not think that it has escalated, they have always been there, but have not been recognized as such,' Dr Snyman told the *Star* newspaper. Inadequate training of detectives and the structure of apartheid may have also contributed to the lack of existing information. 'South Africa has, unfortunately, an exceptionally high rate of violence and it can only be assumed that, proportionally, serial killing will also be higher, but this cannot be proved,' Snyman added.

Dr Pistorius, a slight woman in her late thirties, has become legendary in South Africa for her dead-on profiling of serial killers. Trained under former FBI agent Robert Ressler, Dr Pistorius has enjoyed an astonishing success rate unequaled by any other serial killer profiler in the world. Her work has led to the capture of South Africa's deadliest predators. The list of creeps netted by this former journalist – a veritable 'who's who' of sexual psychopaths in South Africa – includes the 'Station Strangler', the 'Donnybrook Serial Killer', the 'Pine Town River Strangler', the 'Wemmer Pan Killer', the 'Lover's Lane Murderer', the 'Saloon Killer', the 'Gauteng Murderer', the 'Nasrec Strangler' and the 'Phoenix Strangler'.

Before joining the force in 1994, Pistorius never considered a career as a police profiler. Instead, she completed her masters in psychology at the University of Pretoria. 'In my wildest dreams, I never saw myself in the police force, but my interest in Freudian psychology led me to seeing a connection between the theory and serial killers. One thing led to another, and here I am.' Her first assignment was the profiling of the feared Station Strangler, suspected of sodomizing and strangling 21 young boys whom he snatched from the Cape Town train station. Her surprisingly accurate profile led to the quick arrest of Norman Avzal Simon. 'All my cases have been tough ones, but that one made the greatest impression,' she said. 'The strangler was very well-educated, speaking seven languages.' Dr Pistorius, after meeting the convicted killer, said he was 'pleasant, well read . . . Serial killers are very pleasant. I haven't met one who wasn't.' Simon, who was 28 at the time of his arrest, conveniently turned religious while in jail. Though charged initially with twelve murders, eleven charges were dropped for lack of evidence. Simon is serving a 25-year prison sentence for the murder of one boy. In 1998, after numerous appeals from the victim's relatives, his 25-year jail sentence was increased to life.

According to the psychologist, to successfully profile a killer you have to 'focus on the person's sexual fantasy,' she said in an interview with Angella Johnson of the *Electronic Mail & Guardian*. 'You have to try to picture that; no matter how grotesque it is, to relive the most minute detail. You have to decipher it as you would a work of art. You know, things like the position of the body; weaponry, was torture involved, the kinds of wounds, how the body is positioned, is there evidence of a pattern?' But the heart of her profiles lies in the little details that reveal the motivation of the killer. 'You have to reconstruct chronologically what he did and figure out why he did it. If you want to kill someone you only have to shoot them, anything extra will give you characteristics of your killer.'

South Africa's first known serial killer is probably Daisy de Melker who, during the '20s and early '30s, is believed to have poisoned two husbands and possibly five of her children. She was executed in December 1932 after being found guilty of poisoning her son, Rhodes. After her execution there were hardly any other reported instances of serial killing until the demise of apartheid. Since then there has been a serial killing explosion, starting with the arrest of 29-year-old former policeman Kobus Geldenhuys, who was convicted in 1993 of raping and murdering five young women in the Gauteng neighborhood of Norwood.

Next came the arrest of Norman Simon, the Station Strangler. Since then, most serial killers arrested in this multi-ethnic republic have been successfully profiled by Dr Pistorius. Known as the Donnybrook Serial Killer, Christopher Mhlengwa Zikode, 21 at the time of his arrest, murdered eighteen people and attempted to murder another eleven over a period of two years in the rural Natal midlands town of Donnybrook. His *modus operandi* was to kick open the door of his victims' house, shoot the men in the head and drag the women to a nearby plantation where he would rape them repeatedly, sometimes for as long as five hours, then kill them. If they resisted he would kill them first, then rape them post-mortem. He was arrested on 29 September 1995, after being profiled by Dr Pistorius. On 7 January 1997, Zikode was sentenced to 140 years in prison. The judge said during sentencing that Zikode had absolutely no regard for human life and his attitude to women was 'contemptible'. Zikode was convicted on 21 charges, including eight murders, five rapes, five attempted murders and one indecent assault.

Though having committed more murders than Ted Bundy, hardly anyone knows about Moses Sithole. Like Bundy, Sithole, who was known as the Gauteng Murderer, used his charm and intelligence to lure his victims to their deaths. On 5 December 1997, he was convicted of 38 murders and 40 rapes in the Pretoria, Johannesburg and East Rand areas and sentenced to 2,410 years in jail. In a jailhouse videotaped confession shown during his trial – which was made on the condition that Sithole and three other prisoners would get a share of the royalties – he said he hated women and felt he was teaching them 'a very good lesson' by murdering them. Between 1994 and 1995 Sithole lured women to secluded fields, then assaulted, raped and strangled them with their own underwear or belts. Several of the women were left with their hands tied behind their backs. One woman was blindfolded. Some were found with their heads covered with clothing. Several of his victims were found at the same gravesite, suggesting that the women knew they were going to die once he took them to the murder site and they saw themselves surrounded by corpses. Apparently he murdered his first victim because she had shouted at him when he asked her for directions. 'I cannot remember her name,' he said. 'I killed her and left her there. I went straight home and had a shower.'

On 18 October 1995, after a week-long nationwide hunt, police shot, wounded and arrested Sithole. At the time police thought he acted in conjunction with another man, David Selepe, who was also in custody. Strangely, authorities had no evidence indicating that the men knew each other. Selepe, who was known as the Cleveland Strangler, was arrested in

December 1994 and charged with the murders of eleven black women who were found in a mine dump in Cleveland. Unfortunately for justice, he was killed while in custody on 17 December 1994, when police took him to one of the crime scenes to point out the location of a body. At an inquest following his death police alleged he had attacked one of the detectives with a stick before he was shot. At the time police claimed Selepe had been 'positively linked' to six of the Cleveland Strangler victims. But after Sithole's arrest four of the six Selepe victims were linked to the newly arrested killer. Selepe's wife, Linda, then sued police, declaring that her husband had been wrongfully accused of crimes he did not commit. 'They killed the truth when they killed my husband,' she told the South African media. 'Had they brought him to court then, the South African public would have known the truth that David was not a killer.'

Another serial killer, Samuel Bongani Mfeka, was arrested on 8 September 1996, on a rape charge. While in custody Samuel, who was known as the Kranskop Serial Rapist-Killer, pointed out different locations where the bodies of six women who had been raped and strangled had been hidden. The first murder dates to 1993 following the discovery of a body in Carletonville. Another body was found in the veldt in Vrede in November 1994. The four other corpses were found in the Kranskop area. The last body was found in an advanced state of decomposition on the day of his arrest. According to authorities, four of the bodies were found within easy distance of the suspect's house in a rural area in KwaZulu Natal. A police spokesman said that Mfeka was also being questioned in relation to sixteen murders attributed to the still at large Nasrec Strangler. As of this writing he has not been charged with any of the murders.

On 15 August 1997, after being profiled by Dr Pistorius, Sipho Agmatir Thwala was arrested during an early morning raid in the Besters shantytown near Phoenix. Thwala, who was thirty at the time of his arrest, was charged with being the feared Phoenix Strangler. The killer allegedly promised his victims a job, then asked them to accompany him. Saying they were taking a short cut, Thwala would walk the women through a sugar cane plantation in the Dunbar suburb of Phoenix where he raped and strangled at least sixteen women. The killings are believed to have started in August 1994. The latest victim is believed to have died on 5 August 1997. Nearly all the victims were black and between twenty and thirty years old. They were found within a two-mile radius in the plantation, with some within a few yards of each other. They were all bound, gagged, strangled with their own underwear and buried in shallow graves. Thwala, who had been acquitted of rape and murder in 1994, was arrested after a survivor identified him and DNA-samples from the crime scenes matched his own.

Only one woman escaped from his clutches. She told the court that Thwala had promised her a job and asked her to accompany him. After raping her the killer allegedly asked her to be his girlfriend. The woman said he started throttling her again but when she pleaded for her life she was spared. State prosecutor Garry Williams told the judge: 'No words can describe the horror and the trauma that his victims faced.' Dr Pistorius's profile described the killer as an intelligent Zulu man between thirty and forty years old who gained the confidence of his victims by offering them employment. 'He will not have any outstanding features which would attract any attention. He knows the Phoenix area very well and could therefore be a local resident.'

In 1997 Captain Piet Byleveld of the Brixton Murder and Robbery Unit thought he was investigating at least three different serial killers operating in southern Johannesburg. One, known as the Wemmer Pan Killer, was considered responsible for the murder of five couples in a recreational park south of the city. Four of the victims were bludgeoned to death, six were shot. The women were also raped. In a second seemingly unrelated serial cluster, authorities thought there was a killer responsible for the rape–murders of four women in the Claremont area. A third serial killer, known as the Hammer Killer, was believed to have targeted tailor shops in the inner city, killing seven people in thirteen similar-style attacks. Three survivors described the assailant as a short, well-spoken, slightly built black man. He was well-dressed and had 'a thick crop of hair'. In two of the assaults the attacker carried hardware tools in a plastic bag and claimed to be a plumber.

Police first focused on the Wemmer Pan killings, linking at least five of the cases. Police spokesman Captain Andy Pieke said: 'We believe these attacks may be connected to different killers. There is the possibility more than one serial killer is behind this, but we cannot rule out that all these murders are unrelated. The area is generally a dangerous one.'

Dr Pistorius, who was called in to profile the possible killers, pointed out several links that suggested a connection between the Wemmer Pan and Claremont serial clusters. 'It could be two serial killers operating in the same area. There is what is called linkage blindness. The police sit with dozens of dockets persons and do not always know about the cases which their colleagues are investigating. Serial murders are about patterns in the mind of the killer. They are not always obvious. Serial killers are very conscious of their own patterns. Police have to decipher these patterns; they're incredibly difficult to detect.'

Elmarie Myburgh, the investigative psychologist assigned to the case, said authorities suspected that two men were linked to 'a number of murders' in the Wemmer Pan area. 'If the men are not working together, each has an accomplice,' she said. A single profile was drawn for both killers because they used the same *modus operandi*. According to Myburgh, the suspects were black males, between thirty and forty years old, who may live or work in the Wemmer Pan area.

By early 1998, serial killer expert Captain Piet Byleveldt noticed that evidence from one serial cluster started overlapping with evidence from the two others, suggesting that in fact the same person or group of people could be responsible for the three separate serial patterns. By a stroke of luck Maupa Shadrick Maake, 33 at the time, was arrested as a suspect after a string of rapes and robberies throughout the Wemmer Pan area. Once in custody it became clear he was a viable suspect in all three serial murder cases. 'We regard the arrest of the Wemmer Pan suspect as one of the best breakthroughs in the world. And Byleveldt's success is due to his incredible experience and professionalism in follow-up and interviewing the suspect,' said Superintendent Philip Heydenrych of the Detective Academy in Pretoria.

Maake was arrested near Jeppe railway station on 23 December. By 12 January, after police found a receipt from a pawnshop linking him to a bicycle he stole from one of his victims, he became the prime suspect in more than 55 cases of murder, rape and robbery. Police came to believe Maake could be linked to as many as sixty murders committed between September 1995 and December 1997. Eventually he was charged with 37 murders and a total of 129 criminal offences. In March 2000 the Johannesburg High Court found Maake responsible for 27 deaths. He was also found guilty of 26 attempted murder charges, fourteen rape charges and 41 charges of robbery with aggravating circumstances.

Surprising all investigators, Maake proved to be an exceptionally active serial killer who, uncharacteristically, followed different patterns without fixating on the type of victim or method of killing. During the week Maake targeted tailors in and around Johannesburg and killed them with a hammer. According to the prosecution the Wemmer Pan killings were like 'weekend jobs' in which he used a gun. He also went for women on their own whom he raped and bludgeoned to death with rocks. Then he attacked people in their homes using knives and blunt objects. His victims ranged from a 74-year-old Fordsburg tailor to a fifteen-year-old teenager whom he raped and then shot between the eyes. He killed early in the morning, during the day, and late at night. And he showed no racial predilection during his assaults: he killed Asians, blacks and whites.

The next serial killer to be brought to justice was David Mmbengwa, known as the Lover's Lane Murderer, who was arrested on 19 July 1998. A fanatical Christian fundamentalist, Mmbengwa believed he was on a divine mission each time he ambushed and murdered an amorous couple making love. Mmbengwa allegedly underlined every reference to sex in his worn copy of the Bible, which he carried while he committed his killings. Mmbengwa, 34, was charged with eight murders in the Northern Province. He was arrested at a rented Kagiso township shack on the West Rand after a seven-day manhunt. Arresting officers used a profile drawn by forensic psychologist Elmarie Myburgh and Dr Pistorius. 'Mmbengwa is a very religious person and appears to know the Bible like the back of his hand. His major problem appears to be that he is uncontrollably aggressive, but also very shy. He is highly intelligent,' Myburgh said, adding, 'Survivors of his attacks say he never tried to communicate with his victims before he shot them.'

In January 1999 Pretoria police spokesperson Inspector Gideon Thessner announced the arrest of 36-year-old Samuel Sadano who was suspected of being the feared Pretoria Strangler. 'Dr Micki Pistorius, police psychologist and an expert on serial killers, confirmed that Sadano's psychological and physical profile linked him to the bodies found,' said Thessner. The first of six victims attributed to Sadano was found on 14 December 1998, in an area behind Pretoria Zoo. While analyzing the crime scene, police discovered three more bodies, one of a twelve-year-old boy and two of young men, in various stages of decomposition. The first murder case was investigated separately until police confirmed that all cases were linked. The body of the fifth victim, a twenty-year-old woman, was found on a hill in the area by police. The sixth and final victim, a man, was found in the same area as the five other ones shortly after Sadano's arrest.

Though Dr Pistorius and Captain Byleveldt have, together and separately, tracked down more than thirty serial killers, there are still between five and ten predators on the loose. Possibly the most active of killers at large in South Africa is the Cape Town Strangler. To date the strangler has killed at least twenty prostitutes and dumped their bodies in undeveloped areas of the Western Cape. Operating since 1992, the killer picks up his victims in the Sea Point and Wynberg areas and does not appear to have raped any of his victims. In three cases police found that the victims were tortured. One of the prostitutes was buried alive upside down with her legs and buttocks protruding above the ground. Another corpse had a glass bottle shoved between her legs. The police have a number of suspects but nobody has yet been arrested. Like

Peter Sutcliffe, Britain's Yorkshire Ripper, the killer seems to be on a 'mission to kill prostitutes'. The police, stepping up their manhunt, formed a task force to meet with prostitutes and invited them to visit police stations to have their fingerprints and photos taken, and give personal details that will be used to track them and help to identify any subsequent victims.

Authorities in KwaZulu Natal have been looking for the Pinetown River Strangler who is suspected of having killed three women since 1994. He is believed to be a black man in his twenties who attacks petite young white women, whom he rapes and murders before dumping their bodies in a river. His first attack was on a twenty-year-old woman on 9 August 1994. He then raped and murdered Kim Boddington, fourteen, on 12 February 1995, and threw her body into a river. His next victim, whom he tried to drown on 17 March 1995, escaped. But twelve days later, he raped and killed Kate Willy, fifteen. His next attack was nine months later when he attacked another young girl who managed to flee from his clutches. No more information is available on other Pinetown killings.

Since May 1995 the feared Nasrec Strangler has been preying on women commuting between Soweto and Johannesburg. He is believed to have killed at least fifteen women and a teenager and has left many of their bodies in the Nasrec Township south of Johannesburg. The killer was profiled by Police Captain Piet Byleveldt and Dr Pistorius as a well-dressed, suave and intelligent man with a deep-seated hatred of women. His victims have been mostly black females, between the ages of twenty and 35, who were lured to their deaths from minibus taxis. Authorities suspect the killer could be a minibus driver. Though police have failed to arrest the prime suspect, their investigations have led to the arrest of Samuel Mfeka, the Kranskop Serial Rapist-Killer, and the Booysens serial rapist.

In 1997 Transkei region authorities reported that a 'river monster' is believed to have killed at least seven people crossing the Mzintlava River to Rubaleko village in the Mount Ayliff area. Though the monster has been described as 'half-fish, half-horse', there are growing fears that a serial killer is actually responsible for the killings. Police Inspector Maphelo Ngame confirmed that they were investigating the possible existence of the serial killing monster. 'The matter has been reported to the police by several people in Mount Ayliff and while the monster is said to have struck on different occasions, the affected families have given similar accounts of how the victims were attacked. So we have no reason to dismiss the monster story as a myth and we are duty bound to investigate.' Thozama Fikeni, a local businesswoman, told the *Mercury* newspaper that though she did not want to dismiss the story as a myth, she had a feeling the so-called monster was actually some maniac in disguise.

Maritzburg Police investigators believe they have a serial killer and rapist in their area who might be responsible for the gruesome murders of at least eleven women since September 1997. Captain Lionel Holder of the Maritzburg Murder and Robbery Unit said the victims were mostly sex-trade workers in Johannesburg aged between twenty and forty. Their naked or half-naked bodies have been found dumped alongside the N3 highway around the Hilton, Howick, Mkondeni and Town Hill areas. Police linked the murders to a serial killer after establishing similarities in the method of the killings and the physical build of the victims. Most of the victims were big-build women. In almost all cases, the victims had been raped or sexually assaulted before being strangled to death with their underwear. In some cases, items of the victims' clothing were found hanging on fences. 'We suspected from about August 1998 that a serial killer/rapist might have been involved in the murders,' Captain Holder told the Johannesburg *Sunday Times*. According to police the killer is a thirty- to forty-year-old black man who could work as a taxi driver operating along the N3 Highway. The suspect uses a car to take his victims to a place where he rapes and kills them, then dumps their bodies along the N3 highway.

In another horrifying development of multiple killings in South Africa, two separate gangs of muti-killers – who sell body parts to witch doctors – are believed to be behind a spate of gruesome murders in poverty-stricken areas south of Johannesburg and the rural Mpumalanga region. Muti is a ritualized religion practiced by South African blacks that uses specific mutilated body parts as powerful charms. Inspector Tinus Oosthuizen, who has been investigating the disappearance of children in the townships of Orange Farm, Finetown and Ennerdale, said that at least five girls killed in the area between February 1997 and January 1998 could be the victims of the same person. 'At this stage we don't suspect that the children were targeted for muti-killings, but the possibility can't be ruled out,' Oosthuizen said. At first, investigators believed the pattern of the attacks suggested they were dealing with an unusual combination of two serial killers working as a team. 'It could be that the killers are curious about how the body works or they want to shock the police and public,' said Detective Inspector Christopher Moultrey. 'Or they are getting arrogant and are sending a message to the police that they are getting better and will never be caught.'

Perhaps related to the case was the discovery of a severely mutilated baby in the area in late 1996. No one ever claimed the body. The five girls – Edith Aaron, Nompumelelo Kgamedi, Nthabiseng Majoe, Zanele Nongiza and Bukeka Mhlonitshwa – were all six years old. Aaron, Kgamedi and Majoe had broken necks and were found under trees. Nongiza and Mhlonitshwa were found decapitated and their torsos were missing. Later that year the police found a child's ribs and intestines in a plastic bag, which authorities said could be linked to the killings. The investigation was triggered by the discovery of the dismembered body of six-year-old Zanele Nongiza near her home. Three days later authorities found a skull and ribs, also believed to be those of a child. The cases were quickly linked to another six-year-old girl who was also found mutilated in nearby Finetown. Authorities said they were also looking into the disappearance of eleven more children in the area whom may have fallen prey to suspected muti-murderers or a serial killer. After announcing the investigation two of the missing children recognized themselves in published photographs and contacted police. Apparently, after being reported missing the two young boys returned home and no one alerted the authorities to their return.

Another muti-related case was uncovered in September 1998 in the rural area of Mpumalanga, in the KwaZulu Natal region, when fishermen found three heads – belonging to two adults and a ten-year-old child – floating in the Wilge River near Botleng. A week later authorities in the town of Delmas found two headless bodies floating in a farm dam about twelve miles away. Another headless body was then found in a field in nearby Sundra. Police initially believed that the killings were the work of a serial killer. In fact, they even had a viable suspect: a mentally deranged man who had recently escaped from a psychiatric institution. The suspect, Johannes Mohale-Monareng, had been sentenced in 1990 to 25 years in Weskoppies Psychological Institute for decapitating a young girl in Delmas and trying to sell her head. He was eventually arrested and questioned about the recent spate of mutilation murders but was found to have been uninvolved in the carnage. Ironically he was then re-arrested in February 1999 after trying to sell another head in the Witbank police station.

Dr Pistorius, who was sent to Delmas to assist with the investigation, determined that the motive of the killings was financial gain from the sale of body parts. According to the psychologist, the decapitations could not have been done by a single serial murderer or a mentally disturbed person. 'I don't have a single shred of evidence pointing to a serial killer,' she told the *Cape Times*. 'The fact that the heads were thrown twenty kilometres away in a river indicates a rational attempt at preventing the identification of the victims. It is not the work of a mentally disturbed person. There is probably more than one person involved in this case, and they use a vehicle.' The victims, police determined, were abducted from Thembisa and Vosloorus on the East Rand, killed and dumped in the Delmas area. Furthermore, they all had their necks removed – indicating the murders were carried out by professional body-snatchers looking for specific body parts.

'It's the only part missing in all cases and is the strongest indication that this may be the work of muti-killers. All the bodies have had their necks, from the shoulders to the chin, chopped off,' said Captain Danie Hall. 'We still haven't found out what the necks are used for.'

As of this writing the muti-murders remain unsolved. Whether it's muti-murderers, river monsters or sexual predators, South Africa is being flooded with the blood of innocents. As the bodies have piled up throughout the republic serial killing has become part of its national character. One can blame it on the generational effects of apartheid or the lingering problems that come with poverty, but still neither explanation fully accounts for the epidemic level of its serial killer crisis. Such easy rationalization just cheapens the tragedy of all the lives lost. Just as another sexual predator is arrested and sentenced to life in jail, a new boogieman is detected snatching someone else's life away. And the horror will continue unchecked and unstopped even if Dr Pistorius, Captain Byleveldt and their colleagues keep working miracles profiling and arresting emerging serial killers.

EPILOGUE

Science and technology have made huge strides in the detection and identification of serial killers. In fact, DNA examinations have become a mainstay in all serious crime investigations. In the State of Illinois the governor has imposed a moratorium on all executions until convicts are DNA-tested to confirm their guilt in the crime for which they were convicted. In fact, high-profile solved and unsolved cases from the past are now being reopened and re-examined at an exponential rate to DNA-test evidence to determine the real identities of the killers.

In current investigations throughout the US detectives are relying heavily on DNA-databanks and computerized systems like VICAP to shift out possible serial killers. But the slaughter continues unabated. New serial patterns are emerging in Denver, Pittsburgh, Brooklyn and France, while many other spots in the globe are grappling with uncaught serial predators. Is there any way to stop the mayhem? How many more roaming maniacs lusting for blood are still out there undetected and unknown?

Though Chicago police have successfully solved all but two of the killings the Southside Task Force was investigating, there is no reason not to believe a new killer will soon pick up where the others were stopped. With the arrest of Andre Crawford, Chicago authorities have had to repeal the death sentence of Hubert Geralds after both men confessed to the same murder and Crawford demonstrated to have more intimate knowledge of the crime. As of this writing, one more victim has been added to the Crawford hit list, bringing his total to eleven killings.

In California, police announced that they hoped to identify the elusive Zodiac Killer by comparing DNA recovered from a 1966 crime scene in Riverside and genetic material recovered from a Vallejo man who died in 1992. In between 1968 and 1969 the Zodiac terrorized the San

Francisco Bay Area by killing six people and sending taunting letters to the police and newspapers. In one of the letters the killer claimed to have killed 37 people. In another, he referred to a Riverside, California killing: 'I do have to give them credit for stumbling across my Riverside activity, but they are only finding the easy ones, there are a hell of a lot more down there.' The killing, the 1966 stabbing of Cheri Jo Bates, is believed to be the first murder attributed to the feared killer.

Authorities say that Bates fought with her attacker, providing authorities with DNA material that was collected from under her fingernails. A hair was also found in the palm of Bates's dead hand and is also believed to be the killer's. Authorities want to DNA-test the evidence and compare it with a DNA-sample from longtime Zodiac suspect, Arthur Leigh Allen. A convicted child molester, Allen was considered the prime suspect in the Zodiac case due to circumstantial evidence, but was never charged with any of the killings. Allen died at age 59 of natural causes.

In Oakland County, Michigan, authorities said they were going to exhume the body of David Norberg, who died in a car wreck in 1981, to determine whether he was a serial child killer known as the 'Babysitter'. Authorities hope to match DNA from Norberg's body with a hair found on the body of one of his six victims. The killer got his nickname because of the lavish care he provided the youngsters before murdering them. After one disappearance, the child's grieving mother went on television promising her son his favorite chicken dish if he returned home. He never made it back home alive, but the killer did feed him a chicken dinner before suffocating him. Of the six suspected Babysitter victims the corpses of four were washed clean and carefully laid on fresh snow. In the 1980s, suspicion focused on Norberg posthumously, when relatives found among his belongings a cross inscribed with Kristine – the first name of one of the victims.

Through DNA-testing, police in Glasgow, Scotland, believe they solved a 26-year-old murder mystery and traced the identity of 'Bible John', the area's most infamous serial killer. In 1998 police reopened the case of Helen Puttock, one of Bible John's victims, to re-examine a pair of tights she was wearing at the time of her death. A DNA-sample extracted from the tights was then compared with samples taken from several suspects in the case. Because one of the suspects had already died, police took a sample from a relative. Surprisingly, that very sample was the one that matched with the DNA from the tights. Police then exhumed the body of the unnamed man and confirmed the DNA match. The man, a former Scots Guard, was married and had three children. He is said to have committed suicide in 1980. Bible John earned his moniker by leaving passages from the Scriptures next to his victim's bodies and reading from the Bible after each killing.

DNA-testing, in all its permutations, has indeed revolutionized every aspect of crime-fighting investigations. In the near future perhaps many more solved and unsolved cases will be put to the test to either identify the killer or exonerate the person who was charged with the crime. In Massachusetts the son of Albert DeSalvo wanted to reopen the Boston Strangler investigation and DNA-test the remains of his father. The courts did not allow it, citing that reopening the investigation would be too painful for the victim's relatives. In Atlanta a lawyer for Wayne Williams said the suspected 'Atlanta Child Murderer' was pushing for DNA-testing to exonerate himself of all charges after spending eighteen years in prison. Lawyer Lynn Whatley said Williams was trying to raise the money to have tests conducted on the hair and blood samples that linked Williams to two murders. As of this writing no new developments have been made public in the Williams case.

However, as old investigations are being re-examined, new serial patterns are being discovered throughout the globe. In Denver five transients were brutally pummeled to death in similar fashion within a six-block area during a two-month period in 1999. Although police did not officially link any of the killings, they acknowledged the possibility that the attacks could be the work of one individual or a group of thrill-killers. Criminologist James Alan Fox said the circumstances in these five deaths were too similar to be coincidence. 'You have five people killed in a short period of time in a similar fashion in the same general area fitting the same general description,' he said.

A month after the last of the five transients was found dead two more homeless men were discovered separately in a nearby field. Both men were decapitated. Their heads have yet to be found. 'The deaths of seven homeless men have left our community in a state of disbelief,' Denver Mayor Wellington Webb said. 'We thought it was over . . . But in reality, we have two more homeless bodies, and we don't know if it's a copycat or related.'

The spate of murders has unnerved Denver's homeless community. 'This is the worst thing I have seen in eighteen years on the street,' Dave Roy, a transient, told the *Denver Post*. 'Somebody has something against the homeless. I don't think this is the end. I don't think it's over.' Two men and a sixteen-year-old boy have been charged with first-degree murder for one of the fatal beatings. The six other murders remain unsolved.

In 1999, Pittsburgh police announced they were working on a theory that a serial killer has, since 1992, killed at least one woman every year. In an all too familiar profile, all victims were young, had problems with drugs and worked as prostitutes. While police insist there are no strong threads connecting the cases, they pointed out intriguing similarities. 'There could be a link. Anybody who looks at a number of cases of young females who just turn up dead would have to say so,' said Inspector Ken Fulton, head of the Allegheny County homicide department. 'Some of the women were prostitutes, but not all of them. Several were killed and then dumped in remote areas. One or two were strangled; one was dismembered . . . We don't even know the cause of death in some of the cases.'

In Minnesota and North Dakota a serial killer is suspected in the disappearances of three mentally retarded women over a nine-year period. Floyd Tapson, who has been charged in Montana with the rape and attempted murder of a 22-year-old mentally retarded woman, is a possible suspect in the case. Investigators in Maryland are also reviewing cases of several women who disappeared in the late 1980s when

Tapson was working at a group home in the Baltimore area. Tapson pleaded not guilty in the Montana case and is free on bail. He was arrested after allegedly driving the woman to a remote area outside Billings and shooting her in the face at close range. The woman, miraculously, survived the attack and fingered Tapson. 'An inch or two over, she could be dead, and we'd never know about this guy,' said Detective Seth Weston of the Yellowstone County Sheriff's Office in Montana.

Over the last three decades the FBI has chronicled the deaths of at least 32 women along a 50-mile stretch, between Houston and Galveston, of the Interstate 45. 'It appears that there may be multiple serial killers,' said Don K. Clark, Special Agent in charge of the FBI's Houston division. The latest victim was discovered early in 1999 by a little boy while he was walking his dog. The dog came up with a bone, then the boy saw a skull. Nearby, police found earrings, shreds of clothing and a belt tied around a tree. Investigators believe the killer used it to bind the young woman while she was sexually assaulted. Evidence pointed to a serial killer in the area long ago. Now, after a computerized analysis of the evidence, new subtle data patterns have emerged suggesting there are at least two separate killers at work. One killer, investigators said, likes short, slim, brown-haired women, while the other has demonstrated distinctive habits at his dumpsites.

In France police linked a Salvador Dali painting of a dismembered woman to the murder of two young women and the disappearance of a third. The three victims were last seen near the Perpignan railway station, which since the 1960s was a focus of obsession for the famed surrealist painter. The first mutilated victim, Moktaria Chaib, a pretty nineteen-year-old student, was found near the station just before Christmas 1997. Chaib had been stabbed to death and her sexual organs were amputated with such surgical precision that police thought only somebody with medical training could have been responsible. Within weeks a Peruvian-born surgeon living near the station was arrested. Denounced by the press as 'a Latin Jack the Ripper', the surgeon was linked to the 1995 disappearance of Tatiana Andujar, a seventeen-year-old student who, like Chaib, was last seen getting off a train at Perpignan.

But the case against the surgeon fell apart on 26 June 1998, when the mutilated body of Marie-Hélène Gonzalez was discovered. Like Chaib, her anus had been excised with a scalpel. The 22-year-old office worker had disappeared after catching a train to Perpignan. Her head and hands were missing like in the Dali painting, 'The Specter of Sex Appeal', where a female torso is depicted. The missing body parts were found six months later in a ditch outside Perpignan. And the monstrous killer is still on the loose, plotting his next hit.

And there are many more just like him. Undetected and unknown. Hunting for men, women and children. Out there, lusting for blood. Don't be their next victim.

NEWSFLASH 2001

Since the first edition of *Killers on the Loose* was published in January 2000, suspects have been arrested in three cases featured in the book. In Spokane, Robert Lee Yates plea-bargained his way to confessing to thirteen murders in exchange for a 408-year sentence. Trials are still pending for Andre Crawford, accused of killing eleven women in Chicago, and Juan Juárez Rosales, suspected of at least six murders in Ciudad Juárez.

New serial killer patterns have emerged in the Hawaiian paradise island of Kauai, as well as in Swaziland, Guatemala and, of all places, Mashad, one of Iran's holiest cities. Other suspected serial killers have been arrested in New York, Texas, South Carolina, Kansas, Yemen, and Detroit. Of the new batch of serial killers in custody, two had US Navy connections, one trolled Internet chat rooms in search for victims, and another worked at the morgue of a university.

Over the last year New York police have arrested two suspected serial killers. One, Vincent Johnson, a homeless crack addict, confessed to being the feared 'Brooklyn Strangler', responsible for strangling five women. The other suspect, Richard Rogers, is believed to be the 'Last Call Killer', suspected of killing and mutilating between two and five gay or bisexual men.

The two suspected serial killers with US Navy backgrounds are John Eric Armstrong and Reinaldo Rivera. Armstrong, a refueler, who served for seven years abroad the *USS Nimitz*, was arrested by Detroit police on 12 April 2000 for the murder of five area prostitutes. In custody, the 300-pound former sailor confessed to committing eighteen murders throughout the world over an eight-year period.

According to police, Armstrong, 28, said he started his killing spree in Raleigh, North Carolina, when he joined the Navy in 1992. For the next seven years he continued murdering women during port stops while serving a tour of duty on the *Nimitz*. He confessed to committing three murders in Seattle, two in Hong Kong, two in Hawaii, and one each in Virginia, North Carolina, Thailand and Singapore. Police believe that – other than the five murders he committed in Detroit – the rest of Armstrong's confession was a figment of his imagination.

In April 1999 Armstrong was honorably discharged from the Navy and relocated with his wife and infant child to the Dearborn Heights area of Detroit. There he worked as a refueler in the Detroit Metropolitan Airport and committed five murders in less than four months. At the time of his arrest his wife, Katie, was pregnant with their second child.

Police said Armstrong was questioned following the January death of a prostitute in Dearborn Heights, whom he allegedly found dead in a stream. Police suspected him of the murder but did not have enough evidence to arrest him. About four months later a prostitute called Detroit Police to report she had been assaulted by a man and gave a description of the suspect and his vehicle. Two days later a Conrail worker spotted a body near the tracks. Investigators found two other women's bodies nearby. All three women were prostitutes killed at different times, then dumped in the same area. Police theorize that Armstrong strangled them in his car, then dumped near the tracks. The first body had been dumped four weeks before, the second three weeks before, and the third two days before Armstrong's arrest.

Another former sailor, 37-year-old Reinaldo Rivera, has been charged with killing four women around the area of

Aiken County, South Carolina and Augusta, Georgia. Rivera, who worked for the US Joint Chiefs of Staff in Washington, DC, was arrested 16 October 2000 in a blood-splattered motel room in Augusta after he tried to kill himself by slashing his wrists. A woman who survived an attack by Rivera gave police a description of him which, a week later, led to his arrest. The woman said she went to her house with her attacker, who then allegedly raped her, knocked her unconscious and stabbed her three times in the neck with a steak knife.

Investigators believe Rivera approached his victims – mostly young and blonde women – at malls and parking lots saying he was opening a modeling agency and asking them about their sex lives. Though several dozen women have told police they were propositioned by him, at least four fell prey to his trick: Melissa Dingess, seventeen, of Graniteville, South Carolina, who disappeared 17 July 1999; Tiffaney Wilson, seventeen, of Jackson, South Carolina, whose body was found in the woods near Bettis Academy Road in Graniteville, 29 December 1999; Tabatha Leigh Bosdell, eighteen, who disappeared 29 June 2000; and Fort Gordon Sergeant Marni Glista, 21, of Augusta, who was found raped and strangled at her home on 7 September 2000.

Like many other suspects featured in this book, Rivera hid his sexual psychopathy behind a seemingly normal, middle-class family life. The son of a doctor, Rivera was born in Madrid, Spain, where he lived until he was seven, when his family moved to Puerto Rico. At nineteen he joined the Navy and reported for basic training in Orlando, Florida. From December 1986 to March 1991, Rivera worked for the Joint Chiefs of Staff in Washington where he was arrested but not charged with a knife attack on an eighteen-year-old prostitute. Several other incidents of conduct unbecoming to an officer led to his eventual dismissal from the Navy, then to jail for four rape and murder counts.

Another 'pillar of the community' who turned out to be a sadistic serial killer was John Edward Robinson. In what is arguably the first cyber-sex serial killer case in history, Robinson, 56, trolled S&M Internet chat rooms in search of victims. Authorities believe between five and eight women over a sixteen-year period fell prey to his deadly schemes. The case against the Internet bondage killer broke when authorities, who had been investigating Robinson for fraud, arrested him on 6 July 2000, for sexually assaulting two women that he met separately in Internet chat rooms. Following his arrest, authorities unearthed two 55-gallon barrels with two corpses inside, from a property he owned. Next, police found three more drums with three dead women in a storage locker he rented 30 miles away in Raymore, Missouri.

There was nothing in Robinson's childhood that would signal his future as a serial predator. In fact, he was a more-than-remarkable child who grew up near Chicago. Some considered him a child prodigy who, as an Eagle Scout, traveled to England to sing for the Queen and developed a friendship with Judy Garland.

But as an adult, he honed his skills as a scam artist living from one con to the next. Robinson's varied schemes, which border on the unthinkable for their sheer mind-bending deviancy, were true exercises in the manipulation of unsuspecting victims.

One of the more outrageous projects he embarked on involved nineteen-year-old Lisa Stasi and her five-month-old baby daughter, Tiffany. In 1985 Robinson allegedly met Stasi in a shelter for battered women and recruited her for his fraudulent 'Outreach' program for young single mothers. On 8 January 1985, she and her baby checked in to an Overland Park Rodeway Inn using a credit card issued to Equi-II – a bogus consulting company set up by Robinson. After Stasi informed her family of her sudden stroke of good fortune, she was never heard from again. That is, until Robinson was arrested.

More than fifteen years later authorities located Tiffany – Lisa Stasi's daughter – alive and living under the name Heather Robinson. Robinson allegedly arranged the fake adoption of Tiffany by his older brother soon after she and her mother disappeared. Unaware that the adoption was illegal, or that the girl's mother had presumably been killed by Robinson, his brother raised the little girl in a seemingly normal fashion. According to authorities the brother never suspected any wrongdoing, and had been given fake legal documents concerning the adoption.

On the other side of the world, a morgue worker at Sanaa University in Yemen used his position at the university to kill at least sixteen women. Mohammad Adam Omar, 48, was arrested 17 May 2000 following the persistent complaining by the mother of an Iraqi student who mysteriously disappeared December 1999. After his arrest, the lethal morgue worker confessed to killing 51 women throughout the Middle East over a 25-year period. In Yemen, Omar confessed to killing sixteen women, eight of whom were students at the university. He added that he cut off the hands and feet of his victims, dissolved them in chemicals and kept their bones as mementos.

Yemeni police reported they discovered the remains of fifteen women around the medical faculty of Sanaa University. Nine of the corpses were skeletons, six headless corpses. Two additional heads were found that did not match any of the bodies. Some of the remains were found buried and others were in the university's sewage system. In custody, Omar said he regretted his murder spree but added he had been unable to resist the urge to kill beautiful women.

'I regret what I did and executing me will purify me from my sins,' Omar said. 'Sometimes I used to hate what I did, but when I saw women, especially beautiful ones, something happened inside me that I could not resist at all.'

On 20 November Omar was convicted of killing two women and sentenced to death. The court ordered that the former morgue worker be executed by firing squad in the main square of the medical school.

In New York, Vincent Johnson, a homeless crack addict, confessed to being the feared Brooklyn Strangler, responsible for the death of five women over a year-long strangulation spree. Johnson was arrested 5 August 2000, after another homeless man pointed him out to officers as he walked back from Manhattan over the Williamsburg Bridge. In custody,

Johnson confessed to five murders, adding that 'Thoughts of my childhood and foster care and mom came into my mind' as he choked his last victim to death.

In the videotaped confession, Johnson admitted to killing Patricia Sullivan, Rhonda Tucker, Joanne Feliciano, Vivian Caraballo and Laura Nusser. Police believe he also killed Katrina Niles. All six murdered women had arrest records for prostitution and/or drugs, all were found nude or partly clothed, and all were strangled. The killer used whatever he found at hand to kill: two were strangled with their own sneaker laces; one with the drawstring from a pair of sweatpants; two with an electrical cord and one with a piece of cloth. The first three victims had sex with him before they were killed; two were found on rooftops. Three of the victims – Caballero, Feliciano and Sullivan – were killed on a Thursday, and a fourth – Tucker – was found dead in her apartment on a Saturday, but was last seen on a Thursday.

Johnson was identified as the killer by another homeless man who had originally been suspected of being guilty of the crimes. The man was cleared because his DNA did not match, but he then fingered Johnson. He called officers when he saw Johnson crossing the Williamsburg Bridge. Police surreptitiously obtained a DNA sample from Johnson after he was interrogated but had refused to give a sample. As he left the police station, one of the interrogating officers saw him spit in a cup and ran out the station to retrieve it. On 10 March 2001, Johnson pleaded guilty to strangling five women and was sentenced to life in prison without the possibility of parole.

Another pending serial killer case in New York has Nurse Richard W. Rogers Jr accused of the 1992 murder of Thomas Mulcahy and the 1993 murder of Anthony Marrero. Both victims were found carefully dismembered, packed in plastic bags and dumped near rest stops on New Jersey highways. Manhattan's district attorney office said the suspect is believed to be the feared 'Last Call Killer', who is thought to have murdered five gay and bisexual men whom he met in Manhattan bars between 1991 and 1993. Rogers, 50, was arrested 30 May 2001 at Mount Sinai Medical Center in

Manhattan – his workplace for the last 20 years. The break in the case came when fingerprints from the bags were matched with prints of Rogers from a manslaughter charge he beat in Maine 27 years ago.

Rogers, who was 22 at the time, became a suspect in the death of a Frederic A. Spencer, who lived in his apartment building in Orono. Spencer's body was found a few days after his death by two cyclists riding along a deserted road near Old Town. After his arrest, Rogers told police he caught Spencer in his apartment and that Spencer had come at him with a hammer. He said he managed to get the hammer away and beat Spencer to death. Six months later, Rogers was acquitted of manslaughter in Penobscot County Superior Court.

The killing of Michael Sakara, 56, of New York, was a defining moment in what was later termed the 'Last Call Killer' case. His murder marked the fifth unsolved killing of middle-aged gay or bisexual men whose bodies were later found dismembered and dumped outside New York City. Sakara's head and arms were found 31 July 1993, carefully washed and triple bagged in a garbage can at a rest area known as 'The Lookout' along the Hudson River about thirty miles north of Manhattan. His legs and torso were recovered a week later in a garbage container about eight miles away. He was last seen two days before stumbling out of a Greenwich Village gay piano bar with a new friend. Sakara, who was the fifth victim in the serial pattern, proved beyond doubt that a killer was stalking Manhattan gay bars, killing middle-aged men, and dumping their dismembered remains in rural New York and New Jersey.

The first victim of the five grisly murders in the 'Last Call' file was Peter Stickney Anderson, a 54-year-old Philadelphia socialite and Republican city council candidate. He was found 5 May 1991, stuffed in several plastic bags at a rest stop on the Pennsylvania Turnpike. Anderson was last seen two days earlier at the Townhouse Bar & Restaurant, an upscale bar popular with gay men on the Upper East Side of Manhattan.

Fourteen months later, a state crew emptying garbage cans from a rest area on New Jersey's Route 72 in Woodland

Township, Burlington County, found the head of Thomas Mulcahy, 57, a bisexual computer executive who had disappeared from Manhattan two days earlier. Mulcahy's legs and torso were found twenty miles away. Mulcahy, who had a wife of 34 years and four children in Sudbury, Massachusetts, had been staying in Manhattan on business. His body was sawn into seven parts and carefully washed. The head and arms were dumped at Woodland, along with his clothes, briefcase, presentation materials, wallet and identification. Police described the killer as 'a medic, nurse or hunter, at least moderately familiar with anatomy and cutting'.

One week after Mulcahy's head was discovered, the limbs and torso of Guillermo Mendez, 56, of Schenectady, NY were found in garbage bags in Rotterdam, NY. His head was later found in a garbage bag in a cemetery. Then, on 10 May 1993, the head of Anthony Marrero, a 43-year-old gay prostitute who performed sex acts for $10 in the restrooms of the Port Authority Bus Terminal in Manhattan, was found in a plastic bag on Crow Hill Road in Manchester Township, Ocean County. The rest of his body was found in the nearby woods. The last dismembered body to be found was Sakara's.

Since his arrest, Rogers has been charged only with the murders of Mulcahy and Marrero. But police in New York, New Jersey and Pennsylvania contend the two killings fit the pattern of the 'Last Call Killer' and are trying to find enough evidence to charge him with the other murders. Friends of the suspect told the *New York Times* that Rogers was an antique aficionado and 'do-gooder' who would not hurt anyone. He was also described as 'the kind of guy you could trust with your ATM card'. Little did they know about his skillful use of the saw.

On the Hawaiian island of Kauai, police believe there is a serial killer hunting petite, middle-aged, Caucasian women. To date, the maniac has killed two victims. A third survived a brutal attack that left her stabbed and badly beaten. The first victim of the Kauai Serial Killer was found 30 August 2000, at a remote campsite at Pakala Point Beach near Waimea. The woman, 42-year-old

Daren Singer, 42, was raped and stabbed, and her face was severely beaten. On 7 April the battered body of Lisa Bissell, 38, was found in a ditch near Polihale State Park. She too had been raped, stabbed and beaten. On 22 May a 52-year-old woman was stabbed and badly beaten and left for dead in a remote area of Kekaha. All three cases bear striking similarities, suggesting they are the work of the same individual. Previous to this sudden rash of murders there has not been a homicide in Kauai for more than two and a half years.

In the tiny African mountain kingdom of Swaziland, authorities have announced that there is a serial killer on the loose who has claimed the lives of at least 21 women and three children. Their bodies were uncovered in a mass grave in April 2001 in a forest near Swaziland's traditional capital, Lobamba. Initial investigations revealed that the victims were killed over a period of several months up to a couple of years. Police Commissioner Edgar Hillary described the murders as a 'national disaster'. Police and soldiers stumbled from one body to another after a herdsman discovered the first victim. All bodies were either in an advanced stage of decomposition or skeletal. Senior police detective Jomo Mavuso said that all the victims had been killed in a similar way and were found stripped naked lying face down.

In Guatemala City, a serial killer dubbed 'Jack the Ripper' has killed five prostitutes during the first half of 2001. The suspect has been writing messages for the police on the backs of his victims with a red marker. He has also marked his victims with the letters MS, the initials of the Salvadoran gang 'Mara Salvatrucha'. Police believe the unidentified killer may have previously killed prostitutes in Log Angeles and might have moved to El Salvador, where he is still killing. According to witnesses who say they saw the suspect enter various hotels with prostitutes who were later found dead, the killer is a short, tan-skinned, 35-year-old man with closely cut black hair and sunken brown eyes. Police say he goes by the last name Blanco and speaks with a Salvadoran accent. Investigators believe the suspect may have fled back to El Salvador after police closed in on his trail. 'We have been in close contact with authorities there because we are convinced this man will kill again,' said Enio Rivera, director of Guatemala's national police force.

The killings began 27 January 2001 when police discovered the body of an unidentified prostitute who had been strangled in a dingy hotel in downtown Guatemala City. In a note to police, written on his victim's back, the killer said he 'didn't like it, but couldn't help killing', and that he had already killed two prostitutes in Los Angeles. Authorities in California were unable to confirm the killings. Two weeks later, police found the strangled body of Roxana Jamileth Molina in a hotel room on the western outskirts of the Guatemalan capital. Then, on 6 March, the owner of a nearby hotel discovered the strangled body of another unidentified prostitute. The killer's fourth victim was found four days later, also near downtown Guatemala City. The woman's body had 'Death to all the dogs. Seven down, three to go' etched in flowery handwriting on her back.

On 29 March, the body of a fifth strangled prostitute was discovered in the town of Huehuetenango, about 180 miles northwest of Guatemala City.

In Mashad, one of Iran's holiest cities, a suspect has been arrested in connection with the murders of at least sixteen 'truck women' – a local euphemism for prostitutes who service truckers and delivery men. The murders, which started in July 2000, were dubbed 'Spider Killings' because of the way the killer left the victims wrapped in their head-scarves. All victims were found strangled to death, their bodies dumped into local streets and canals, and their chadors knotted twice to the right side of the neck. Police noted that all victims had previous drug and prostitution convictions. They were all killed on Sundays, leading investigators to believe the killer was motivated by religious fervor.

Curiously, the killings posed a complex problem for Iran's secular leadership who fervently denied the existence of prostitution and drugs in their society. Even more difficult was the fact that the killings were being committed in the city center of Mashad, next to the burial site of Imam Rex, the eighth grandson of the prophet Muhammad, in an area crawling with heroin addicts and prostitutes.

Following the discovery of a nineteenth dead prostitute in Mashad, police rounded up 500 prostitutes in an attempt to protect them from a mysterious killer and to clean up the city. On 26 July police arrested Said Hanoi, a 39-year-old construction worker, and charged him with killing sixteen women. 'I killed the women for the sake of God, and for the protection of my religion because they were prostitutes and (were) corrupting other people', he told reporters at the site of one of the murders. 'I wouldn't have bothered even if I had killed a hundred and fifty women because I wanted to clean the holy city of Mashad from corrupt women and prostitutes.' Three other suspects were arrested for copycat killings.

For updates and new serial patterns, check the Newsflash section of the website – www.mayhem.net

Look out for other compelling True Crime titles coming from
Virgin Books in 2002

February 2002

CROSSING TO KILL – THE TRUE STORY OF THE SERIAL-KILLER PLAYGROUND
by Simon Whitechapel

Since 1993 over 180 women have been raped and brutally murdered
in Ciudad Juárez, a Mexican border town notorious for its pollution
and overcrowding. Despite a number of arrests, the killing won't
stop. Authorities suspect that killers are coming from all over Mexico
– and even crossing the border from the USA – to rape and kill with
impunity. Simon Whitechapel conducts a detailed analysis of the
contributory factors surrounding these brutal slayings and looks at
the turbulent cultural history of this often-violent country. Is there
any way to protect women from this playground for serial killers?
£6.99   ISBN: 07535 0686 6

March 2002

JACK THE RIPPER, THE FINAL CHAPTER
by Paul H. Feldman

A haunting journal that came to light in 1991 and was published in
1993 as *The Diary of Jack the Ripper* was believed to be a hoax. Yet
no one was able to explain how it was forged, or by whom. The
reason, as Paul Feldman explains, is because the journal is genuine.
In this exhaustively researched and most extensive Ripper investigation ever undertaken, Paul Feldman cuts through the cover-ups and
wild theories surrounding the Ripper mystery to undoubtedly prove
that James Maybrick was Jack the Ripper. As well as uncovering
crucial new evidence about the murders, Feldman presents sensa-
tional revelations from the Ripper's living descendants.

'. . . my own feeling was that Feldman has taken game, set and match.'   Colin Wilson
£6.99   ISBN: 0 7535 0637 8

April 2002

LONE WOLF – TRUE STORIES OF SPREE KILLERS
by Pan Pantziarka
Revised and updated edition

Cases of loner gunmen embarking on slaughter sprees have begun to occur with frightening regularity since the late 1980s. People like Timothy McVeigh, Thomas Hamilton and Michael Ryan. What drives these mass murderers to turn on friends, family and strangers in acts of senseless rage and slaughter? Is there any way to stop this growing tide of violence that devastates entire communities? Pan Pantziarka conducts an in-depth look at the disturbed personalities and the brutal trend of seemingly indiscriminate killing that blights our 'civilised' society.
£6.99   ISBN: 0 7535 0617 3

May 2002

I'LL BE WATCHING YOU – TRUE STORIES OF STALKERS AND THEIR VICTIMS
by Richard Gallagher

Stalking is on the increase – and it isn't only celebrities who become the targets of irrational individuals. Men and women with everyday jobs who lead ordinary lives can just as easily become someone else's obsession. Each year, hundreds of people fall victim to terrifying harassment by people they may have never even met. Richard Gallagher has exhaustively researched this disturbing phenomenon to provide a serious investigation into this unsettling but fascinating crime. Featuring interviews with victims, police, psychologists – and those who 'stalk the stalkers' – he has unearthed remarkable accounts of obsession and delusion. It's a book whose time has definitely come.

'A carefully researched collection of case histories of stalking . . . a compelling picture of a disturbing trend.'   *Books Magazine*
£6.99   ISBN: 0 7535 0696 3

UNSOLVED MURDERS – WHEN KILLERS ESCAPE JUSTICE
by Russell Gould

The Black Dahlia. JonBenét Ramsay. PC Keith Blakelock. Rachel Nickell. Their killers have never been brought to justice. These, and several other compelling cases, make up this study of the most puzzling murders of the late twentieth century. Could six-year-old beauty queen JonBenét Ramsay have been killed by a member of her own family? Were British government agencies responsible for the murder of activist Hilda Murrell? How could the so-called Zodiac killer's reign of terror continue unchecked for so long? Russell Gould draws upon all of the evidence – and all of the theories – to bring together the definitive, uncensored account of these unsolved crimes.
£6.99   ISBN: 0 7535 0632 7

MY BLOODY VALENTINE – COUPLES WHOSE SICK CRIMES SHOCKED THE WORLD
Edited by Patrick Blackden

Good-looking Canadian couple Paul Bernardo and Karla Homolka looked the epitome of young, wholesome success. No one could have guessed that they drugged, raped and murdered young women to satisfy Bernardo's deviant lusts. Nothing inspires more horror and fascination than couples possessed of a single impulse – to kill for thrills. Obsessed by and sucked into their own sick and private madness, their attraction is always fatal, their actions always desperate. The book covers a variety of notorious killer couples: from desperados Starkweather and Fugate, on whom the film *Natural Born Killers* was based, right through to Fred and Rose West, who committed unspeakable horrors in their semi-detached house in Gloucester, England. With contributions from a variety of leading true crime journalists, *My Bloody Valentine* covers both the world-famous cases and also lesser-known but equally horrifying crimes.
£7.99   ISBN: 0 7535 0647 5

Karin
Hunter

626 Riverside
Dr.

Apt 23 I

NYC
10031

(212) 862-
9120